CU00766056

The Mathematical And Philosophical Works Of The Right Rev. John Wilkins, Late Lord Bishop Of Chester: Iii. An Abstract Of His Essay Towards A Real Character, And A Philosophical Language...

John Wilkins

Nabu Public Domain Reprints:

You are holding a reproduction of an original work published before 1923 that is in the public domain in the United States of America, and possibly other countries. You may freely copy and distribute this work as no entity (individual or corporate) has a copyright on the body of the work. This book may contain prior copyright references, and library stamps (as most of these works were scanned from library copies). These have been scanned and retained as part of the historical artifact.

This book may have occasional imperfections such as missing or blurred pages, poor pictures, errant marks, etc. that were either part of the original artifact, or were introduced by the scanning process. We believe this work is culturally important, and despite the imperfections, have elected to bring it back into print as part of our continuing commitment to the preservation of printed works worldwide. We appreciate your understanding of the imperfections in the preservation process, and hope you enjoy this valuable book.

Thank you for your order

ORDER ID   203-5131419-6030703 (WWW.AMAZON.CO.UK)

ORDER DATE   2013-02-03T22:55:28+00:00

203-5131419-6030703

Order Details	
Title	**The Mathematical and Philosophical Works of the Right REV. J**
Code	APC9781276333627
Quantity	1
Unit Price	GBP 11.06
Shipping	GBP 2.80
Vat INCL.	GBP 0.00

Goodridge Avenue, Gloucester, GL2 5EB, United Kingdom | AMAZONUK@BOOKDEPO:

hn Wilkins, Late Lord Bishop of Chester: III. an Abstract of His Essay Towards a Real Cha

Total GBP 13.86

NEW JERSEY
COLLEGE LIBRARY

THE

MATHEMATICAL AND PHILOSOPHICAL

WORKS

OF THE

RIGHT REV. JOHN WILKINS,

LATE LORD BISHOP OF CHESTER.

TO WHICH IS PREFIXED

THE AUTHOR's LIFE,

AND

AN ACCOUNT OF HIS WORKS.

IN TWO VOLUMES.

VOL. II.

CONTAINING,

I. Mercury: or, the Secret and Swift Messenger. Shewing how a Man may with Privacy and Speed communicate his Thoughts to a Friend at any Distance.

II. Mathematical Magic: or the Wonders that may be performed by Mechanical Geometry.

III. An Abstract of his Essay towards a Real Character, and a Philosophical Language.

LONDON:

PRINTED BY C. WHITTINGHAM,
Dean Street, Fetter Lane,

FOR VERNOR AND HOOD, POULTRY; CUTHELL, AND MARTIN, MIDDLE-ROW; HOLBORN; AND J. WALKER, PATERNOSTER-ROW.

1802.

CONTENTS.

VOL. II.

MERCURY,
THE SECRET AND SWIFT MESSENGER.

CHAP. I.

8012
974
.11
v.2   32719

ARCHIMEDES; OR, MECHANICAL POWERS.

BOOK I.

DÆDALUS; OR, MECHANICAL MOTIONS.

BOOK II.

MERCURY:

OR, THE

SECRET AND SWIFT MESSENGER.

SHEWING

**HOW A MAN MAY WITH PRIVACY AND SPEED COMMUNICATE
HIS THOUGHTS TO A FRIEND AT A DISTANCE.**

TO

THE RIGHT HONOURABLE

GEORGE LORD BERKLEY,

BARON OF BERKLEY, MOBRAY, SEGRAVE, AND BRUCE,

AND KNIGHT OF THE NOBLE ORDER OF THE BATH.

My Lord,

I Do here once more present your Lordship with the fruit of my leisure studies, as a testimony of my readiness to serve you in those sacred matters, to which I devote my more serious hours. I should not have presumed to this dedication, had I not been encouraged by that generousness and sweetness of disposition, which does so eminently adorn your Lordship's place and abilities.

If your Lordship please to excuse this boldness, and to vouchsafe this pamphlet a shelter under your favourable patronage, you shall thereby encourage me in those higher studies, which may be more agreeable to that relation wherein I stand, as being

Your Lordship's servant and chaplain,

J. W.

THE READER.

THAT which first occasioned this discourse, was the reading of a little pamphlet, stiled *Nuntius Inanimatus*, commonly ascribed to a late reverend bishop; wherein he affirms, that there are certain ways to discourse with a friend, though he were in a close dungeon, in a besieged city, or a hundred miles off.

Which promises, at the first perusal, did rather raise my wonder than belief, having before that time observed nothing that might give any satisfaction in these particulars. And I should have esteemed them altogether fabulous, had it not been for the credit of their reputed author.

After this, I did collect all such notes to this purpose, as I met with in the course of my other studies.

From whence when I have received full satisfaction, I did for mine own farther delight compose them into this method.

I have already attained mine own ends, both in the delight of composing this, and the occasion of publishing it: and therefore need not either fear the censure of others, or beg their favour. I could never yet discern, that any reader hath shewed the more charity for the author's bespeaking it.

Farewell.

J. W.

TO MERCURY THE ELDER:

ON THE

MOST LEARNED MERCURY THE YOUNGER.

REST Maia's son, sometimes interpreter
   Of gods, and to us men their messenger:
Take not such pains as thou hast done of old,
To teach men hieroglyphics, and to unfold
Egyptian hidden characters, and how
Men writ in dark obscurity: for now
Trithemius and Selenus both are grown
Such cryptographers, as they scarce will own
Thee for their master; and decipherers know
Such secret ways to write, thou ne'er didst show,
These are but artists which thou didst inspire;
But now thou of a Mercury art sire
Of thine own name, a post with whom the wind,
Should it contend, would be left far behind.
Whose message, as thy metal, strikes the gold
Quite through a wedge of silver uncontrol'd;
And in a moment's space doth pass as far
As from the arctic to th' antarctic star
So proving what is said of influence,
May now be said of his intelligence,
They neither of them having such a quality
As a relation to locality:
No places distance hindering their commerce,
Who freely traffic through the universe;
And in a minute can a voyage make
Over the ocean's universal lake.
This son of thine, could any words or praise,
His learning, worth, or reputation raise,
We should be suitors to him to bestow
Encomiums on himself, which we do owe
Unto his worth, and use that eloquence,
Which as his own, must claim pre-eminence:
For thee, 'tis glory enough thou hast a son
Of art, that hath thyself in art outdone.

Sir FRANCIS KINASTON, Knt.

TO THE UNKNOWN AUTHOR.

OF old, who to the common good apply'd
 Or mind or means, for it were deified:
But chiefly such who new inventions found;
Bacchus for wine, Ceres that till'd the ground.
I know no reason time should breed such odds,
(W' have warrant for't) men now may be stil'd gods.
By hiding who thou art, seek not to miss
The glory due to such a work as this;
But set thy name, that thou may'st have the praise,
Lest to the unknown God we altars raise.

ANTHONY AUCHER, Esq.

TO MY FRIEND THE AUTHOR.

TO praise thy work, were to anticipate
 Thy reader's judgment, and to injure fate;
Injustice to thyself; for real worth
Needs not arts flattery to set it forth.
Some chuse selected wits to write as friends,
Whose verses, when the work fails, make amends,
So as the buyer has his pennyworth,
Though what the author write prove spumy froth.
Thou, of a humour cross to that, hast chose
A friend or two, whose verse hops like rough prose;
From whose inexpert vein thou canst not look
For lines that may enhance the price o'th' book.
Let it commend itself, all we intend
Is but to shew the world thou art our friend.

RICHARD HATTON, Esq.

TO THE READER.

READER, this author has not long ago
 Found out another world to this below:
Though that alone might merit great renown,
Yet in this book he goes beyond the moon:
Beyond the moon indeed, for here you see
That he from thence hath fetched down Mercury;
One that doth tell us things both strange and new,
And yet believe 't they're not more strange than true.
I'm loth to tell thee what rare things they be,
Read thou the book, and then thou'lt tell them me.

TOB. WORLRICH, J. C. Doct.

TO HIS HONOURED FRIEND J. W.

THE SECRET AND SWIFT MESSENGER.

INIMITABLE Sir, we here discern
  Maxims the Stagirite himself might learn.
Were Plato now alive he'd yield to you,
Confessing something might be known anew.
Fresh heresies (new-nothings) still appear
As almanacks, the births of every year.
This Dutchman writes a comment; that translates;
A third transcribes; your pen alone creates
New necessary sciences: this art
Lay undiscovered as the world's fifth part.
But secrecy's now publish'd; you reveal
By demonstration how we may conceal.
  Our legates are but men, and often may
Great state affairs unwillingly betray ;
Caught by some sifting spies, or tell-tale wine,
Which dig up secrets in the deepest mine.
Sometimes, like fire pent in, they outward break,
And 'cause they should be silent, therefore speak.
  Nor are kings' writings safe: to guard their fame,
Like Scævola they wish their hand i'th' flame.
Ink turns to blood; they oft participate
By wax and quill sad Icarus's fate.
Hence noblemen's bad writing proves a plot;
Their letters are but lines, their names a knot.
  But now they shall no more seal their own fall;
No letters prove killing, or capital.
Things pass unknown, and each ambassador's
Strict as the breast of sacred confessors:
Such as the inquisition cannot see;
Such as are forc'd neither by rack, nor fee.
Swift secrecy descends to human powers;
That which was Pluto's helmet, now is ours.
We shall not henceforth be in pay for air,
Transported words being dear as precious ware;
Our thoughts will now arrive before they're stale;
They shall no more wait on the carrier's ale
And hostess, two land-remoraes, which bind
All to a tortoise pace, though words be wind.

This book's a better ark; we brook no stay,
Maugre the deepest flood, or foulest way.
Commerce of goods and souls we owe to two,
(Whose fames shall now be twins) Noah and You.
Each bird is turn'd a parrot, and we see
Esop's beasts made more eloquent by thee.
Wooers again may wing their fetter'd love
By Noah's trusty messenger the dove.
Torches which us'd only to help our sight,
(Like heavenly fires) do give our reason light.
Death's harbingers, arrows, and bullets prove
Like Cupid's darts, ambassadors of love.
Then your diviner hieroglyphics tell,
How we may landskips read, and pictures spell.
You teach how clouds inform, how smokes advise;
Thus saints with incense talk to deities.
Thus by dumb creatures we instructed are,
As the wise men were tutor'd by a star.
    Since we, true serpents like, do little wrong
With any other member but the tongue;
You tell us how we may by gestures talk;
How feet are made to speak, as well as walk;
How eyes discourse, how mystic nods contrive;
Making our knowledge too, intuitive.
A bell no noise but rhetoric affords;
Our music notes are speeches, sounds are words.
Without a trope there's language in a flow'r,
Conceits are smelt without a metaphor.
Dark subtilties we now shall soon define,
Each organ's turn'd the sense of discipline.
'Tis to your care we owe that we may send
Business unknown to any but our friend.
That which is English friendship to my brother,
May be thought Greek or nonsense to another.
We now may Homer's Iliads confine,
Not in a nut-shell, but a point, or line.
Which art though't seem to exceed faith, yet who
Tries it will find both truth and reason too.
'Tis not like jugglers tricks, absurd, when shown;
But more and more admir'd, the more 'tis known.
Writing's an act of emanation,
And thoughts speed quick and far as day doth run.

RICHARD WEST, C. C. Ox.

MERCURY,

THE SECRET AND SWIFT MESSENGER.

CHAP. I.

The dependance of this knowledge in nature. The authors that have treated of it. Its relation to the art of grammar.

EVERY rational creature, being of an imperfect and dependent happiness, is therefore naturally endowed with an ability to communicate its own thoughts and intentions ; that so by mutual services, it might the better promote itself in the prosecution of its own well-being.

And because there is so vast a difference betwixt a spirit and a body, therefore hath the wisdom of Providence contrived a distinct way and means, whereby they are each of them enabled to discourse, according to the variety of their several natures.

The angels or spiritual substances, *per insinuationem specierum,* (as the schoolmen speak *) by insinuating of the species, or an unveiling of their own natures in the knowledge of such particulars as they would discover to another. And since they are of an homogeneous and immaterial essence, therefore do they hear, and know, and speak, not with several parts, but with their whole sub-

---

* Aquinas part 1. Quæst. 107. Zanch. de operibus Dei, part 1. l. 3. c. 19.

stance. And though the apostle mentions the tongue of angels*, yet that is only *per concessionem, et ex hypothesi.*

But now, men that have organical bodies, cannot communicate their thoughts so easy and immediate a way. And therefore have need of some corporeal instruments, both for the receiving and conveying of knowledge. Unto both which functions, nature hath designed several parts. Amongst the rest, the ear is chiefly the sense of discipline or learning, and the tongue the instrument of teaching. The communion betwixt both these, is by speech or language, which was but one at first, but hath since been confounded into several kinds. And experience now shews, that a man is equally disposed for the learning of all, according as education shall direct him †. Which would not be, if (as some fondly conceive) any one of them were natural unto us. For *intus existens prohibet alienum.*

Or suppose that a man could be brought up to the speaking of another tongue ‡, yet this would not hinder, but that he should still retain his knowledge of that which was natural. For if those which are gotten by art do not hinder one another, much less would they be any impediment to that which is from nature. And according to this it will follow, that most men should be of a double language, which is evidently false. Whence likewise you may guess at the absurdity of their enquiries, who have sought to find out the primitive tongue, by bringing up infants in such silent solitary places, where they might not hear the speech of others.

Languages are so far natural unto us, as other arts and sciences. A man is born without any of them, but yet capable of all.

Now, because words are only for those that are present both in time and place ; therefore to these there hath been added, the invention of letters and writing, which are such a

* 1 Cor. xiii. 1.   † Vallesius Sacr. Phil. cap. 3.
‡ Cæl. Rhod. Ant. lect. l. 2. 9. c. 14.

representation of our words (though more permanent) as our words are of our thoughts. By these we may discourse with them that are remote from us, not only by the distance of many miles, but also of many ages. *Hujus usu scimus maxime constare humanitatem vitæ, memoriam, ac hominum immortalitatem,* saith Pliny*. *Quid hoc magnificentius? Quid æque mirandum? in quod ne mortis quidem avida rapacitas jus ullum habeat,* saith Rhodiginus. This being the chiefest means both for the promoting of human society, and the perpetuating our names unto following times.

How strange a thing this art of writing did seem at its first invention, we may guess by the late discovered Americans, who were amazed to see men converse with books, and could scarce make themselves believe that a paper should speak; especially, when after all their attention and listening to any writing (as their custom was) they could never perceive any words or sound to proceed from it.

There is a pretty relation to this purpose, concerning an Indian slave; who being sent by his master with a basket of figs and a letter, did by the way eat up a great part of his carriage, conveying the remainder unto the person to whom he was directed; who when he had read the letter, and not finding the quantity of figs answerable to what was spoken of, he accuses the slave of eating them, telling him what the letter said against him †. But the Indian (notwithstanding this proof) did confidently abjure the fact, cursing the paper, as being a false and lying witness. After this, being sent again with the like carriage, and a letter expressing the just number of figs that were to be delivered, he did again, according to his former practice, devour a great part of them by the way; but before he meddled with any, (to prevent all following accusations) he first took the letter, and hid that under a great stone,

* Nat. Hist. l. 14. c. 11. Antiq. lect. l. 4. c. 3.
† Hermannus Hugo de Orig. Scribendi Præf.

assuring himself, that if it did not see him eat the figs, it could never tell of him; but being now more strongly accused than before, he confesses the fault, admiring the divinity of the paper, and for the future does promise his best fidelity in every employment.

Such strange conceits did those wilder nations entertain, concerning this excellent invention. And doubtless it must needs argue a vast ability both of wit and memory in that man who did first confine all those different sounds of voice, (which seem to be almost of infinite variety) within the bounds of those few letters in the alphabet.

The first inventor of this was thought to be the Egyptian Mercury*, who is therefore stiled the messenger of the Gods. To which purpose the poets have furnished him with wings for swiftness and dispatch in his errands. And because the planet of that name was thought to observe a more various and obscure revolution than any of the rest, therefore likewise did they attribute unto him such secret and subtle motions, as might make him a trusty and private messenger, and so the fitter for that preferment to which for this invention they had advanced him.

There is yet another way of discoursing, by signs and gestures; and though it be not so common in practice as either of the other, yet in nature perhaps it is before them both, since infants are able this way to express themselves, before they have the benefit of speech.

But now, because none of these ways in ordinary use, are either so secret or swift as some exigencies would require; therefore many of the ancients have busied themselves in a further enquiry, how both these deficiencies may be remedied; as conceiving that such a discovery would be of excellent use, especially for some occasions that are incident to statesmen and soldiers.

That the ignorance of secret and swift conveyances, hath often proved fatal, not only to the ruin of particular

* Cic. l. 3. de Nat. Deor. Polyd. Vir. de Inventor. l. 1. c. 6. Vossius de Grammatica, l. 1. c. 9. Natal. Comes Mytho. L 5. c. 5.

persons, but also of whole armies and kingdoms, may easily appear to any one that is but little versed in story. And therefore the redressing of these may be a subject worth our enquiry.

Amongst the ancients that have most laboured in these particulars, Æneas[1], Cleomenes, and Democritus, (as they are cited by Polybius[2]) were for their inventions of this kind, more remarkably eminent. And that author[3] himself hath given us such an exact relation of the knowledge of antiquity in these things, that it is a wonder these following ages should either take no more notice, or make no more use of it. Besides these, there is also Julius Africanus, and Philo Mechanicus, two ancient Grecians, who have likewise treated of this subject.

The military significations in use amongst the Romans, are handled by Vegetius[4] and Frontinus[5].

Their notes of secrecy, and abbreviation in writing, are largely set down by Valerius Probus[6], and Pet. Diaconus. There is likewise a volume of these set forth by Janus Gruterus, which for their first invention are commonly ascribed unto Cicero and Seneca[7].

In latter times these particulars have been more fully handled by the Abbot Trithemius[8], Theodorus Bibliander[9], Baptista Porta[10], Cardan. Subtil. l. 17. de var. C. 12. 6. Isaac Casaubon[11], Johannes Walchius[12], Gustaphus Selenus[13], Gerardus Vossius[14], Hermannus Hugo[15], and divers others in particular languages.

Amongst the rest, our English Aristotle, the learned Verulam, in that work truly stiled the advancement of learning, hath briefly contracted the whole substance of what may be said in this subject. Where he refers it to the art of Grammar, noting it as a deficient part. And in refe-

---

[1] Poliorcetica. [2] Hist. l. 10. [3] Polybius, ib. juxta finem. [4] De re militar. l. 3. c. 5. [5] De Strat. [6] L. de notis antiquus. [7] The father. [8] L. de Polygraph. item de Stenograph. [9] Tract de ratione commun. linguarum. [10] Lib. de Zyphris. [11] Notis in Æneæ Polyorcetica. [12] Fab. 9. [13] De Cryptog. [14] De Gram. L. 1. c. 40. [15] L. de Or. Scrib. de Augm. Scientiar. l. 6. c. 1.

rence to this is it handled by most of those authors who have treated of it.

That art, in its true latitude comprehending a treaty, concerning all the ways of discourse, whether by speech, or by writing, or by gesture, together with the several circumstances pertaining to them. And so this subject belongs to the mint of knowledge; expressions being current for conceits, as money is for valuations.

Now as it will concern a man that deals in traffic, to understand the several kinds of money, and that it may be framed of other materials besides silver and gold : so likewise does it behove them who profess the knowledge of nature or reason, rightly to apprehend the several ways whereby they may be expressed.

So that besides the usefulness of this subject for some special occasions, it doth also belong unto one of the liberal arts.

From which considerations we may infer, that these particulars are not so trivial, as perhaps otherways they would seem ; and that there is sufficient motive to excite any industrious spirit unto a further search after them.

In this following discourse I shall enquire,

1. Concerning the secrecy of means, whereby to communicate our thoughts.

2. Concerning their swiftness, or quick passing at any great distance.

3. How they may be both joined together in the conveyance of any message.

In the prosecution of which, I shall also mention (besides the true discoveries) most of those other ways, whether magical, or fabulous, that are received upon common tradition.

CHAP. II.

The conditions requisite to secrecy : the use of it in the matter of speech, either

By { FABLES OF THE HEATHEN.
{ PARABLES OF SCRIPTURE.

TO the exactness of secrecy in any way of discourse, there are these two qualifications requisite.

1. That it be difficult to be unfolded, if it should be doubted of, or examined.

2. That it be (if possible) altogether devoid of suspicion; for so far as it is liable to this, it may be said to come short in the very nature of secrecy; since what is once suspected, is exposed to the danger of examination, and in a ready way to be discovered; but if not, yet a man is more likely to be disappointed in his intentions, when his proceedings are mistrusted.

Both these conditions together are to be found but in few of the following instances; only they are here specified, to shew what a man should aim at, in the inventions of this nature.

The art of secret information in the general, as it includes all significatory signs, may be stiled *cryptomeneses,* or private intimations.

The particular ways of discoursing, were before intimated to be threefold.

1. By speaking.
2. By writing.
3. By signs or gestures.

According to which variety, there are also different ways of secrecy.

1. *Cryptologia.*
2. *Cryptographia.*
3. *Semæologia.*

Cryptologia, or the secrecy of speaking, may consist either,

    1. In the matter.
    2. In the words.

1. In the matter : when the thing we would utter is so concealed under the expression of some other matter, that it is not of obvious conceit. To which purpose are the metaphors, allegories, and divers other tropes of oratory ; which, so far as they concern the ornament of speech, do properly belong to rhetoric ; but as they may be applied for the secrecy of speech, so are they reducible unto this part of grammar.

To this likewise appertains all that ænigmatical learning, unto which not only the learned heathen, but their gods also were so much devoted, as appears by the strange and frequent ambiguities of the oracles and sybils. And those were counted the most profound philosophers amongst them, who were best able for the invention of such affected obscurities.

Of this kind also were all those mysterious fables, under which the ancients did veil the secrets of their religion and philosophy, counting it a prophane thing to prostitute the hidden matters of either, unto vulgar apprehension. *Quia sciunt inimicam esse naturæ, opertam nudamque expositionem sui ; quæ, sicut vulgaribus hominum sensibus, intellectum sui, vario rerum tegmine operimentoque subtraxit, ita a prudentibus arcana sua voluit per fabulosa tractari,* saith Macrobius*. The gods and nature would not themselves have hidden so many things from us, if they had intended them for common understandings, or that others should treat of them after an easy and perspicuous way : hence was it that the learned men of former times were so generally inclined to involve all their learning, in obscure and mysterious expressions. Thus did the Egyptian priests, the Pythagoreans, Platonicks, and almost all other sects and professions.

---

* In Somn. Scip. lib. 1. cap. 2.

And to this general custom of those ages (we may guess) the Holy Ghost does allude, in the frequent parables both of the Old and New Testament. *Parabola est sermo similitudinarius, qui aliud dicit, aliut significat*, saith Aquinas *. It is such a speech of similitude, as says one thing and means another. The disciples do directly oppose it to plain speaking †, Behold now speakest thou plainly and no parables.

And elsewhere it is intimated, that our Saviour did use that manner of teaching for the secrecy of it: that those proud and perverse auditors, who would not apply themselves to the obedience of his doctrine, might not so much as understand it ‡. To whom it is not given to know the mysteries of the kingdom of God, to them all things are done in parables, that seeing they may see and not perceive, and hearing they may hear and not understand.

The art of these was so to imply a secret argument §, that the adversary might unawares be brought over to an acknowledgment and confession of the thing we would have. Thus did Nathan unexpectedly discover to David, the cruelty and injustice of his proceedings in the case of Uriah ‖. Thus did another prophet make Ahab condemn himself, for suffering the king of Syria to escape ¶. And by this means did our Saviour in the parable of the vineyard, and the unjust husbandman **, force the unbelieving Jews to a secret acknowledgment of those judgments they had themselves deserved.

Of this nature was that argument of an ancient orator, who when the enemies had proposed peace upon this condition, that the city should banish their teachers and philosophers, he steps up and tells the people a tale, of certain wars betwixt the wolves and the sheep, and that the wolves promised to make a league, if the sheep would put away

---

* Commen. in Isaj. xiv.   † John xvi. 29.

‡ Mat. xiii. 10, 11.   Mark. iv. 11, 12.   § Glos. Phil. l. 2. par. 1.
par. 1. Tract. 2. Sect. 5.   ‖ 2 Sam. xii.   ¶ 1 Kings xx. 39.
** Mat. xxi. 31.

their mastiff-dogs. By this means better instructing them of the danger and madness there would be, in yielding to such a condition.

The jewish doctors do generally in their Talmud, and all their other writings, accustom themselves to a parabolical way of teaching; and it is observed, that many of those horrid fables that are fathered upon them, do arise from a misapprehension of them in this particulars: whilst others interpret that according to the letter*, which they intended only for the moral. As that which one rabby relates, concerning a lion in the forest of Elay, that at the distance of four hundred leagues, did with his roaring shake down the walls of Rome, and make the women abortive. Wherein he did not affirm the existence of any such monster, but only intimate the terribleness and power of the divine majesty. But this by the way.

By this art many men are able in their ordinary discourses, so secretly to convey their counsels, or reproofs, that none shall understand them, but those whom they concern. And this way of teaching hath a great advantage above any other, by reason it hath much more power in exciting the fancy and affections. Plain arguments and moral precepts barely proposed, are more flat in their operation, not so lively and persuasive, as when they steal into a man's assent, under the covert of a parable.

To be expert in this particular, is not in every man's power; like poetry, it requires such a natural faculty as cannot be taught. But so far as it falls under the rules and directions of art, it belongs to the precepts of oratory.

In the general it is to be observed, That in these cases a man must be very careful to make choice of such a subject, as may bear in it some proper analogy and resemblance to the chief business. And he must before-hand in his thoughts, so aptly contrive the several parts of the similitude, that they may fitly answer unto those particular passages which are of greatest consequence.

---

* Srickard Examen. Commen. Rabbin. dis. 7.

CHAP. III.

Concerning that secrecy of speech, which consists in the words, either

By inventing new ones, { CANTING.
as in . . . . { CONJURING.

Or by a changing (INVERSION.
of the known) TRANSMUTATION.
language, whe-) DIMINUTION.
ther. . . . . (AUGMENTATION.

THE secret ways of speaking, which consist in the matter of discourse, have been already handled. Those that are in the words are twofold. Either,

1. By inventing new words of our own, which shall signify upon compact.

2. Or by such an alteration of any known language, that in pronunciation it shall seem as obscure, as if it were altogether barbarous.

To the first kind we may refer the canting of beggars; who though they retain the common particles, yet have imposed new names upon all such matters as may happen to be of greatest consequence and secrecy.

And of this nature the charms of witches, and language of magicians seem to be. Though of these it may well be doubted, whether they have any signification at all. And if they have, whether any understand them, but the devil himself. It is probable he did invent such horrid and barbarous sounds, that by them he might more easily delude the weak imaginations of his credulous disciples. Martinus de Arles*, an archdeacon in Navar, speaking of a conjuring-book, that was found in a parish under his visitation,

* Tract. de superstitionibus.

†

repeats out of it these forms of discoursing with the devil. *Conjuro te per ælim, per ælion, per seboan, per adonay, per allelujah, per tanti, per archabulen,* &c. And a little after, *Sitis allegati & constricti per ista sancta nomina Dei, hir, ælli, habet, sat, mi, filisgæ, adrotiagundi, tat, chamileram,* &c. And in another place, *Coriscion, Matatron, Caladafon, Ozcozo, Yosiel,* &c.

In which forms the common particles and words of usual sense, are plainly set down in ordinary Latin; but many of the other, which seem to have the greatest efficacy, are of such secret sense, as I think no linguist can discover.

The inventions of this kind do not fall under any particular rule or maxim, but may be equally infinite to the variety of articulate sounds.

The second way of secrecy in speech*, is by an alteration of any known language, which is far more easy, and may prove of as much use for the privacy of it, as the other. This may be performed four ways.

1. By inversion, when either the letters or syllables are spelled backwards.

Mitto tibi METULAS *cancros imitare legendo,* where the word SALUTEM is expressed by an inversion of the letters. Or as in this other example, *Stisho estad, veca biti,* which by an inversion of the syllables, is *Hostis adest, cave tibi.*

2. By transmutation, or a mutual changing of one letter for another in pronunciation; answerable to that form of writing, mentioned in the seventh chapter. And though this may seem of great difficulty, yet use and experience will make it easy.

3. By contracting some words, and leaving part of them out; pronouncing them after some such way as they were wont to be both written and printed in ancient copies. Thus *ā ā* stands for *anima, Arl's* for *Aristoteles.* But this can be but of small use in the English tongue, because that does consist most of monosyllables.

---

* Porta de furi. lit. l. 1. cap 5. Selenus de Cryptographia, l 2. c. 1.

4. By augmenting words with the addition of other letters. Of which kind is that secret way of discoursing in ordinary use, by doubling the vowels that make the syllables and interposing G. or any other consonant, K. P. T. R. &c. or other syllables, as Porta lib. 1. cap. 5. de furtiv. liter. notis. Thus if I would say, Our plot is discovered, it must be pronounced thus, *Ougour plogot igis digiscogovegereged.* Which does not seem so obscure in writing, as it will in speech and pronunciation. And it is so easy to be learnt, that I have known little children, almost as soon as they could speak, discourse to one another as fast this way, as they could in their plainest English.

But all these latter kinds of secrecy in speech, have this grand inconvenience in them, that they are not without suspicion*.

There are some other ways of speaking by inarticulate sounds, which I shall mention afterwards.

CHAP. IV.

Concerning the secret conveyances of any written message in use amongst the ancients.

Either by $\left\{\begin{array}{l}\text{LAND.} \\ \text{WATER.} \\ \text{THE OPEN AIR.}\end{array}\right.$

THE secrecy of any written message $\left\{\begin{array}{l}\text{Conveyance.} \\ \text{Writing.}\end{array}\right.$ may consist either in the

1. In the conveyance, when the letter is so closely concealed in the carriage of it, as to delude the search and suspicion of the adversary. Of which kind ancient historians do furnish us with divers relations, reducible in the general unto these three heads. Those that are

* Chap. 17, 18.

1. By Land.
2. By Water.
3. Through the open Air.

1. The secret conveyances by land, may be of numberless variety; but those ancient inventions of this nature, which to my remembrance are most obvious and remarkable, are these.

That of Harpagus the Mede (mentioned by Herodotus and Justin*) who when he would exhort Cyrus to a conspiracy against the king his uncle, (and not daring to commit any such message to the ordinary way of conveyance, especially since the king's jealousy had stopped up all passages with spies and watchmen) he puts his letters into the belly of a hare, which, together with certain hunters nets, he delivered unto a trusty servant, who under this disguise of a huntsman, got an unsuspected passage to Cyrus. And Astyages himself was by this conspiracy bereaved of that kingdom which was then the greatest monarchy in the world.

To this purpose likewise is that of Demaratus†, king of Sparta, who being banished from his own country, and received in the Persian court, when he there understood of Xerxes his design and preparation for a war with Greece, he used these means for the discovery of it unto his countrymen. Having written an epistle in a tablet of wood‡, he covered over the letters with wax, and then committed it unto a trusty servant, to be delivered unto the magistrates of Lacedæmon; who when they had received it, were for a long time in a perplexed consultation what it should mean; they did see nothing written, and yet could not conceive but that it should import some weighty secret; till at length the king's sister did accidentally discover the writing under the wax: by which means the Grecians

---

* Herod. l. 1. cap. 123. Justin. l. 1.

† Justin. l. 2. See the like related of Hamuear. Ib. l. 21.

‡ Such as formerly they were wont to write upon, whence the phrase *Rasa tabula*, and *litera a litura*.

were so well provided for the following war, as to give a defeat to the greatest and most numerous army that is mentioned in history.

The fathers of the council of Ephesus *, when Nestorius was condemned, being strictly debarred from all ordinary ways of conveyances, were fain to send unto Constantinople by one in the disguise of a beggar.

Some messengers have been sent away in coffins as being dead: some others in the disguise of brute creatures, as those whom Josephus mentions in the siege of Jotapata †, who crept out of the city by night like dogs.

Others have conveyed letters to their imprisoned friends, by putting them into the food they were to receive, which is related of Polycrita.   Laurentius Medicus ‡ involving his epistles in a piece of bread, did send them by a certain nobleman in the form of a beggar.   There is another relation of one, who rolled up his letters in a wax-candle, bidding the messenger tell the party that was to receive it, that the candle would give him light for his business. There is yet a stranger conveyance spoken of in Æneas ||, by writing on leaves, and afterwards with these leaves covering over some sore or putrid ulcer, where the enemy would never suspect any secret message.

Others have carried epistles inscribed upon their own flesh, which is reckoned amongst those secret conveyances mentioned by Ovid.

Caveat hoc custos, pro charta, conscia tergum
Præbeat, inque suo corpore verba ferat §.

But amongst all the ancient practices in this kind, there is none for the strangeness, to be compared unto that of Hystiæus, mentioned by Herodotus, and out of him in Aulus Gellius ¶ ; who whilst he resided with Darius in Per-

* Isaac Casa. Notis in Æneæ Polior. c. 31.
† De Bello Judaic. l. 3. c. 8.
‡ Herm. Hugo de Orig. Scrib. c. 15.   Solemn. de Crytographia, l. 8.
c. 7. || Poliorcet. c. 31.   § De Arte Amand.
¶ Herod. l. 5. c. 35. Noctes Atti. l. 17. c. 10.

sia, being desirous to send unto Aristagoras in Greece, about revolting from the Persian government (concerning which they had before conferred together) but not knowing well how at that distance to convey so dangerous a business with sufficient secrecy, he at length contrived it after this manner: he chose one of his houshold-servants that was troubled with sore eyes, pretending that for his recovery his hair must be shaved, and his head scarified; in the performance of which Hystiæus took occasion to imprint his secret intentions on his servant's head; and keeping him close at home till his hair was grown, he then told him, that for his perfect recovery, he must travel into Greece unto Aristagoras, who by shaving his hair the second time, would certainly restore him. By which relation you may see what strange shifts the ancients were put unto, for want of skill in this subject that is here discoursed of.

It is reported of some fugitive Jews* at the siege of Jerusalem, who more securely to carry away their gold, did first melt it into bullets, and then swallow it down, venting it afterwards amongst their other excrements†. Now if a man had but his faculty, who could write Homer's Iliads in so small a volume as might be contained in a nut-shell; it were an easy matter for him, by this trick of the Jews, securely to convey a whole pacquet of letters.

When all the land-passages have been stopped up, then have the ancients used other secret conveyances by water; writing their intentions on thin plates of lead, and fastening them to the arms or thighs of some expert swimmer. Frontinus § relates, that when Lucullus would inform a besieged city of his coming to succour them, he put his letters into two bladders, betwixt which a common soldier in the disguise of a sea-monster, was appointed to swim into the city. There have been likewise more exquisite inventions to pass under the water, either by a man's self, or in a boat, wherein he might also carry provision, only

---

* Joseph. de Bello Juda. l. 6. c. 15.   † Solin. Polyhist. c. 5.
§ De Stratag. l. 3. c. 13.

having a long trunk or pipe, with a tunnel at the top of it, to let down fresh air. But for the prevention of all such conveyances, the ancients were wont in their strictest sieges, to cross the rivers with strong nets*, to fasten stakes in several parts of the channel with sharp irons, as the blades of swords, sticking upon them.

3. Hence was it that there have been other means attempted through the open air, either by using birds, as pigeons and swallows, instead of messengers, of which I shall treat more particularly in the sixteenth chapter. Or else by fastening a writing to an arrow, or the weight that is cast from a sling.

Somewhat of this nature, was that intimation agreed upon betwixt David and Jonathan †, though that invention does somewhat savour of the ancient simplicity and rudeness. It was a more exact invention mentioned by Herodotus ‡ concerning Artábazus and Timoxenus, who when they could not come together, were wont to inform one another of any thing that concerned their affairs, by fastening a letter unto an arrow, and directing it unto some appointed place, where it might be received.

Thus also Cleonymus ‖ king of Lacedæmon, in the siege of the city Trezene, enjoined the soldiers to shoot several arrows into the town, with notes fastened unto them having this inscription, ‘Ηκω τον πολιν ελευθερωσαν. I come that I may restore this place to its liberty. Upon which the credulous and discontented inhabitants were very willing to let him enter.

When Cicero was so straightly besieged by the Gauls, that the soldiers were almost ready to yield; Cæsar being desirous to encourage him with the news of some other forces that were to come unto his aid, did shoot an arrow into the city, with these words fastened unto it, *Cæsar Ciceroni fiduciam optat, expecta auxilia.* By which means

---

* Plin. l. 10. c. 37.　　† 1 Sam. xx.

‡ Urania, sive l. 8. c. 128.　‖ Polyænus, l. 2. See Plutarch in Cimon.

the soldiers were persuaded to hold out so long, till these new succours did arrive and break up the siege.

The same thing might also be done more securely, by rolling up a note within the head of an arrow, and then shooting of it to a confederate's tent, or to any other appointed place.

To this purpose is that which Lypsius * relates out of Appian, concerning an ancient custom for the besieged to write their minds briefly in a little piece of lead, which they could with a sling cast a great distance, and exactly hit any such particular place as should be agreed upon, where the confederate might receive it, and by the same means return an answer.

Of this nature likewise are those kind of bullets, lately invented in these German wars, in which they can shoot, not only letters, corn, and the like, but (which is the strangest) powder also into a besieged city.

But amongst all other possible conveyances through the air, imagination itself cannot conceive any one more useful, than the invention of a flying chariot, which I have mentioned elsewhere †. Since by this means a man may have as free a passage as a bird, which is not hindered, either by the highest walls, or the deepest rivers and trenches, or the most watchful centinels. But of this perhaps I may have occasion to treat more largely in some other discourse.

* Poliorcet. L 4. c. Dialog, 2. mentioned also by Heliodor. Hist. Æthio. l. 9. † World in the Moon, chap. 14.

CHAP. V.

Of that secrecy which consists in the materials of writing,
whether the paper or ink.

THE several inventions of the ancients, for the private conveyance of any written message, were the subject of the last chapter.

The secrecy of writing may consist,

Either in { THE MATERIALS,
or,
THE FORM.

1. The materials of writing, are, the paper and ink * (or that which is instead of them), both which may be so privately ordered, that the inscribed sense shall not be discoverable, without certain helps and directions.

1. The chief contrivance of secrecy by the paper in use among the ancients, was, the Lacedemonian scytale; the manner of which was thus: there were provided two round staves, of an equal length and size, the magistrates always retaining one of them at home, and the other being carried abroad by the general, at his going forth to war. When there was any secret business to be writ by it, their manner was, to wrap a narrow thong of parchment about one of these staves, by a serpentine revolution, so that the edges of it might meet close together; upon both which edges they inscribed their epistle; whereas, the parchment being taken off, there appeared nothing but pieces of letters on the sides of it, which could not be joined together into the right sense, without the true scytale. Thus is it briefly and fully described by Ausonius †.

Vel Lacedemoniam scytalen imitare libelli,
Segmina pergamei, tereti, circumdata ligno,
Perpetuo inscribens versu, deinde solutus,
Non respondentes sparso dabit ordine formas.

---

* Selenus de Cryptogra. l. 8. c. 1. 4.   † Ausonius ad Paulinum.

You may read in Plutarch, how by this means Pharna-
baz did deceive Lysander *.

It is true, indeed, that this way was not of such inextricable secrecy, but that a litfle examination might have
easily discovered it (as Scaliger † truly observes); however, in those ages, which were less versed in these kinds
of experiments, it seemed much more secret than now it
does unto us; and in these times, there are such other
means of private discoursing, which even Scaliger's eyes
(as good as they were) could not discover ‡. And therefore it was too inconsiderate and magisterial a sentence of
him, from thence to conclude all this kind of learning to
be vain and useless, serving only for imposture, and to per-
plex the enquirer.

It is certain, that some occasions may require the exactest privacy; and it is as certain, that there may be some
ways of secrecy, which it were madness for a man to think
he could unfold. *Furori simile esse videtur, sibi aliquem
persuadere, tam circumspectum hominem esse posse, ut se à
furtivo quodam scripto, abditaque machinatione tueri possit;
nam astans quilibet, vel procul distans loquitur, & factum
nunciat, ut non solum à nemine percipiatur, sed ne sic quidem significare quippiam posse existimet,* saith Vegetius §.
And Baptista Porta ‖, who had a strange and incredible ability in discovering of secret writings, yet doth ingeniously
confess, *Multa esse posse furtiva scripta, quæ se interpre-
taturum quenquam polliceri, furorem ac delirium plane
existimarem.*

So that though the ancient inventions of this kind were
too easily discoverable, yet Scaliger had no reason to conclude this to be a needless art, or that therefore he could
unfold any other way that might be invented. But this by
the by.

2. The other material of writing, is, the ink, or that li-

---

* In Vita Lysandri.   † Exerc. 327.
‡ Vossius de Arte Gram. l. 1. c. 40.   § Veget. de re milit. l. 3.
‖ Proœm. l. 3. de furtivis notis.

quor which is used instead of it; by which means also there are sundry ways of secrecy, commonly mentioned in natural magic *.

Thus, if a man write with salt armoniac dissolved in water, the letters will not appear legible, till the paper be held by the fire: this others affirm to be true also in the juice of onions, lemons, with divers the like acid and corroding moistures.

And on the contrary; those letters that are written with dissolved alum, will not be discernible, till the paper be dipped in water.

There are some other juices, that do not appear, till the paper be held betwixt a candle and the eye.

That which is written with the water of putrified willow, or the distilled juice of glow-worms, will not be visible but in the dark; as Porta affirms from his own experience †.

There is also a secret way of writing with two several inks, both of them alike in colour, but the one being of that nature, that it will easily be rubbed or washed off, and the other not.

A man may likewise write secretly with a raw egg, the letters of which being thoroughly dried, let the whole paper be blacked over with ink, that it may appear without any inscription; and when this ink is also well dried, if you do afterwards gently scrape it over with a knife, it will fall off from those places, where before the words were written.

Those letters that were described with milk, or urine, or fat, or any other glutinous moisture, will not be legible, unless dust be first scattered upon them; which, by adhering to those places, will discover the writing. This way is mentioned by Ovid ‡:

Tuta quoque est, fallitque oculos è lacte recenti
Litera, carbonis pulvere tange, leges.

---

* Porca Magiæ, l. 16. Wecker. de Secret. l. 14. Joach. Fortius Experient. Cardan. Subt. l. 17. Item de varietate, l. 12. c. 61.

† Bibliander de Ratione com. linguarum. De furtiv, lit. l. 1. c. 15.

‡ De Arte Amandi.

And it is thought that Attalus made use of this device, the better to excite the courage of his soldiers. Being before the battle to sacrifice to the gods for success, as he pulled out the entrails of the beast, he described upon them these words, *Regis victoria*, which he had before written backward in his hand with some gummy juice. The entrails being turned up and down by the priest, to find out their signification, the letters did by that means gather so much dust as to appear legible. By which omen the soldiers were so strangely heightened in their hopes and valour, that they won the day.

Unto these experiments of secrecy in the materials of writing, some add those other ways of expressing any private intimation, by drawing a string through the holes of a little tablet or board * ; these holes should be of the same number with the letters, unto which by compact they should be severally applied. The order of the threads passing through them, may serve to express any words, and so consequently any sense we would discover.

To this purpose likewise is that other way of secret information, by divers knots tied upon a string, according to certain distances, by which a man may as distinctly, and yet as secretly, express his meaning, as by any other way of discourse. For who would mistrust any private news or treachery to lie hid in a thread, wherein there was nothing to be discerned, but sundry confused knots, or other the like marks?

The manner of performing it is thus: let there be a square piece of plate, or tablet of wood like a trencher, with the twenty-four letters described on the top of it, at equal distances, and after any order that may be agreed upon before-hand; on both the opposite sides let there be divers little teeth, on which the string may be hitched or fastened for its several returns, as in the following figure.

* Gust. Selenus de Cryptographia, l. 8. c. 3.

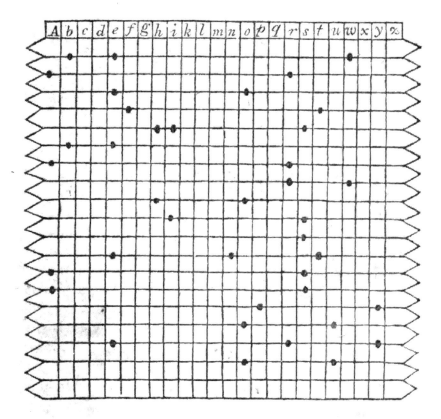

Where the string is supposed to be fastened by a loop on the first tooth, towards the letter A, and afterwards to be drawn successively over all the rest. The marks upon it do express the secret meaning: *Beware of this bearer, who is sent as a spy over you.* When it is taken off, and sent to a confederate, he may easily understand its intention, by applying it to his own tablet, which must be answerable unto this. The instrument may be made much longer than is here expressed: but if the matter to be revealed should happen to be more than the tablet would bear, then may it be supplied either by another string, or else by beginning again with that part of the same string wherein the last letter was terminated.

There may be divers other inventions of this kind, but I have not observed any more remarkable than those which are already mentioned.

CHAP. VI.

Secret writing with the common letters, by changing of their places.

THAT secrecy which does consist in the form of writing, is when the words or letters are so framed by compact, that they are not of ordinary signification *. The inventions of this kind may, both for their pleasure and benefit, justly challenge a place amongst our other studies †.

St. Austin speaking of such human inventions as are to be embraced or avoided, and rejecting all magical institutions and commerce with the devil, he adjoins, *Ea verò quæ homines cum hominibus habent, assumenda, & maxime literarum figuræ, &c. Ex eo genere sunt etiam notæ, quas qui didicerunt, proprie notarii appellantur. Utilia sunt ista, nec discuntur illicite, nec superstitiose implicant, nec luxu enervant, si tantum occupent, ut majoribus rebus, quibus inservire debent, non sint impedimento* ‡.

This way of secret writing may be contrived, either,

1. By the common letters.

2. Or by some invented notes and characters instead of them.

Both these being distinguishable into those kinds that contain either,

1. Equal.

2. Or more.

3. Or fewer signs than are naturally required to the true framing of the word.

The particulars of these may be altered to such great variety as cannot be reckoned, and therefore I shall specify

---

* Selenus de Cryptographia, l. 2. c. 5.

† Ars notarum occultandi inter artes subtilitate præstantes annumeranda est. Cardan. Subtil. l. 17.   ‡ De Doctrin. Christiana, l. 2. c. 26.

those only which seem most remarkable, either for their antiquity or usefulness.

The way of secret writing by equal letters, is, either by changing of

1. Their places, or
2. Their powers.

1. By altering of the places;

Either of the
{
LINES.
LETTERS.
BOTH,
}

1. A man may obscure the sense, by perplexing the order of the lines. If they be written, not only from the left hand to the right, but also from the right hand to the left, as in the eastern languages; or from the top to the bottom, and so upward again, as is commonly related to be usual amongst the inhabitants of Taprobana in the South Sea, with those in China and Japan *: according to this following example.

```
e   r   f   d   l   e   e   l   l   t
i   e   t   o   o   s   w   i   i   h
l   s   u   u   h   h   s   n   t   e
p   h   o   t   o   a   v   c   s   p
p   a   h   t   t   l   t   r   h   e
u   n   t   h   e   l   s   e   t   s
s   d   i   e   l   n   g   a   o   t
y   s   w   s   b   o   n   s   d   i
d   p   e   i   a   t   o   e   c   l
e   e   g   e   e   b   m   a   n   e
```

In the reading of which, if you begin at the first letter towards the right hand, and so downwards, and then upwards again, you may find these words expressed:

The pestilence doth still increase amongst us; we shall not be able to hold out the siege without fresh and speedy supply.

---

* Diodor. Sic. Biblioth. l. 2. Herman. Hugo de Orig. Scrib. c. 8.

2. A man may obscure the sense of his writing, by transposing each letter, according to some unusual order. As, suppose the first letter should be at the latter end of the line, the second at the beginning, or the like.

3. The meaning of any written message may be concealed, by altering the order both of the letters and the lines together. As if a man should write each letter in two several lines, thus:

T e o l i r a e l m s f m s e s p l v o w e u t e l
h s u d e s r a l o t a i h d, u p y s r e m s y i d

The souldiers are almost famished; supply us, or we must yield.

This way may be yet further obscured, by placing them in four lines *, and after any discontinuate order. As, suppose that the first letter be in the beginning of the first line, the second in the beginning of the fourth line, the third in the end of the first, the fourth in the end of the fourth, the fifth in the beginning of the second line, the sixth in the beginning of the third, the seventh in the end of the second, the eighth in the end of the third; and so of the rest: as in this example.

W m r p i t a h h s c t e i a p k e
h a t h f o n o i h k f t o e n i l
a n o e r r o c g t t t h m n v r l
e a u o m h t e i n l e n e t t e s

Which in its resolution is this:
We shall make an irruption upon the enemy from the north, at ten of the clock this night.

This way will yet seem more obscure, if each line be severed into such words as may seem barbarous †.

All these kinds may be varied unto divers other more in-

---

* Or as many more as the length of the epistle shall require.
† Walchius, Fab. 9.

tricate transpositions, according as a man's fancy or occasion shall lead him.

CHAP. VII.

Concerning secret Writing with equal letters, by changing their powers. The use of this amongst the Jews and Romans. The key-character.

AS a written message may be concealed by changing the places of the letters, so likewise by changing of their powers, putting one of them for another, as suppose L for A, and A for L, or the like: answerable to that kind of cabalism in the Jewish learning, which the rabbies call צירוף, or *combinatio*; when the letters of the alphabet are severally transposed, and taken one for another, after any known order *. Of which there be as many kinds, as there may be several combinations of the letters: but amongst the rest, they observe two of more frequent use. The first is stiled from the four first correspondent letters אלבם *albam;* in which they are thus opposite to one another.

א ב ג ד ה ו ז ח ט י כ
ל מ נ ס ע פ צ ק ר ש ת

The other is from the same reason called אתבש *athbash,* wherein the letters are thus mutually opposed:

א ב ג ד ה ו ז ח ט י כ
ת ש ר ק צ כ ע ס נ מ ל

Both these kinds of secret writing, the Jewish doctors think to be frequently used by the sacred penmen of holy writ; amongst whom, the prophet Isaiah and Jeremiah are observed to be of more especial note for their skill in cabalisms.

---

* Schickard in Bechinath, Haperus. Disp. l. 4. Glassius Philolog. l. 2. par. tract. 2.

By the first of these combinations, called *Albam*, that place of Isaiah vii. 6. is usually interpreted ; where there is a person mentioned, under the unknown name of טבאל *Tabeal*, whom the prophet affirms to aspire unto the crown of Judah ; meaning, by a secret transmutation of the letters, רמלה Remaliah the king of Israel, whom he was loth more expressly to nominate ; and therefore he veils it by this kind of secrecy, instead of ר writing the letter above it ט ; for מ, the correspondent letter ב ; and so ל for א, and א for ל. Which being joined together, do make טבאל, instead of רמלא.

By the second of these combinations, called *Athbash*, is that place, Jerem. li. 1. translated ; where by the original לב קמי *Cor insurgentium contra me*, is meant כשרים the Chaldæans : and therefore both the Targum, and the Septuagint do unanimously translate it so * ; as if in their version of it, they had chiefly respect unto this kind of cabalism. So likewise in 41 verse of the same chapter, by the feigned name of ששך, is meant בבל.

This way of secret writing hath been also in use amongst the ancient Romans : thus Suetonius † relates of Julius Cæsar, when he would convey any private business, he did usually write it, *per quartam elementorum literam;* that is D for A, E for B, and so of the rest, after this order.

```
d e f g h i k l m n o p q r s t u w x y z a b c
a b c d e f g h i k l m n o p q r s t u w x y z
```

Hasten unto me.
Ldwxhq yqxr ph.

And the same author reports of Octavius Augustus, that in the writing of his secrets, he did *secundum elementum proprii loco substituere*, set down the second letter for the first, as B for A, C for B, and for A a double x x.

---

* Item c. 25. v. 26. fide Hieron. com. in eundem locum.
† Sueton. in vita ejus.   A. Gellius Noct. Attic. l. 17. c. 9.

But now, because such an epistle might be easily unfolded, being altogether written by the same way; therefore this kind of secrecy hath, by later invention, been further obscured, by writing each several word, or line, or
letter, by a diverse alphabet.

For the performance of this, two friends must before-
hand, by compact, agree upon some certain form of words,
that may be instead of a key, serving both to close, and
to unlock the writing; which words would be less discoverable, if they be barbarous, and of no signification.

But for the easier apprehending of this, I shall explain
it in an example.

Suppose the key agreed upon, were only this one word
prudentia.

Having first framed several alphabets, according to each
of its letters, thus:

A	b	c	d	e	f	g	h	i	k	l	m	n	o	p	q	r	s	t	u	w	x	y	z
P	q	r	f	t	v	w	x	y	z	a	b	c	d	e	f	g	h	i	k	l	m	n	o
R	s	t	u	w	x	y	z	a	b	c	d	e	f	g	h	i	k	l	m	n	o	p	q
U	w	x	y	z	a	b	c	d	e	f	g	h	i	k	l	m	n	o	p	q	r	s	t
D	e	f	g	h	i	k	l	m	n	o	p	q	r	s	t	u	w	x	y	z	a	b	c
E	f	g	h	i	k	l	m	n	o	p	q	r	s	t	u	w	x	y	z	a	b	c	d
N	o	p	q	r	s	t	u	w	x	y	z	a	b	c	d	e	f	g	h	i	k	l	m
T	u	w	x	y	z	a	b	c	d	e	f	g	h	i	k	l	m	n	o	p	q	r	s
I	k	l	m	n	o	p	q	r	s	t	u	w	x	y	z	a	b	c	d	e	f	g	h
A	b	c	d	e	f	g	h	i	k	l	m	n	o	p	q	r	s	t	u	w	x	y	z

I may write each line, or word, or letter, according as
the order of these alphabets shall direct. As in these.

1. In the lines.

Ixt hdkasytgh bkiycn
xfi nrel fx matlmrck;
npkkfs pn, im oczs qdff
uhyrox xr xlh hqmpmh.

2. In the words.

Ixt kfmcuawik gpodhs
iru aery bs oiwnotem;
bdyytg, vs, dg lzwp qdff
uhyrox ys gur ygcfcy.

3. In the letters.

Izz wshemitin in pzgcwy
vfm zean xf kaxxznebr
skgkoc hm, xr izzb awet
rtm iox gh cht whmqwy.

Which examples being unfolded, do each of them express this inward meaning:

> *The souldiers mutiny*
> *For want of victuals;*
> *Supply us, or they will*
> *Revolt to the enemy.*

These ways may be yet further obscured, if the first alphabet, (according to which the rest are described) be contrived after any mixed order. As, suppose instead of the ordinary A b c, &c. there be written these letters, after this manner.

R z k m p s e b l a u f t c y g w h x o q i n d.

And then will they be liable to all those other differences of secrecy, that are usually invented by the wheel character, which you may see largely described by Porta.

There may be divers other ways to this purpose, but by these you may sufficiently discern the nature of the rest.

CHAP V.

*Of secret writing by more letters than are requisite
to the intended meaning.*

THE different kinds of secrecy by equal letters have
been already handled. The next particular to be dis-
cussed, is concerning the ways of hiding any private sense
under more letters than are required to the words of it.

Of which kind there may be divers particulars, some of
them in use amongst the ancients.

1. A writing may be so contrived, that only one letter in
a verse shall be significant. As it was in those remarkable
acrosticks made by a Sybil concerning our Saviour*;
where the lettters at the beginning of each verse, being
put together, made up these words, Ιησυς Χριστος Θευ υιος
σωτηρ. Jesus Christ the son of God, a Saviour.

The translation of these you may see in St. Augustin de
Civit. Dei, lib. 18. cap. 23 †. And the original are mentioned by Ludovicus Vives, in his notes upon that place.

According unto this doth Plautus contrive the names of
his comedies in the first letters of their arguments. But
this way is so ordinary in practice, that it needs not any
further explication.

2. The inward sense hath likewise been conveyed by
some single letters of several words in the same verse.
As in that common distich.

> *Mitto tibi caput Veneris, ventremque Dianæ
> Latronisque caput, posteriora canE.*

3. Sometimes one letter in each word was only significant. By which way of secret expression, the Holy Ghost
(say the rabbies) hath purposely involved many sacred mysteries in scripture. When these significant letters were at

* Sybilla Erythræa.　　　　† Beda, l. de Sybillis.

the beginning of each word, the cabalists in their learning, called such an implicit writing ראשי תיבות *capita dictionum.* When they were at the latter end, then was it stiled סופי תיבות *fines dictionum.* Both being reckoned as species of that cabalism which they called נוטריקון *notaricon,* imposed by some later rabbies from the Latin word *notarius.*

Of the first sort, is that collection from those eminent words, Gen. xlix. 10. יבא שילה ורו. Shilo shall come, and in him, &c. where the capital letters make up the word ישו Jesu.

So Psal. lxxii. 17. ינין שמו ויתברכרבו His name shall continue, and in him shall be blessed, &c. which place does expressly treat concerning the Messias his name, and therefore seems unto the Jews, to be of strong consequence for the proof of christianity. For so much is that nation befooled in their absurd dotage upon these trivial literal collections, that a reason of this nature is of greater force unto them, than the most evident solid demonstration that may be urged. Ludovicus Carret*, a famous Jew, physician to the French king, being himself converted, and writing an epistle to this purpose, unto those of his own nation, he does chiefly insist upon the arguments of this kind, as being in his opinion of greatest efficacy to prove the truth of christian religion.

Of the other sort is that passage, Gen. i. 1. היס את ברא אל where the final letters make up the word אמח or truth. Which kind of cabalism is six times repeated in the history of the creation. As if Moses by such an artificial contrivance of the letters at the beginning of his writings, did purposely commend unto our belief his following books. Unto this David is thought to allude, Psal. cxix. 160. The beginning of thy word is אמח truth. Of this nature likewise is that observation from Exod. iii. 13. לי מה שמו מה. When they shall say unto me, what

---

* Lib. Visorum Divinorum.

is his name, &c. Where the final letters answer יהוה Jehovah.

It were an easy matter for a man that had leisure and patience for such enquiries, to find out sundry arguments of this kind for any purpose.

4. There is another way of hiding any secret sense under an ordinary epistle, by having a plate * with certain holes in it, through which (being laid upon the paper) a man may write those letters or words, that serve to express the inward sense; the other spaces being afterwards filled up with such other words, as in their conjunction to these former, shall contain some common unsuspected business.

5. There is also another intricate way to this purpose, much insisted on by Trithemius, Porta, and Sylenus. When each usual word or form of an epistle, is varied to as many differences as there are letters, unto which they must all of them be severally assigned. But these two latter inventions (though they be of great secrecy, yet) because they require so much labour and trouble in the writer, I shall therefore pass them over without any further enlargement.

* Cardan de subtil. l. 17. Porta de furt. l. 2, c. 18.

CHAP. IX.

*Of concealing any written sense under barbarous words,
and such as shall not seem to be of any signification.
How all the letters may be expressed by any five, three,
or two of them. Of writing with a double alphabet.
How from these two last ways together, there may be
contrived the best kind of secret writing.*

ALL the ways of secrecy by more letters, already specified, do make the writing appear under some other
sense, than what is intended, and so consequently are
more free from suspicion: there are likewise some other
inventions to express any inward sense by barbarous words,
wherein only the first, and middle, and last letters shall be
significant. As in this example.

Fildy, fagodur wyndeeldrare discogure rantibrad.

Which in its resolution is no more than this:

Fly for we are discovered.

To this purpose likewise is that other way of expressing
the whole alphabet by any five, or three, or two of the
letters repeated. And though such a writing, to ordinary
appearance, will seem of no signification at all, and so may
seem of less use; yet because a right apprehension of these
ways may conduce to the explication of some other particulars that follow, it will not be amiss therefore to set them
down more distinctly.

All the letters may be expressed by any five of them
doubled. Suppose A B C D E.

A B C D E F G H I K L M N
aa ab ac ad ae ba bb bc bd be ca cb cc

O P Q R S T V W X Y Z. &
cd ce da db dc dd de ea eb ec ed ee

According to which, these words, *I am betrayed*, may
be thus described.

Bd aacb abaedddbaaecaead.

Three letters being transposed through three places, do give sufficient difference, whereby to express the whole alphabet.

A   B   C   D   E   F   G   H   I
aaa aab aac baa bba bbb bbc caa cca

K   L   M   N   O   P   Q   R   S
ccb ccc aba abb abc aca acb acc bca

T   V   W   X   Y   Z   &.
bcb bcc bab cba cbb cbc bac

Hasten unto me.

Caa aaa bca bcb bba abb bcc abb bcb abc aba bba.

Two letters of the alphabet being transposed through five places, will yield thirty-two differences, and so will more than serve for the four and twenty letters; unto which they may be thus applied.

A.   *B.*   *C.*   *D.*   *E.*   *F.*   *G.*
aaaaa.   aaaab.   aaaba.   aaabb.   aabaa.   aabab.   aabba.

H.   *I.*   *K.*   *L.*   *M.*   *N.*   *O.*
aabbb.   abaaa.   abaab.   ababa.   abaab.   abbaa.   abbab.

P.   *Q.*   *R.*   *S.*   *T.*   *V.*   *W.*
abbba.   abbbb.   baaaa.   baaab.   baaba.   baabb.   babaa.

X.   *Y.*   *Z.*
babab.   babba.   babbb.

aababababababba.   aaaaababaaaaaaababba.

f   l   y   a   w   a   y.

There is yet another way of secrecy by more letters than are naturally required to the inward sense; if we write with a double alphabet, wherein each letter shall in the fashion of it, bear some such small distinction from the other of the same kind, as is usual in common mixed writing. For example.

The first Alphabet.

D 2

Aa.Bb.Cc.Dd.Ee.Ff.gg. Ḥ h
Ji.Kk.LLMm.Nn.Oo.Pp. Qq.
Rr.S∫s.Tt.Vuv.Ww.Xx. Yy.Zz.

the second Alphabet.

Aa.Bb.Cc.Dd.Ee.ff.Gg.Hh
Ji.Kk.LL.MmXn.Oo.Pp.Qq.
Rr.S∫s. Tt.Vuv.Ww.Xx.Yy.Zz.

1. Write an epistle of an ordinary matter, or (if it be needful) contrary to what you intend. Let the body of it consist chiefly of the first alphabet, only inserting (as you have occasion) such letters of the second, as may express that inward meaning which you would reveal to a confederate.

For example, from those that are besieged.

Wee prosper still in our af=
faires. and shall (without
hauing any further helpe)
endure the siege.

In which clause, the letters of the second alphabet are only significant, expressing this inward sense. ·

Weeperiſh with hunger helpe us

But because the differences betwixt these two alphabets may seem more easily discoverable, since they are both generally of the same kind, the letters of the second being all of them more round and full than the other ; therefore for their better secrecy in this particular, it were safer to mix them both by compact, that they might not in themselves be distinguishable.

Now if this kind of writing be mixed with the latter way of secrecy, by two letters transposed through five places, we may then write *omnia per omnia,* (which as a learned man speaks *) is the highest degree of this cyphering.

For supposing each letter of the first alphabet to be instead of the letter A, and those of the other for B, we may easily inscribe any secret sense in any ordinary letter, only by a quintuple proportion of the writing infolding to the writing infolded.   As for example.

* Bacon. Augment. Scient. l. 6. c. 8.

All things do happen ac cording to our desires, the particulars you shall vnder stand when wee meete at the appointed time and place of which you must not faile by any means The success of our affairs dos much depend, vpon the meeting that wee have agreed vpon.

The involved meaning of which clause is this:

Fly, for we are discovered, I am forced to write this.

If you suppose each letter of the first alphabet to be instead of A, and those of the second for B, then will the former clause be equivalent to this following description.

Aabab	ababa	babba	aabab	abbab	baaaa	babaa
F	l	y	f	o	r	w
aabaa	aabaa	aaaaa	baaaa	aabaa	aaabb	abaaa
e	e	a	r	e	d	i
baaab	aaaba	abbab	baabb	aabaa	baaaa	aabaa
s	c	o	v	e	r	e
aaabb	abaaa	aaaaa	ababb	aabab	abbab	baaaa
d,	I	a	m	f	o	r
aaaba	aabaa	aaabb	baaba	abbab	babaa	baaaa
c	e	d	t	o	w	r
abaaa	baaba	aabaa	baaba	aabbb	abaaa	baaab.
i	t	e	t	h	i	s.

This way of secrecy may be serviceable for such occasions as these. Suppose a man were taken captive, he may by this means discover to his friends the secrets of the enemy's camp, under the outward form of a letter persuading them to yield. Or, suppose such a man were forced by his own hand-writing to betray his cause and party, though the words of it in common appearance may express what the enemy does desire; yet the involved meaning (which shall be legible only to his confederates), may contain any thing else which he has a mind to discover to them: as in the former example.

But now if there be a threefold alphabet (as is easy to contrive), then the inward writing will bear unto the outward but a triple proportion, which will be much more convenient for enlarging of the private intimations.

And this way of writing is justly to be preferred before any of the other, as containing in it more eminently, all those conditions that are desirable in such kind of inventions. As,

1. It is not very laborious either to write or read.
2. It is very difficult to be decyphered by the enemy.
3. It is void of suspicion.

But by the way, it is to be generally observed, that the mixture of divers kinds of secret writing together (as suppose this with the key-character) will make the inward sense to be much more intricate and perplexed.

CHAP. X.

Of writing any secret sense by fewer letters than are re-quired to the words of it. The use of this amongst the Jews and Romans.

AS the sense may be obscured by writing it with more letters than are required to the words of it, so like-wise by fewer. Abbreviations have been anciently used in all the learned languages, especially in common forms, and phrases of frequent use. Sometimes by contracting words, when some parts of them did stand for the whole*. So in the Hebrew, וכו׳ for וכולו *et totum illud*, which is all one with our *et cetera*, &c. כל׳ for כלומר *secundum dicere*, equivalent to our *viz.* or *v. g. verbi gratia*. So likewise in the Greek, Χϛ for Χριστος, and ανΘ for ανΘρωπος. And in the Latin, *Dns* for *Dominus*; *āā* for *anima*, and the like. But these were rather for the speed of writing, than the secrecy.

Sometimes words were expressed only by their first let-ters. Thus did the Jews write all their memorials, and common forms, which are largely handled by Buxtorf. Hence was it, that their captain Judas had his name of Maccaby; for being to fight against Antiochus, he gave that saying for his watch-word, Exod. xv. מי כמכה באלהים יהוה. Who is like unto thee (O Lord) amongst the gods? in-scribing in his ensigns the capital letters of it, מכב׳ Mac-cabi. Whereupon after the victory, the soldiers stiled their captain by that name.

It is observed by the Rabbies, that many grand mysteries are this way implied in the words of Scripture. Thus, where

* Buxtorf. de Abbreviat. in initio.

it is said, Psalm iii. רבמ Many rise up against me, it is interpreted from the several letters, Resh the Romans, Beth the Babylonians, Jod the Ionians or Grecians, Mem the Medes. Answerable unto which, that place in Gen. xlix, 10. (speaking of Shilo, unto whom יקהת the gathering of the people shall be) is by another Rabby applied to the Jews, Christians, Heathens, and Turks.

Upon these grounds likewise, is that argument to prove the trinity, from the first verse of Genesis. ברא אלהים The word אלהים Elohim, being of the plural number, is thought to be that divine name which denoteth the persons of the deity; which persons are more particularly intimated in the letters of the verb ברא, that answers unto it: ב Beth being put for מ the Son, ר Resh for רוח the Holy Ghost, א Aleph for אב the Father. And if you will believe the Jews, the holy spirit hath purposely involved in the words of scripture, every secret that belongs to any art or science, under such cabalisms as these. And if a man were but expert in unfolding of them, it were easy for him to get as much knowledge as Adam had in his innocency, or human nature is capable of.

These kind of mysterious interpretations from particular letters, do seem to be somewhat favoured, by God's addition of the letter ה unto the name of Abraham and Sarah *, upon the renewing of his covenant with them; which in all likelihood was not without some secret mystery. That being the chief letter of the tetragrammaton, might perhaps intimate that amongst their other posterity, with the promise of which he had then blessed them, they should also be the parents of the Messias, who was Jehovah.

This likewise others have confirmed from the example of Christ †, who calls himself Alpha and Omega. Rev. i. 8.

But though such conjectures may be allowable in some particulars, yet to make all scriptures capable of the like secrets, does give such a latitude to men's roving and corrupt fancies, as must needs occasion many wild and strange

---

* Gen. xvii. 5. 15.   † Vide Tertul. l. de præscr. c. 50.

absurdities. And therefore Irenæus* does fitly observe, that from such idle collections as these, many heresies of the Valentinians and Gnostics had their first beginnings.

As this way of short writing by the first letters, was of ancient use among the Jews, so likewise amongst the Romans, which appears from many of their contractions yet remaining, as *S. P. D. Salutem plurimum dicit. S. Pq. R. Senatus populusque Romanus.   C. R. Civis Romanus. U. C. Urbs condita.*   And the like.

These single letters were called *syglæ, per syncopen,* from the obsolete word *sigillæ,* whence *sigillatim.*   They were usually inscribed in their coins, statues, arms, monuments, and public records.   You may see them largely treated of by Valerius Probus †, where he affirms the study of them to be very necessary for one that would under-stand the Roman affairs.   *His enim exprimebant nomina curiarum, tribuum, comitiorum, sacerdotiorum, potestatum, magistratuum, præfecturarum, sacrorum ludorum, rerum ur-banarum, rerum militarium, collegiorum, decuriarum, fas-torum, numerorum, mensurarum, juris civilis, & similium.*

They were first used by their notaries, at senates and other public assemblies, and from thence retained in their statutes and civil laws: whence Manilius makes it the note of a good lawyer.

> ———*Qui legum tabulas & condita jura*
> *Noverit, atque notis levibus pendentia verba.*

Thus (saith Isidor ‡) (A) inversed ɐ did formerly stand for *pupilla,* and M inversed ꟽ for *mulier.*   By these letters *D. E. R. I. C. P.* is signified, *De ea re ita censuerunt patres.*

When the judges were to inscribe their several opinions on a little stone or tessera, to be cast into the urn; by the note Λ, they did absolve, by K § condemn; by *N. L. Non*

---

* Iren. l. 1. c. 13.

† Lib. de liter. antiquis.   As it is set forth by Jacobus Mazochius.

‡ Isidor. Bibliand. de ratione com. ling.   Pet. Crinit. Honest. Disc. l. 6. c. 8.

§ From the Greek καταδικαζειν.

liquet, they did intimate that they could not tell what to make of the business, and did therefore suspend their judgments.

But because of those many ambiguities which this contracted way of writing was liable unto, and the great inconveniences that might happen thereupon in the misinterpretation of laws; therefore the emperor Justinian did afterward severely forbid any further use of them, as it were, calling in all those law-books that were so written *. *Neque enim licentiam aperimus ex tali codice in judicium aliquid recitari.*

The chief purpose of these ancient abbreviations amongst the Romans, was properly for their speed. But it is easy to apprehend how by compact they may be contrived also for secrecy.

CHAP. XI.

Of writing by invented characters.

The distinction of these into such as signify, either, { LETTERS. WORDS. NOTIONS. }

The general rules of unfolding and obscuring any letter-characters. How to express any sense, either by points, or lines, or figures.

BESIDES the ways of secret writing by the common letters, there may likewise be divers others by invented notes.

The difference of characters, whereby several languages are expressed, is part of the second general curse in the confusion of tongues; for as before there was but one way of speaking, so also but one way of writing. And as now, not only nations, but particular men, may discover their

* Lib. 1. Cod. Tit. 17. leg. 1, 2.

thoughts by any different articulate sounds, so likewise by any written signs.

These invented characters in the general, are distinguishable into such as signify, either

    1. *Letters.*

    2. *Words.*

    3. *Things, and notions.*

First, concerning those that signify letters : to which kind some learned men* refer the Hebrew character that is now in use ; affirming, that Ezra first invented it, thereby the better to conceal the secrets of their law, and that they might not have so much as their manner of writing common with the Samaritans and other schismatics.

It were but needless to set down any particulars of this kind, since it is so easy for any ordinary man to invent or vary them at pleasure.

The rules that are usually prescribed for the unfolding of such characters, are briefly these.

1. Endeavour to distinguish betwixt the vowels and consonants. The vowels may be known by their frequency, there being no word without some of them. If there be any single character in English, it must be one of these three vowels, *a, i, o.*

2. Search after the several powers of the letters : for the understanding of this, you must mark which of them are most common, and which more seldom used. (This the printers in any language can easily inform you of, who do accordingly provide their sets of letters.) Which of them may be doubled, and which not, as *H, 2, X, Y.* And then, for the number of vowels or consonants in the beginning, middle, or end of words, a man must provide several tables, whence he may readily guess at any word, from the number and nature of the letters that make it : as, what words consist only of vowels ; what have one vowel, and one consonant ; whether the vowel be first, as in these

* Hieronym. præf ad lib. Regum. Joseph Scal. notis ad Euseb.

words, *am, an, as, if, in, is, it, of, on, or, us*; or last, as in these words, *Be, he, me, by, dy, ly, my, ty, do, to, so,* &c. And so for all other words, according to their several quantities and natures.

These tables must be various, according to the difference of languages. There are divers the like rules to be observed, which are too tedious to recite; you may see them largely handled by Baptista Porta, and Gustavus Selenus.

The common rules of unfolding being once known, a man may the better tell how to delude them; either by leaving out those letters that are of less use, as *H, K, 2, X, Y*; and putting other characters instead of them, that shall signify the vowels: so that the number of this invented alphabet will be perfect; and the vowels, by reason of their double character, less distinguishable. Or a man may likewise delude the rules of discovery, by writing continuately, without any distinction betwixt the words, or with a false distinction, or by inserting nulls and non-significants, &c.

These characters are besides liable to all those other ways whereby the common letters may be obscured, whether by changing their places, or their powers.

The particulars of this kind, may be of such great variety, as cannot be distinctly recited: but it is the grand inconvenience of all these ways of secrecy by invented characters, that they are not without suspicion.

For the remedying of which, there have been some other inventions of writing by points, or lines, or figures; wherein a man would never mistrust any private message, there being nothing to be discerned in these kinds of intimation, but only either some confused and casual, or else some mathematical descriptions; as you may see in these following examples.

NEW JERSEY COLLEGE LIBRARY

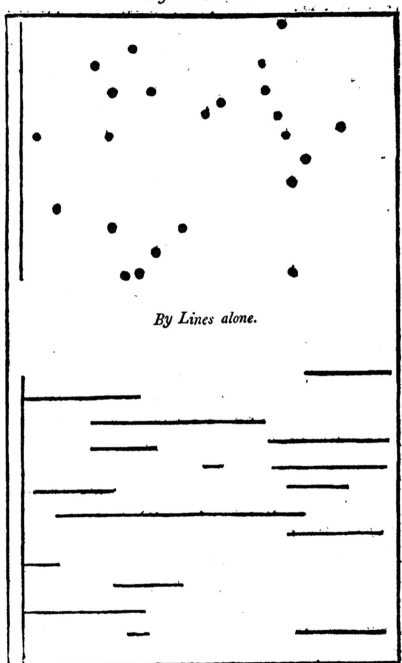

By Points alone.

By Lines alone.

By Mathematical Figures.

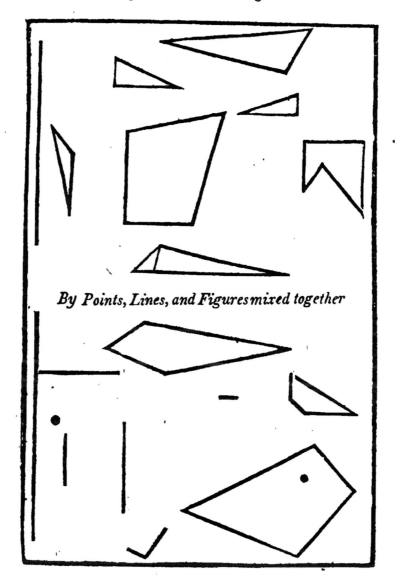

By Points, Lines, and Figures mixed together

Each of which figures do express these words :

There is no safety but by flight.

The direction both for the making and unfolding of these descriptions, is this : let the alphabet be described at equal distances, upon some thin and narrow plate, pasteboard, or the like, thus:

A b c d e f g h i k l m n o p q r s t u w x y z

Let the sides of the paper which you are to write upon, be secretly divided into equal parts, according to the breadth of the plate; and then by application of this to the epistle, it is easy to conceive how such a writing may be both composed and resolved. The points, the ends of the lines, and the angles of the figures, do each of them, by their different situations, express a several letter.

This may likewise be otherwise performed, if the alphabet be contrived in a triangular form, the middle part of it being cut out.

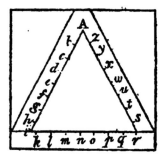

The larger these directories are, by so much the less liable unto error will the writing be, that is described from them.

It is easy to apprehend by these particulars, how a man may contrive any private saying in the form of a landscape, or other picture*. There may be divers the like ways, whereby this invention of secrecy may be further obscured; but they are in themselves so obvious, that they need not any larger explication.

* Joh. Walchius, Fab. 9.

CHAP. XII.

Of characters that express words. The first invention of these. Of those that signify things and notions, as hieroglyphics, emblems.

THE next particular to be discoursed of, is, concerning characters that express words. The writing by these is properly stiled Stenography, or short-hand; *Scripturæ compendium, cum verba non perscribimus, sed signamus,* saith Lypsius *. The art of them is, to contrive such figures for several syllables, as may easily be joined together in one form, according as different words shall require. Thus it is ordinary to represent any proper name by some such unusual character, as may contain in it all the letters of that name for which it is intended. Of this nature was that angular figure so much used by the Grecians of old, which might be resolved into the letters υγιεα †.]

This mark was esteemed so sacred amongst the ancients, that Antiochus Soter, a perpetual conqueror, did always instamp it upon his coin, and inscribe it on his ensigns; unto which he did pretend to be admonished in a dream, by an apparition of Alexander the Great. And there are many superstitious women in these times, who believe this to be so lucky a character, that they always work it upon the swaddling clothes of their young children, thinking thereby to make them more healthful and prosperous in

* Cent. 1. ad Belg. Epist. 27.   † Schikard Happer. Disp. 5.

their lives. Unto this kind also, some refer the characters that are used in magic, which are maintained to have, not only a secret signification, but likewise a natural efficacy.

This short-hand writing is now so ordinary in practice (it being usual for any common mechanic both to write and invent it) that I shall not need to set down any particular example of it. In ancient times it was not so frequently used; but then there was a twofold kind of it.

PRIVATE.

PUBLIC.

These private characters were practised by the Roman magistrates, and others of eminent favour amongst them; who being often importuned to write in the commendation of those persons they knew not, were fain to agree upon some secret notes, whereby their serious epistles might be distinguished from those of form *. Whence the proverb arose, *De meliori nota commendare.*

The other characters of public and common use, are many of them explained by Valerius Probus, in his book *de Literis Antiquis*; and there is a whole volume, or dictionary of them, set forth by Janus Gruterus. From the practice of these came the word *notarius*, as St. Austin † observes.

The first invention of them is commonly ascribed to Tyro, who was a servant unto Cicero. So Eusebius ‡, and Polydore Virgil §. But Trithemius affirms, that Cicero himself writ a treatise on this subject, which was afterwards augmented by St. Cyprian: and that he had found in an old library, the copy of a psalter written in these characters, inscribed by some ignorant man with this title, *Psalterium in Lingua Armenica.*

That Cicero ‖ was not unacquainted with these notes,

---

* And therefore Pancirollus reckons it amongst these later inventions, l. de Repert. tit. 14. Casaubon. notis in Æne. Poliorcet. c. 31. De notis Tyronis & Senec.

† De Doct. Christ. l. 2. c. 26.   ‡ In Chron.

§ De invent. rerum, l. 2. c. 8   De Polygr.

‖ Lib. 13. ad Attic. Ep. 32.

may be evident from that passage to Atticus: *Quod ad te de legatis scripsi, parum intellexit, credo, quia διὰ σημειων scripseram.*

Pet. Diaconus * attributes the first invention of these to the old poet Ennius; whose beginnings in this kind, did afterwards receive successive addition from the works of Tyro, Philargirus, Aquila, and Seneca the father; by whom they were increased to the number of 5000.

But Hermannus Hugo †, a late jesuit, will have this short-hand writing to be of far more ancient use; affirming, that David alludes to the practice of it, in that phrase, Psalm xlv. 1. The pen of a ready writer. And that the writing upon the wall, in Dan. v. 25. which so puzzled the Chaldean wizards, was described in such kind of characters. But whether this were so, or not, is not much material: it is sufficiently pertinent to the present enquiry, that the use of these word-characters may well enough conduce to the secrecy of any written message.

The third and last sort of signs, that have been anciently used for the expression of things and notions, are either hieroglyphics, or emblems.

1. Concerning hieroglyphics. The word signifies sacred sculptures, which were engraven upon pillars, obelisks, pyramids, and other monuments, before the invention of letters. Thus the Egyptians ‡ were wont to express their minds, by the pictures of such creatures as did bear in them some natural resemblance to the thing intended §. By the shape of a bee, they represented a king; intimating, that he should be endowed with industry, honey, and a sting. By a serpent, with his tail in his mouth, the year, which returns into itself: and (which was a kind of prophetical hieroglyphic) by the sign of a cross, they did anciently denote *spem venturæ salutis,* or *vitam eternam,* as

---

* Prolog. not. Conrad. Imp. Isidor. Orig. l. 1. c. 21.
† De Orig. scribendi, c. 18. juxta finem.   ‡ Tacit. Annal. l. 11.
§ Pol. Virgil. de Invent. l. 3. c. 11.

Pet. Crinitus relates out of Ruffinus *. Philo † reckons up the knowledge of these amongst those other abstruse Egyptian arts, wherein Moses is said to be so expert. And Clemens relates of Pythagoras, how he was content to be circumcised, that so he might be admitted to the understanding of those many and great mysteries which were this way delivered by the ancient priests, who did conceal all their learning under such kind of magical expressions, as the poet ‡ stiles them.

> *Nondum flumineas Memphis contexere byblos*
> *Noverat, & saxis tantum volucresque feræque,*
> *Sculptaque servabant magicas animalia linguas.*

Plutarch § speaks of a temple in Egypt dedicated to Minerva, in the front of which there was placed the image of an infant, an old man, a hawk, by which they did represent God; a fish, the expression of hatred; and a sea-horse, the common hieroglyphic of impudence: the construction of all being this; O ye that are born to die, know that God hateth impudence.

Of this nature were those presents sent unto Darius ‖, when he was almost wearied in his war against the Scythians; which were, a bird, a mouse, a frog, and certain arrows; intimating, that unless the Persians could fly as birds, or hide themselves under water as frogs, or inhabit the caverns of the earth as mice, they should not escape the Scythian arrows. Of this kind likewise were some military signs amongst the Romans. When any thing was to be carried with silence and secrecy, they lifted up the representation of a minotaur ¶; thereby teaching the captains, that their counsels and contrivances must be as inextricable as a labyrinth, which is feigned to be the habitation of that monster.

---

* De honesta disciplina, l. 7. c. 2.
† Lib. de vita Mosis.   Lib. 1. Stromat.   ‡ Lucan, l. 3.
§ Lib. de Isid. & Osiride.
‖ Herodot. Melpom. l. 4. c. 130.   Cl. Alex. Strom. 5.
¶ Pierius Hieroglyph. l. 3. c. 38.

2. Like unto these hieroglyphics, are the expressions by emblems *. They were usually inserted as ornaments upon vessels of gold, and other matters of state or pleasure. Of this nature are the stamps of many ancient medals, the impresses of arms, the frontispieces of books, &c.

The kinds of them are chiefly twofold.

1. Natural. Which are grounded upon some resemblance in the property and essence of the things themselves. So a dolphin, which is a swift creature, being described upon an anchor, which serves for the stay and rest of a ship, signifies *festina lente*, deliberation in counsel, and dispatch in execution: a young stork carrying the old one, filial gratitude.

2. Historical. Those that refer to some common relation. So the picture of Prometheus gnawed by a vulture, signifies the desert of over-much curiosity. Phaeton, the folly of rashness. Narcissus, the punishment of self-love.

It was formerly esteemed a great sign of wit and invention, handsomely to convey any noted saying under such kind of expressions.

CHAP. XIII.

Concerning an universal character, that may be legible to all nations and languages. The benefit and possibility of this.

AFTER the fall of Adam, there were two general curses inflicted on mankind: the one upon their labours, the other upon their language.

Against the first of these we do naturally endeavour to provide, by all those common arts and professions about

---

* Emblems, from the Greek word εμβαλλεσθαι, interserere, injicere.

which the world is busied; seeking thereby to abate the sweat of their brows in the earning of their bread.

Against the other, the best help that we can yet boast of, is the Latin tongue, and the other learned languages, which by reason of their generality, do somewhat restore us from the first confusion. But now if there were such an universal character to express things and notions, as might be legible to all people and countries, so that men of several nations might with the same ease both write and read it, this invention would be a far greater advantage in this particular, and mightily conduce to the spreading and promoting of all arts and sciences: because that great part of our time which is now required to the learning of words, might then be employed in the study of things. Nay, the confusion at Babel might this way have been remedied, if every one could have expressed his own meaning by the same kind of character. But then perhaps the art of letters was not invented.

That such a manner of writing is already used in some parts of the world, the kingdoms of the high Levant, may evidently appear from divers credible relations. Trigaultius affirms, that though those of China and Japan* do as much differ in their language as the Hebrew and the Dutch; yet either of them can, by this help of a common character, as well understand the books and letters of the others, as if they were only their own.

And for some particulars, this general kind of writing is already attained amongst us also.

1. Many nations do agree in the characters of the common numbers, describing them either the Roman way by letters, as I. II. V. X. C. D. M. or else the Barbarian way by figures, as 1. 2. 3. 10. &c. So likewise for that which we call philosophical number, which is any such measure whereby we judge the differences betwixt several substances, whether in weight, or length, or capacity; each of

---

* Histor. Sinens. l. 1. c. 5.   Bacon Augment. Scient. l. 6. c. 13.
Voss. Gr. l. 1. c. 41.   Herm. Hugo de Orig. scrib. c. 4.

these are expressed in several languages by the same character. Thus Ə signifies a scruple, ʒ a drachm, and so of
the rest.

2. The astronomers of several countries do express both
the heavenly signs, and planets, and aspects by the same
kind of notes, as ♈, ♉, ♊, ♋, &c. ♄, ♃, ♂, ♀,
&c. ☌, ✳, △, ☐, ☍. Which characters (as it is
thought) were first invented by the ancient astrologers for
the secrecy of them, the better to conceal their sacred and
mysterious profession from vulgar capacity.

3. The chymical treatises that are written in different
languages, do all of them agree in the same form of writing their minerals. Those that are attributed to any of the
planets, are decyphered by the character of the planet to
which they belong. The rest by other particular signs, as
△ for salt ammoniac, ♂ for arsenic, &c.

4. Musical notes in most countries are the same : nor is
there any reason why there may not be such a general
kind of writing invented for the expression of every thing
else as well as these particulars.

In the contrivance of this there must be as many several
characters as there are primitive words. To which purpose the Hebrew is the best pattern, because that language
consists of fewest radicals.

Each of these primitives must have some particular
marks to distinguish the cases, conjugations, or other necessary variations of those derivatives that depend upon it.

In the reading of such a writing, though men of several countries should each of them differ in their voices, and
pronouncing several words, yet the sense would be still the
same. As it is in the picture of a man, a horse, or tree ;
which to all nations do express the same conceit, though
each of these creatures be stiled by several names, according to the difference of languages.

Suppose that astronomical sign ♉ were to be pronounced, a Jew would call it שׁור ; a Grecian ταυρον ; an Ita-

lian, toro; a Frenchman, *taureau*; a German, *stier*; an Englishman, *a bull*.

So likewise for that character, which in Tiro's notes signifies the world, a Jew would read it תבל; a Grecian Κοσμῷ; an Italian, *il monde*; a Frenchman, *le monde*; a German, *belt*. Though several nations may differ in the expression of things, yet they all agree in the same conceit of them.

The learning of this character will not be more difficult than the learning of any one language, because there needs not be more signs for the expression of things, than there is now for the expression of words. Amongst those in China and Japan, there is said to be about seven or eight thousand.

The perfecting of such an invention were the only way to unite the seventy-two languages of the first confusion; and therefore may very well deserve their endeavours who have both abilities and leisure for such kind of enquiries.

CHAP. XIV.

Concerning the third way of secret discoursing by signs and gestures, which may signify, either

$$\text{Ex} \begin{cases} \text{Congruo.} \\ \text{Placito.} \end{cases}$$

THE third way of discoursing was by signs and gestures, which (as they are serviceable to this purpose) may be distinguished into such as are significant, either

1. Ex congruo.
2. Or ex placito.

1. *Ex congruo*, when there is some natural resemblance and affinity betwixt the action done, and the thing to be

exprest. Of which kind are all those outward gestures, whereby not only dumb creatures, but men also do express their inward passions, whether of joy, anger, fear, &c. For,

Sæpe tacens vocem verbaque vultus habet.

And the wise man notes it of the scorner, That he winketh with his eyes, he speaketh with his feet, he teacheth with his fingers *.

Of this kind likewise are many religious actions, and circumstances of divine worship, not only amongst the ancient heathen, but some that were particularly enjoined the priests and levites of the old law; and some too that are now in use in these times of the gospel. For by such bodily gestures and signs, we may as well speak unto God as unto men.

To this kind also are reducible those actions of form, that are required as necessary circumstances in many civil affairs and public solemnities, which are usually such, as in themselves are apt to signify the thing for which they are meant.

But now sometimes the intended meaning of these gestures is concealed under a secret similitude. As it was in that act of Thrasybulus, who being consulted with, how to maintain a tyranny that was newly usurped: he bid the messenger attend him in the field; where with his wand he whipt off those higher ears of corn that did over-top the rest; intimating, that it consisted in cutting off the peers and nobility, who were likely to be most impatient of subjection. This I may call a parabolical way of speaking by gestures.

2. *Ex placito*, when these signs have their signification from use and mutual compact; which kind of speaking, as it refers to lascivious intimations, is largely handled by *Ovid, de Arte amandi.*

---

* Prov. vi. 13.

Verba superciliis sine voce loquentia dicam,
Verba leges digitis, &c.

By the help of this it is common for men of several nations, who understand not one another's languages, to entertain a mutual commerce and traffic. And it is a strange
thing to behold, what dialogues of gestures there will pass
betwixt such as are born both deaf and dumb ; who are
able by this means alone, to answer and reply unto one
another as directly if they had the benefit of speech. It is
a great part of the state and majesty belonging to the Turkish emperor, that he is attended by mutes, with whom
he may discourse concerning any private business, which
he would not have others to understand.

It were a miserable thing for a rational soul to be imprisoned in such a body as had no way at all to express its
cogitations ; which would be so in all that are born deaf,
if that which nature denied them, were not in this respect
supplied by a second nature, custom and use.

But (by the way) it is very observable which Valesius *
relates of Pet. Pontius a friend of his, who by an unheard-
of art taught the deaf to speak. *Docens primum scribere,
res ipsas digito indicando, quæ characteribus illis significa-
rentur ; deinde ad motus linguæ, qui characteribus respon-
derent provocando.* First learning them to write the name
of any thing he should point to ; and afterwards provoking
them to such motions of the tongue as might answer the
several words. It is probable that this invention well fol-
lowed, might be of singular use for those that stand in
need of such helps. Though certainly that was far beyond it, (if true) which is related of an ancient doctor,
Gabriel Neale, that he could understand any word by the
mere motion of the lips, without any utterance.

The particular ways of discoursing by gestures, are not
to be numbered, as being almost of infinite variety, according as the several fancies of men shall impose significations

* Sacra Philos. c. 3.

upon all such signs or actions as are capable of sufficient difference.

But some there are of more especial note for their use and antiquity. Such is that upon the joints and fingers of the hand, commonly stiled *arthrologia*, or *dactylologia*; largely treated of by the venerable Bede[*], Pierius[†], and others. In whom you may see, how the ancients were wont to express any number by the several postures of the hands and fingers: the numbers under a hundred, were denoted by the left hand, and those above, by the right hand. Hence Juvenal[‡], commending Rylias for his old age, says, that he reckoned his years upon his right hand.

> *Fœlix nimirum qui tot per sæcula vitam*
> *Distulit, atque suos jam dextra computat annos.*

There are divers passages in the ancient authors, both sacred and profane, which do evidently allude to this kind of reckoning.

Hence it is easy to conceive, how the letters as well as the numbers, may be thus applied to the several parts of the hand, so that a man might with divers touches, make up any sense that he hath occasion to discover unto a confederate.

This may be performed, either as the numbers are set down in the authors before-cited; or else by any other way of compact that may be agreed upon.

As for example: let the tops of the fingers signify the five vowels; the middle parts, the five first consonants; the bottoms of them, the five next consonants; the spaces betwixt the fingers the four next. One finger laid on the side of the hand may signify T, two fingers V the consonant, three W, the little finger crossed X, the wrist Y, the middle of the hand Z.

But because such various gesticulations as are required to this, will not be without suspicion, therefore it were a bet-

---

[*] Lib. de loquelâ per gestum digitorum sive de indigitatione.
[†] Hieroglyphic. l. 37. c. 1. &c. Cælius antiq. lect. l. 23. c. 12.
[‡] Satyr. 10.

ter way, to impose significations upon such actions as are of more common unsuspected use; as scratching of the head, rubbing the several parts of the face, winking of the eyes, twisting of the beard, &c. Any of which, or all of them together, may be as well contrived to serve for this purpose, and with much more secrecy.

In which art, if our gaming cheats, and popish miracle-impostors, were but well versed, it might much advantage them, in their cozening trade of life.

CHAP. XV.

Concerning the swiftness of informations, either by quali-
ties, as the impression of imagination, and the sensitive
species; or by spiritual substances, as angles.

HAVING already treated concerning the several ways of secrecy in discoursing, I shall in the next place enquire, how a man may with the greatest swiftness and speed, discover his intentions to one that is far distant from him.

There is nothing (we say) so swift as thought, and yet the impression of these in another, might be as quick almost as the first act, if there were but such a great power in imagination, as some later philosophers * have attributed to it.

Next to the acts of thought, the species of sight do seem to be of the quickest motion. We see the light of the east will in a moment fill the hemisphere, and the eye

* Marsil. Ficin. Theolog. Platon. l. 3. c. 1. Pomponatius de Incantat. Paracelsus.

does presently discern an object that is very remote. How we may by this means communicate our thoughts at great distances, I shall discourse afterwards.

The substances that are most considerable for the swiftness of their motion, are

Either $\begin{cases} \text{SPIRITUAL.} \\ \text{CORPOREAL.} \end{cases}$

Amongst all created substances, there are not any of so swift a motion as angels or spirits. Because there is not either within their natures, any such indisposition and reluctancy, or without them in the medium, any such impediment as may in the least manner retard their courses. And therefore have the ancient philosophers employed these as the causes of that mad celerity of the celestial orbs; though according to their suppositions, I think it would be a hard match, if there were a race to be run betwixt the *primum mobile* and an angel. It being granted that neither of them could move in an instant, it would be but an even lay which should prove the swifter.

From the fitness of spirits in this regard to convey any message, are they in the learned languages called messengers [*].

Now if a man had but such familiarity with one of these, as Socrates is said to have with his tutelary genius [†]; if we could send but one of them upon any errand, there would be no quicker way than this for the dispatch of business at all distances.

That they have been often thus employed, is affirmed by divers relations. Vatinius being at Rome, was informed by an apparition of that victory which Paulus their general had obtained over king Perses in Macedon, the very same day wherein the battle was fought; which was a long time before any other messenger could arrive with the news [‡].

[*] מלאך, αγγελος, Angelus.
[†] Plutarch. Maximus Tyrius. Dissertat. 26. 27,
[‡] Lactant. Inst. l. 2. ep 8. Val. Max. l. 1. c. 8. Florus, lib. 2. c. 12.

And it is storied of many others, that whilst they have resided in remote countries, they have known the death of their friends, even in the very hour of their departure; either by bleeding, or by dreams, or some such way of intimation. Which, though it be commonly attributed to the operation of sympathy; yet it is more probably to be ascribed unto the spirit or genius. There being a more especial acquaintance and commerce betwixt the tutelary angels of particular friends, they are sometimes by them informed (though at great distances) of such remarkable accidents as befall one another.

But this way there is little hopes to advantage our enquiry, because it is not so easy to employ a good angel, nor safe dealing with a bad one.

The abbot Trithemius, in his books concerning the several ways of secret and speedy discoursing, does pretend to handle the forms of conjuration, calling each kind of character by the name of spirits, thereby to deter the vulgar from searching into his works. But under this pretence, he is thought also to deliver some diabolical magic. Especially in one place, where he speaks of the three saturnine angels, and certain images, by which, in the space of twenty-four hours, a man may be informed of news from any part of the world*. And this was the main reason, why by Junius his advice, Frederic the second, prince palatine, did cause the original manuscript of that work to be burned. Which action is so much (though it should seem unjustly) blamed by Selenus†.

* Vossius Gram. l. 1. c. 41.   Polygraph. l. 3. c. 16.
† Cryptogr. l. 3. c. 15.

CHAP. XVI.

Concerning the swiftness of conveyance by bodies, whether inanimate, as arrows, bullets; or animate, as men, beasts, birds.

THE bodies that are most eminent for their swiftness, may be distinguished into such as are

Either { INANIMATE.
{ ANIMATE.

These inanimate bodies, as arrows, bullets, &c. have only a violent motion; which cannot therefore be continued to so great a distance, as some occasions would require: but for so much space as they do move, they are far swifter than the natural motion of any animated body. How these have been contrived to the speedy conveyance of secret messages, hath been formerly discoursed, in the fourth chapter, which I now forbear to repeat.

Those living bodies that are most observable for their speed and celerity in messages, are either men, beasts, birds: though I doubt not, but that fishes also may be serviceable for this purpose, especially the dolphin, which is reported to be of the greatest swiftness, and most easily circurated, or made tame.

Amongst the ancient footmen, there are some upon record for their incredible swiftness. Lædas is reported to be so quick in his running, *Ut arenis pendentibus & cavo pulvere, nulla indicia relinqueret vestigiorum**; that he left no impression of his footsteps on the hollow sands. And it is related of a boy amongst the Romans, being but eight years old, that did run five and forty miles in an afternoon. Anistius and Philonides, two footmen unto Alexander the Great, are said to have run 1200 stadia in

---

* Solinus Polyhist. c. 5.

a day. Which relations will seem less incredible, if we consider the ancient exercises and games of this kind, together with the public fame and rewards for those that were most eminent.

Amongst the variety of beasts, there are some of more especial note for their strength and swiftness. Scaliger [*] mentions a story, (though he distrusts the truth of it) of a certain beast called ellend, two of which being joined in a little cart, are said to pass three hundred leagues a day upon the ice.

In former ages, and in other countries, the dromedary, and camel, and mule, were of more common use; but in these times and places, the horse (for the most part) serves instead of them all; by the help of which, we have our swiftest means of ordinary conveyance. The custom of riding post, by renewing both horse and man at set stages, is of ancient invention. Herodotus [†] relates it to be used by Xerxes in the Grecian war; and that it was by the Persians called Αγγαρηιον. The particulars that concern these kind of conveyances amongst the ancients, are largely handled by *Hermannus Hugo, Lib.* 3. *de Origine scribendi, c.* 14.

Pliny [‡] tells us of certain mares in Lusitania, which do conceive merely by the west wind; that alone (without the copulation of any male) serving to actuate their heat, and to generate their young. Which are likewise mentioned by Virgil [§]:

Exceptantque auras leves, & sæpe sine ullis
Conjugiis, vento gravidæ, &c.

Methinks these children of the wind should, for their fleetness, make excellent post-horses, and much conduce to the speedy conveyance of any message.

The Paracelsians talk of natural means to extract the metal and spirit out of one horse, and infuse it into

---

[*] Exer. 205.   [†] Lib. 8. 98.
[‡] Nat. Hist. l. 8. c. 42.   [§] Georg. 3.

another; of enabling them to carry a man safely and swiftly through enemies, precipices, or other dangerous places. And such horses (say they) were used by the wise men of the East at our Saviour's nativity; for they had not otherwise been able to have kept pace with a star, or to have passed so great a journey as it was to Jerusalem, which is thought to be five or six hundred miles at the least, from the places of their habitation. If this conceit were feasible, it would much promote the speed of conveyances; but I think it may justly be referred amongst the other dreams of the melancholic chymics.

Amongst all animate bodies, there is not any that have naturally so swift a motion as birds; which if a man could well employ in the dispatch of any errand, there would be but little fear that such messenger should be either intercepted, or corrupted.

That this hath been attempted, and effected by many of the ancients, is affirmed by divers relations. Pliny * tells us of Volaterranus, that he discovered a conquest he had gotten unto the city of Rome, by sending out swallows, which should fly thither, being anointed over with the colour of victory. And of another, who sending one of these birds into a besieged city (whence she was before taken from her young ones), and tying a string unto her with certain knots upon t, did thereby shew, after what number of days their aids would come; at which time they should make an irruption upon the enemy.

And elsewhere, in the same book †, he relates, how Hircius the consul, and Brutus who was besieged in Mutina, did this way maintain mutual intelligence, by tying their letters unto such pigeons, as were taught beforehand to fly from the tents to the city, and from thence to the tents again.

How Thaurosthenes did by this means send the news of

---

* Nat. Hist. l. 10. c. 24.   † Cap. 37.

his victory at Olympia, to his father at Ægina, is related by Ælian *.

Anacreön has an ode upon such a pigeon, which he himself had often used as a messenger, wherein the bird is feigned to say,

> Εγο δ' Αναχριοντι
> Διαχονω τοσαυτα
> Και νυν ὁρας εκεινα
> Επιστολας κομεζω.

Unto this invention also, Juvenal † is thought to allude; where he says,

> ——— *Tanquam è diversis partibus orbis,*
> *Anxia præcipiti venisset epistola penna.*

Lypsius relates out of Varro ‡, that it was usual for the Roman magistrates when they went unto the theatre, or other such public meetings, whence they could not return at pleasure, to carry such a pigeon with them; that if any unexpected business should happen, they might thereby give warning to their friends or families at home.

By which relations you may see how commonly this invention was practised amongst the ancients. Nor hath it been less used in these later times, especially in those countries where by reason of continual wars and dissensions, there have been more particular and urgent necessity for such kind of conveyances. *Nunc vulgatissima res est, columbas habere, ad ejusmodi jussa paratas,* saith Casaubon. *Harum opere, nostrates hoc bello civili, frequenter adjuti sunt,* saith Godesc. Stewechius §.

There are divers other stories to this purpose, but by these you may sufficiently discern the common practices of

---

* Hist. Animalium, l. 6. c. 7.   † Sat. 4. juxta fin.
‡ Saturn. Serm. l. 2. c. 6.
§ Not. in Æneæ Poliorcet. c. 31. Comment. in Veget. l. 3. c. 5. See Nunt. Inanimat. concerning Amiraldus. Porta de furt. lit. l. 2. c. 21. concerning marches. Herm. Hugo de Orig. scribendi, c. 15. Thuanus Hist. L 17.

this kind. As it is usual to bring up birds of prey, as hawks, cormorants, &c. to an obedience of their keepers; so likewise have some attempted it in these other birds, teaching them the art of carrying messages. There is a smaller sort of pigeon, of a light body, and swift flight, which is usually made choice of for such particulars; and therefore the kind of them is commonly called by the name of Carriers.

CHAP. XVII.

Of secret and swift informations by the species of sound.

HAVING in the former chapters treated severally concerning the divers ways of secrecy and swiftness in discourse; it remains that I now enquire (according to the method proposed), how both these may be joined together in the conveyance of any message. The resolution of which, so far as it concerns the particulars already specified, were but needless to repeat.

That which does more immediately belong to the present quære, and was the main occasion of this discourse, does refer to other ways of intimation, besides these in ordinary use, of speaking, or writing, or gestures. For in the general we must note, that whatever is capable of a competent difference, perceptible to any sense, may be a sufficient means whereby to express the cogitations. It is more convenient, indeed, that these differences should be of as great variety as the letters of the alphabet; but it is sufficient if they be but twofold, because two alone may, with somewhat more labour and time, be well enough contrived to express all the rest. Thus any two letters or numbers, suppose A. B. being transposed through five places, will yield thirty-two differences, and so consequently will superabundantly serve for the four and twenty letters, as was before more largely explained in the ninth chapter.

Now the sensitive species, whereby such informations must be conveyed, are, either the species of sound, or the species of sight: the ear and the eye being the only senses that are of quick perception, when their objects are remote.

Vegetius * distinguisheth all significatory signs into these three sorts.

1. *Vocalia.* By articulate sounds.

2. *Semivocalia.* By inarticulate sounds.

3. *Muta.* By the species of sight.

The two last of these are chiefly pertinent to the present enquiry. Concerning which, in the general it may be concluded, that any sound, whether of trumpets, bells, cannons, drums, &c. or any object of sight, whether flame, smoke, &c. which is capable of a double difference, may be a sufficient means whereby to communicate the thoughts.

The particular application of these, to some experiments, I shall treat more distinctly in the remainder of this discourse.

First, Concerning the secrecy and swiftness of any message by the species of sound. Though these audible species be much slower than those of sight, yet are they far swifter than the natural motion of any corporeal messenger. The chief use of these is for such as are within some competent nearness, as perhaps a mile off. But they may also by frequent multiplication be continued to a far greater distance.

There is a relation in Joach Camerarius †, of some that have heard their friends speaking to them distinctly, when they have been many miles asunder. *Habui notos homines, neque leves, & non indoctos, qui affirmabant, se audiisse secum colloquentes diserte, eos quos tunc multorum millium pas-*

* De re milit. l. 3. c. 5.
† Proœm. in lib. Plutar. de defectu oraculorum.

suum abesse certe scirent. But this he justly refers to diabolical magic, and the illusion of spirits.

There are other natural experiments in this kind, of more especial note for their antiquity. Such was that of king Xerxes, related by Cleomenes, as he is cited by Sardus *. *Cleomenes in libro de circulis cœlestibus scribit Xerxem toto itinere à Perside in Græciam stationes statuisse, & in iis homines ita prope, ut vocem alterius alter exaudiret; quo modo quadraginta horarum spatio, ex Græciâ in Persidem res nunciari poterat.* But this invention, besides the great trouble and uncertainty of it, is also too gross for imitation, savouring somewhat of the rudeness of those former and more barbarous ages.

Much beyond it was that experiment of the Romans, in the contrivance of the Picts wall, related by our learned Cambden †; this wall was built by Severus in the north part of England, above a hundred miles long. The towers of it were about a mile distant from one another. Betwixt each of these towers there passed certain hollow pipes or trunks in the curtains of the wall, through which the defendants could presently inform one another of any thing that was necessary, as concerning that place wherein the enemy was most likely to assault them, &c.

Since the wall is ruined, and this means of swift advertisement taken away, there are many inhabitants thereabouts, which hold their land by a tenure in cornage (as the lawyers speak) being bound by blowing of a horn to discover the irruption of the enemy.

There is another experiment to this purpose mentioned by Walchius ‡, who thinks it possible so to contrive a trunk or hollow pipe, that it shall preserve the voice entirely for certain hours or days, so that a man may send his words to a friend instead of his writing. There being al-

---

* De rerum Inventor. lib. 2.

† Britan. de Vallo, sive the Picts Wall, p. 654. Boter. Geog. l. 2. & l. 4. where he mentions also another wall of 8000 furlongs in China.

‡ Fabul. 9

ways a certain space of intermission, for the passage of the voice, betwixt its going into these cavities, and its coming out; he conceives that if both ends were seasonably stopped, whilst the sound was in the midst, it would continue there till it had some vent. *Huic tubo verba nostra insusurremus, & cum probe munitur tabellario committamus,* &c. When the friend to whom it is sent, shall receive and open it, the words shall come out distinctly, and in the same order wherein they were spoken. From such a contrivance as this (saith the same author), did Albertus Magnus make his image, and friar Bacon his brazen head, to utter certain words. Which conceit (if it have any truth) may serve somewhat to extenuate the gross absurdity of that Popish relic, concerning Joseph's [hah] or the noise that he made (as other carpenters use) in fetching of a blow; which is said to be preserved yet in a glass amongst other ancient relics.

But against these fancies it is considerable, that the species of sound are multiplied in the air, by a kind of continuation and efflux from their first original, as the species of light are from any luminous body; either of which being once separated from their causes, do presently vanish and die. Now as it would be a mad thing for a man to endeavour to catch the sun-beams, or inclose the light; upon the same grounds likewise must it needs be absurd, for any one to attempt the shutting in of articulate sounds: since both of them have equally the same intrinsical and inseparable dependance upon their efficient causes.

True, indeed, the species of sound may seem to have some kind of self-continuance in the air, as in echoes; but so likewise is it in proportion with those of sight, as in the quick turning round of a fire-stick, which will make the appearance of a fiery circle: and though the first kind of these be more lasting than the other, by reason their natural motion is not so quick, yet neither of them are of such duration as may be sufficient for the present enquiry.

None of all these inventions already specified, do sufficiently perform the business that is here enquired after;

nor are they either so generally or safely applicable for all places and exigencies.

The discovery that is here promised, may be further serviceable for such cases as these.

Suppose a friend were perfidiously clapped up in some close dungeon, and that we did not know exactly where, but could only guess at the place, within the latitude of half a mile or somewhat more; a man might very distinctly by these other inventions, discourse unto him. Or suppose a city were straitly besieged, and there were either within it or without it, such a confederate, with whom we should necessarily confer about some design ; we may by these means safely discover to him our intentions. By which you may guess that the messenger which is here employed, is of so strange a nature, as not to be barred out with walls, or deterred by enemies.

To the performance of this, it is requisite that there be two bells of different notes, or some such other audible and loud sounds, which we may command at pleasure, as muskets, cannons, horns, drums, &c. By the various sounding of these (according to the former table) a man may easily express any letter, and so consequently any sense.

These tables * I shall again repeat in this place : that of two letters may be contrived thus :

A.	B.	C.	D.	E.	F.	G.
aaaaa.	aaaab.	aaaba.	aaabb.	aabaa.	aabab.	aabba.

H.	I.	K.	L.	M.	N.	O.
aabbb.	abaaa.	abaab.	ababa.	ababb.	abbaa.	abbab.

P.	Q.	R.	S.	T.	V.	W.
abbba.	abbbb.	baaaa.	baaab.	baaba.	baabb.	babaa.

X.	Y.	Z.
babab.	babba.	babbb.

Suppose the word victuals were this way to be expressed, let the bigger sound be represented by A, and the lesser by

---

* Cap. 9.

B, according to which, the word may be thus made up **by** five of these sounds for each letter.

V.   I.   C.   T.   U.   A.   L.
baabb. abaaa. aaaba. baaba. baabb. aaaaa. ababa.

S.
baaab.

That is, the lesser note sounded once, and then the bigger twice, and then again the lesser twice, as (baabb) will signify the letter (V.) So the bigger once, and then the lesser once, and after that the bigger thrice together, as (abaaa) will represent the letter (I.) and so of the rest.

If the sounds be capable of a triple difference, then each letter may be expressed by a threefold sound, as may appear by this other alphabet.

A.   B.   C.   D.   E.   F.   G.   H.   I.   K.   L.
aaa. aab. aac. baa. bab. bba. bbb. bbc. caa. cba. cbb.

M.   N.   O.   P.   Q.   R.   S.   T.   V.   W.   X.
cbc. cca. ccb. ccc. aba. abb. abc. aca. acb. acc. bca.

Y.   Z.
bcb. bcc.

V.   I.   C.   T.   U.   A.   L.   S.
acb. caa. aac. aca. acb. aaa. cbb. abc.

If these sounds do contain a quintuple difference, then may every letter be signified by two sounds only, (which will much conduce to the speed and dispatch of such a message.) As you may see in this other table.

A. B. C. D. E. F. G. H. I. K. L. M. N. O. P.
aa. ab. ac. ad. ae. ba. bb. bc. bd. be. ca. cb. cc. cd. ce.

Q. R. S. T. V. W. X. Y. Z.
da. db. dc. dd. de. ea. eb. ec. ed.

V. I. C. T. U. A. L. S.
de. bd. ac. dd. de. aa. ca. dc.

It is related by Porta *, that when the citizens in the siege of Navarre were reduced to such great extremities

---

* De furt. lit. l. 1. c. 6.

that they were ready to yield, they did discover to their friends the greatness and kind of their wants, by discharging divers cannons and ordnances in the night-time, according to a certain order before agreed upon ; and by this means did obtain such fitting supplies as preserved the city.

CHAP. XVIII.

Concerning a language that may consist only of tunes and musical notes, without any articulate sound.

IF the musical instrument that is used to this purpose, be able to express the ordinary notes, not only according to their different tones, but their times also, then may each letter of the alphabet be rendered by a single sound.

Whence it will follow, that a man may frame a language, consisting only of tunes and such inarticulate sounds, as no letters can express. Which kind of speech is fancied to be usual amongst the lunary inhabitants, who (as Domingo Gonsales * hath discovered) have contrived the letters of the alphabet upon the notes after some such order as this.

Where the five vowels are represented by the min-nums on each of the five lines, being most of them placed according to their right order and consequence, only the

---

* Or the Man in the Moon, written by the same author of *Nuntius Inanimat.*

letters **K.** and **Q.** are left out, because they may be otherwise expressed.

According to this alphabet of notes, these words, *Gloria Deo soli,* must be thus contrived *.

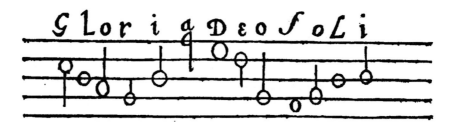

By this you may easily discern how two musicians may discourse with one another, by playing upon their instruments of music, as well as by talking with their instruments of speech. (And which is a singular curiosity) how the words of a song may be contrived in the tune of it.

I suppose that these letters and notes might be disposed to answer one another, with better advantage than here they are expressed. And this perhaps, would be easy enough for those that are thoroughly versed in the grounds of music, unto whose further enquiry I do here only propose this invention.

But now if these inarticulate sounds be contrived for the expression, not of words and letters, but of things and notions (as was before explained, concerning the universal character), then might there be such a general language, as should be equally speakable by all people and nations ; and so we might be restored from the second general curse, which is yet manifested, not only in the confusion of writing, but also of speech,

The utterance of these musical tunes may serve for the universal language, and the writing of them for the universal character. As all nations do agree in the same conceit of things, so likewise in the same conceit of harmonies.

This curiosity (for aught I know) has not yet been men-

* See Dom. Gonsal. 94,

tioned by any author, but it may be (if well considered) of such excellent use, as to deserve a more full and particular enlargement in a treatise by itself.

CHAP XIX.

Of those common relations that concern secret and swift informations by the species of sight; which are either fabulous, or magical.

THE usual relations that concern secret and swift conveyances by the species of sight, may be distinguished into such as are, either

    1. FABULOUS.
    2. MAGICAL.
    3. NATURAL AND TRUE.

First, of those that are fabulous. In which kind, that of the loadstone is most remarkable, as it is maintained by Famianus Strada *, in his imitation of Lucretius's stile, and divers others. The manner that is usually prescribed for the performance of it, is thus: let there be two needles provided, of an equal length and bigness, being both of them touched with the same loadstone: let the letters of the alphabet be placed in the circles on which they are moved, as the points of the compass under the needle of the mariner's chart. Let the friend that is to travel take one of them with him, first agreeing upon the days and hours wherein they should confer together: at which times, if one of them move the needle of his instrument to any letter of the alphabet, the other needle, by a sympathy, will move unto the same letter in the other instrument, though they be never so far distant: and thus by several motions of the needle to the letters, they may easily make up any words or sense which they have a mind to express.

* Lib. 2. Prol. 6,

O utinam hæc ratio scribendi prodeat usu;
Cautior & citior properaret epistola, nullas
Latronum verita insidias, fluviosque morantes,
Ipse suis princeps manibus sibi conficeret rem, &c.

Saith Strada. But this invention is altogether imaginary, having no foundation in any real experiment. You may see it frequently confuted in those that treat concerning magnetical virtues. *Non solum exhibilandi sunt, sed etiam male mulctandi philosophicâ ferulâ, fabularum isti procusores, qui suis portentis deterrent homines à præclarissimo causarum studio;* saith Cabæus to this purpose *.

The first occasion of these relations, was, the proof of that strange immaterial power of the loadstone, whereby it did work through thick and solid bodies, as a table, or wall, or the like; as also of that directive virtue, whereby it always tends to the poles; from whence others have conjectured, that it might be serviceable also for such a business, at so great a distance.

But against this, it is considerable,

1. That every natural agent is supposed to have some certain sphere, which determines its activity.

2. That magnetical operations do not arise (as some fondly conceive) from a sympathetical conformation of natures, which is the same at all distances; but from such a diffusion of these magnetical qualities through the medium, that they may be continued from the agent to the patient. And so these natural powers will not be of so great an extent, as they are supposed in this experiment.

The utmost distance, at which we may discourse with another by these magnetical virtues, is, two or three feet, or thereabouts; and this we may do, though it be through a wall of that thickness. *Fieri enim posse me docuit experientia, ut ope magnetis, & instrumenti ad id aptati, amicus cum amico, in cubiculo proximo, trans crassum murum (puta bipetalem) colloquatur, animi sui sententiam impertiat, & ad quæsita respondeat;* saith a late author †. But

---

* Philosoph. Magnet. l. 4. c. 10.
† S. Ward Magnetis Reduct. c. 40. See Cabæus Phil. Magn. l. 4. c. 11.

in this experiment, it is not only the secondary virtue of the needles that can be thus effectual (as is supposed in the former invention), but there must be the help also of the loadstone itself.

As for the reason why these magnetical powers are able to work through solid bodies; it is considerable, that any quality may be diffused through such a substance, as hath no natural repugnancy unto it. We see, the light does pass as well through hot bodies as cold, through solid as fluid, &c. only opacity keeps it out, because that quality alone is contrary to its nature. So likewise is it with magnetical virtues, which do equally spread themselves through all kind of bodies, whether rare or dense, diaphanous or opacous; there being no quality contrary to this, because it is that general endowment of the whole globe, that universal quality to which all other particulars are naturally subservient.

The second sort of relations to this purpose, are such as refer to diabolical magic; of which kind is that invention thought to be, which is commonly ascribed to Pythagoras; of whom it is reported, that he could write any thing in the body of the moon, so as it might be legible to another at a great distance. Agrippa * affirms this to be naturally possible, and the way of performing it not unknown to himself, with some others in his time. And Fredericus Risner † seems to believe it; for speaking of the strange experiments to be wrought by some glasses, he adds, *Denique certo artificio, depictas imagines, aut scriptas literas, nocte serena, plenæ lunæ sic opponi possunt, ut radiis lunam irradiantibus, ideoque reflexis, videas & legas, quæ Constantinopoli Lutetiam tibi nuncientur.*

There is an experiment in optics, to represent any writing by the sun-beams, upon a wall, or a front of a house: for which purpose, the letters must be first described with wax, or some other opacous colour, upon the surface of the

* Occult. Philosoph. l. 1. c. 6.
† Optic. l. 3. prop. 6. Speculorum persuasio hoc pervasit, &c.

glass, in an inverted form; which glass afterwards reflecting the light upon any wall in the shade, will discover these letters in the right form and order. Unto some such invention I did first (before I had well considered these particulars) attribute the performance of those strange promises in *Nuncius inanimatus* * ; but upon better thoughts it will be found, that the species of reflection in this experiment are so weak, that unless the glass and the letters be very big, and the wall somewhat near, there will be no distinct appearance of the writing. And therefore this way there can be no thoughts of contriving any reflected species, that shall be visible at so great a distance as the moon. Nor is there any other natural means conceivable, by which so strange an effect may be performed; which is the reason that it is so frequently attributed to diabolical magic, by almost all the writers that have occasion to treat of it.

But Agrippa in another place † speaking concerning this invention, affirms that it was performed thus : Pythagoras did first describe with blood any letters which he thought fit, in some great glass, and then opposing the glass against the full moon, the letters would appear through it, as if they were writ in the circumference of her body. *Quæ collibuisset sanguine perscripsit in speculo, quo, ad pleni luminis lunæ orbem obverso, stanti à tergo, res exaratas in disco lunæ commonstravit.* In which passage he seems to intimate, that this writing in the moon could not be visible at any great distance, (as it is related in common tradition) but that it did appear to such only, betwixt whose eyes and the moon this glass might be interposed. And according to this, the wonder of the relation ceases, nor may it truly be referred to diabolical magic.

More properly reducible to this kind, are those inchanted glasses mentioned in divers authors ‡ : in which some magicians are said to contain such familiar spirits, as do inform them of any business they shall enquire after.

---

* World in the Moon, c. 7.   † Agrippa de Vanit. Scient. c. 48.
‡ Joach. Camerar. Procem. in lib. Plut. de defect. Orac.

↑

I have heard a great pretender to the knowledge of all secret arts, confidently affirm, that he himself was able at
that time, or any other, to shew me in a glass what was
done in any part of the world ; what ships were sailing in
the Mediterranean who were walking in any street of
any city in Spain, or the like. And this he did aver with
all the laboured expressions of a strong confidence. The
man, for his condition, was an Italian doctor of physic ;
for his parts, he was known to be of extraordinary skill in
the abstruser arts, but not altogether free from the suspicion of this unlawful magic.

CHAP. XX.

*Of informations by significatory fires and smoke. Their
antiquity. The true manner of using them to this purpose. That these were meant in Nuntius inanimatus.*

THE experiments of this kind that are true, and upon
natural grounds, have been made either by fire in
the night, or smoke and such other signs visible at a distance in the day-time.

These informations by significatory fires, have been of
ancient use. The first invention of them is commonly
ascribed to Sinon in the Trojan wars. *Specularem signi-
ficationem Trojano Bello Sinon invenit*, (saith Pliny *)
This was the sign upon which he agreed to unlock the
wooden horse.

————— *Flammas cum regia puppis
Extulerat* † —————

* Nat. Hist. l. 7. c. 56.   † Virgil

But Diodorus Siculus[*] affirms them to be practised by
Medea in her conspiracy with Jason. And they are frequently mentioned in other ancient historians. Herodotus[†] speaks of them in the Grecian war against Xerxes:
and Thucydides[‡] testifies of them in the onsets that were
made by the Peloponnesians against Salamis, and in the
siege of Corcyra. Appian speaking of Scipio at Numan-
tia, how he divided his camp into divers companies, says,
that he assigned each of them to several tribunes, with
this charge, *Si impeterentur ab hoste, de die, panno rubro
in hasta sublato significarent*[§]; *de nocte, igne.* If the enemy did charge any of them, they should signify it to the
others, in the day-time by holding up a red cloth, in the
night by fires. Vegetius[||] affirms it to be usual, when the
army was divided, to inform one another, in the day by
smoke, in the night by fires. These significatory fires
were by the Grecians called Φρυκτοι (saith Suidas) and
sometimes Πυρσεια. The use of them was chiefly for the
answer of some particular quære[¶], that was before agreed
upon; as concerning the coming of aids or enemies; if
the enemies were coming, they were wont to shake these
torches, if the aids, they held them still (saith the scholiast
upon Thucydides[**]).

But they have by more exact inventions been enlarged
to a greater latitude of signification: so that now, any
thing which we have occasion to discover, may be expressed by them[††].

The ways by which they may be contrived to this purpose, are divers; I shall specify only the chief of them.

That which in ancient times was used by the Grecians,
and is particularly treated of in Polybius[‡‡], adviseth thus.

Let the letters be divided into five tablets or columns.

---

* Biblioth. l. 4,   † Polymn. l. 7. c. 182.   ‡ Hist. l. 2. Item, l. 3.
So Curtius of Alex. M. L 5.   § To this purpose the flags of truce or
defiance. || De re milit. l. 3. c. 5. Lips. de milit. Rom. lib. 5. Dia-
log. 9.   ¶ Æneas Poliorc. c. 31.   ** Schol. in l. 2. Thucyd.
†† Wecker de Secretis, l. 14. c. 1. Port. de Furt. lit. l. 1. c. 10. Cardan.
de Variet. Rerum, l. 12. c. 61.   ‡‡ Hist. l. 10. juxta fin.

I	II	III	IV	V
1	a	f	l	q	w
2	b	g	m	r	x
3	c	h	n	ſ	y
4	d	i	o	t	z
5	e	k	p	u	

Let there be provided ten torches, five being placed on the right hand, and five on the left: let so many torches be lifted up on the right hand, as may shew the number of the table; and so many on the left, as may shew the number of that letter in it which you would express: as in this following example, wherein the several numbers, both at the right and left hand, do signify the word HASTEN.

The right hand.　　　　*The left hand.*

II	H	3
I	A	1
IV	S	3
IV	T	4
I	E	5
III	N	3

That is, two lights being lifted up on the right hand, shew the second column; and at the same time three torches appearing on the left hand, denote the third letter in that column, which is *H*. Thus a single torch being discovered on both sides, doth signify the first letter of the first column, which is *A*; and so of the rest.

There is another way mentioned by Joachimus Fortius *, unto the performance of which there are only three lights required: one torch being shewed alone, shall signify the eight first letters, *A. B. C. D. E. F. G. H.* Two together, the eight next, *I. K. L. M. N. O. P. 2.* And all three the rest, *R. S. T. V. W. X. Y. Z.*

One light being discovered once, signifies *A*; if twice, *B*: two lights being shewed once, do denote the letter *I*; if twice, *K*, &c.

According to this way, if I would express the word ꜰAMIN, the torches must be contrived; one light must be lifted up six times for the letter *F*; one light once for *A*; two lights four times for *M*; two lights once for *I*; two lights five times for *N*.

But here it will be requisite that there be some intermission betwixt the expression of several letters, because otherwise there must needs be a great confusion amongst those that belong to the same number of torches. In which respect, this way is much more tedious and inconvenient than the former invention out of Polybius.

It is easy to conceive, how by the alphabet consisting of two letters transposed through five places, such a manner of discoursing may be otherwise contrived, only by two torches. But then there must be five shews, to express every letter.

There is another way of speaking, by the differences of motion in two lights; which for its quickness and speed, is much to be preferred before any of the rest; the manner of it is thus: provide two torches on long poles: let them be placed so far from one another, that they may

* Lib. de Experiment.

seem unto your confederate to be about four cubits distance. By the divers elevations or depressions of these, inclining of them to the right hand, or to the left, severally or both together, it is easy to express all the alphabet.

One light alone being discovered, must stand for *A*; lifted up, for *E*; depressed, for *I*; inclined to the right hand, for *O*; unto the left hand, for *V*.

Two lights elevated, for *B*; depressed, for *C*; inclined to the right hand, for *D*; to the left hand, for *F*.

Two lights being still discovered, and the torch at the right hand being lifted up, shall signify *G*; being depressed, *H*; inclined to the right hand, *K*; to the left hand, *L*.

The torch at the left hand, being elevated, shall stand for *M*; depressed, for *N*; inclined to the right hand, for *P*; to the left hand for *Q*.

The torch at the right hand being moved towards the left hand, and that at the left hand being at the same time moved towards the right hand, shall signify *R*: the right hand torch being inclined to the left hand, and the other at the same time being elevated, signifies *S*; being depressed, *T*: the left hand torch being inclined to the right hand,. and the other at the same time being elevated, signifies *W*; being depressed, *X*.

The right hand torch being inclined to the right hand, and the other at the same time being elevated, may stand for *Y*; being depressed, for *Z*.

When any thing is thus to be expressed, the two torches being discovered, must remain without any motion, so long, till the confederate shall by other lights shew some sign, that he is ready to take notice. After every one of these particular motions, the torches must be carefully hidden and obscured, that so the several letters expressed by them, may be the better distinguished.

The day-time informations by smoke, cannot so conveniently be ordered according to this latter contrivance, and therefore must be managed by some of those other ways that were specified before: to which purpose there *sternendi, & permeabilem efficiendi.* That is, the greatness of distance can be no impediment, if the space betwixt be fitted with such high mountains, and beacon hills, as may serve for these kind of discoveries. Suppose (I say) this messenger should set forth from London, in the very point of noon, he would notwithstanding arrive at Bristol before twelve of the clock that day: that is, a message may by these means be conveyed so great a distance, in fewer minutes than those which make the difference betwixt the two meridians of those places.

If according to this, we should interpret that passage out of Trithemius*, concerning the three saturnine angels, that in twenty-four hours can convey news from any part of the world; that author might then in one respect, be freed from the aspersion of diabolical magic, which for this very reason hath heretofore been imputed to him. But this by the way.

It may be, the resolution of those great promises in Nuncius Inanimatus, to such easy causes as they are here ascribed unto, will not be answerable to men's expectation; every one will be apt to mistrust some greater matter than is here exprest: but it is thus also in every other the like particular; for ignorance is the mother of wonder, and wonder does usually create unto itself many wild imaginations; which is the reason why men's fancies are so prone to attribute all unusual and unknown events, unto stranger causes than either nature or art hath designed for them.

CONCLUSION.

The poets† have feigned Mercury to be the chief patron of thieves and treachery,

Αρχος Φηλητιων.

* See before cap. 15.

† Horat. l. 1. Od. 10.   Ovid. Metam. l. 11.   Homer. in Hymnis. Nat. Comes. Mytholog. l. 5. c. 5.

To which purpose they relate that he filched from Venus her girdle, as she embraced him in congratulation of a victory; that he robbed Jupiter of his sceptre, and would have stolen his thunderbolt too, but that he feared to burn his fingers. And the astrologers observe, that those who are born under this planet, are naturally addicted to theft and cheating.

If it be feared that this discourse may unhappily advantage others in such unlawful courses; it is considerable, that it does not only teach how to deceive, but consequently also how to discover delusions. And then besides, the chief experiments are of such nature, that they cannot be frequently practised, without just cause of suspicion, when as it is in the magistrates power to prevent them. However, it will not follow, that every thing must be supprest which may be abused. There is nothing hath more occasioned troubles and contention, than the art of writing, which is the reason why the inventor of it is fabled to have sown serpents teeth *. And yet it was but a barbarous act of Thamus, the Egyptian king, therefore to forbid the learning of letters: we may as well cut out our tongues, because that member is a world of wickedness †. If all those useful inventions that are liable to abuse, should therefore be concealed, there is not any art or science which might be lawfully profest.

* Cali. Rho. antiq. lect. l. 22. c. 15.   † James iii.

MATHEMATICAL MAGIC:

OR,

THE WONDERS

THAT MAY BE PERFORMED BY

MECHANICAL GEOMETRY.

IN TWO BOOKS.

CONCERNING

MECHANICAL $\begin{cases} \text{POWERS.} \\ \text{MOTIONS.} \end{cases}$

Being one of the most easy, pleasant, useful (and yet most neglected Part) of the Mathematics.

Not before treated of in this Language.

ARCHIMEDES;

OR,

MECHANICAL POWERS.

BOOK I.

CHAP. I.

*The excellency of these arts.   Why they were concealed by
the ancients.   The authors that have treated of them.*

ALL those various studies about which the sons of
men do busy their endeavours, may be generally
comprised under these three kinds.

> **DIVINE.**
> **NATURAL.**
> **ARTIFICIAL.**

To the first of these, is reducible, not only the speculation of theological truths, but also the practice of those
virtues, which may advantage our minds in the enquiry
after their proper happiness.   And these arts alone may
truly be stiled liberal, *Quæ liberum faciunt hominem, quibus curæ virtus est,* (saith the divine Stoic*) which set a
man at liberty from his lusts and passions.

* Sen. Ep. 88.

To the second may be referred all that knowledge which concerns the frame of this great universe, or the usual course of providence in the government of these created things.

To the last do belong all those inventions, whereby nature is any way quickened or advanced in her defects: these artificial experiments being (as it were) but so many essays, whereby men do naturally attempt to restore themselves from the first general curse inflicted upon their labours.

The following discourse does properly appertain to this latter kind.

Now art may be said, either to imitate nature, as in limning and pictures; or to help nature, as in medicine; or to overcome and advance nature, as in these mechanical disciplines, which in this respect are by so much to be preferred before the other, by how much their end and power is more excellent. Nor are they therefore to be esteemed less noble, because more practical; since our best and most divine knowledge is intended for action; and those may justly be counted barren studies, which do not conduce to practice as their proper end.

But so apt are we to contemn every thing which is common, that the ancient philosophers esteemed it a great part of wisdom to conceal their learning from vulgar apprehension or use, thereby the better to maintain it in its due honour and respect. And therefore did they generally veil all their arts and sciences under such mystical expressions as might excite the people's wonder and reverence; fearing lest a more easy and familiar discovery, might expose them to contempt. *Sic ipsa mysteria fabularum cuniculis operiuntur, summatibus tantum viris, sapientia interprete, veri arcani consciis; contenti sint reliqui, ad venerationem, figuris defendentibus à vilitate secretum,* saith a Platonic *.

* Macrobius Somn. Scip. l. 1. c. 2.

Hence was it, that the ancient mathematicians did place all their learning in abstracted speculations; refusing to debase the principles of that noble profession unto mechanical experiments. Insomuch that those very authors amongst them, who were most eminent for their inventions of this kind, and were willing by their own practice to manifest unto the world those artificial wonders that might be wrought by these arts, as Dædalus, Archytas, Archimedes, &c. were notwithstanding so much infected with this blind superstition, as not to leave any thing in writing concerning the grounds and manner of these operations.

Quintilian * speaking to this purpose of Archimedes, saith thus. *Quamvis tantum tamque singularem geometriæ usum, Archimedes, singularibus exemplis, & admirandis operibus ostenderit, propter quæ non humanæ sed divinæ scientiæ laudem sit adeptus, hæsit tamen in illa Platonis persuasione, nec ullam mechanicam literam prodere voluit.*

By which means, posterity hath unhappily lost, not only the benefit of those particular discoveries, but also the proficiency of those arts in general. For when once the learned men did forbid the reducing of them to particular use, and vulgar experiment; others did thereupon refuse these studies themselves, as being but empty and useless speculations †. Whence it came to pass that the science of geometry was so universally neglected, receiving little or no addition for many hundred years together.

Amongst these ancients, the divine Plato is observed to be one of the greatest sticklers for this fond opinion; severely dehorting all his followers from prostituting mathematical principles, unto common apprehension or practice ‡. Like the envious emperor Tiberius, who is reported to have killed an artificer for making glass malleable, fearing lest thereby the price of metals might be debased. So he, in his superstition to philosophy, would

* Quint. l. 1. c. 10.   † Pet. Ram. Schol. Mathem. l. 1.
‡ Plin. Nat. l. 36. c. 26.

rather chuse to deprive the world of all those useful and excellent inventions which might be thence contrived, than to expose that profession unto the contempt of the ignorant vulgar.

But his scholar Aristotle *, (as in many other particulars, so likewise in this) did justly oppose him, and became himself one of the first authors that hath writ any methodical discourse concerning these arts; chusing rather a certain and general benefit, before the hazard that might accrue from the vain and groundless disrespect of some ignorant persons. Being so far from esteeming geometry dishonoured by the application of it to mechanical practices, that he rather thought it to be thereby adorned, as with curious variety, and to be exalted unto its natural end. And whereas the mathematicians of those former ages, did possess all their learning as covetous men do their wealth, only in thought and notion; the judicious Aristotle, like a wise steward, did lay it out to particular use and improvement; rightly preferring the reality and substance of public benefit, before the shadows of some retired speculation, or vulgar opinion.

Since him there have been divers other authors who have been eminent for their writings of this nature. Such were Hero Alexandrinus, Hero Mechanicus, Pappus Alexandrinus, Proclus Mathematicus, Vitruvius, Guidus Ubaldus, Henricus Monantholius, Galileus, Guevara, Mersennus, Bettinus, &c. Besides many others that have treated largely of several engines, as Augustin Ramelli, Vittorio Zoncha, Jacobus Bessonius, Vegetius, Lipsius.

Most of which authors I have perused, and shall willingly acknowledge myself a debtor to them for many things in this following dicourse.

* Arist. Quæst. Mechan.

CHAP. II.

Concerning the name of this art. That it may properly be stiled liberal. The subject and nature of it.

THE word mechanic is thought to be derived απο τε μηκυς και ανειν, *multum ascendere, pertingere :* intimating the efficacy and force of such inventions. Or else παρα μη χαινειν, (saith Eustathius) *quia hiscere non sinit,* because these arts are so full of pleasant variety, that they admit not either of sloth or weariness *.

According to ordinary signification, the word is used in opposition to the liberal arts : whereas in propriety of speech those employments alone may be styled illiberal, which require only some bodily exercise, as manufactures, trades, &c. And on the contrary, that discipline which discovers the general causes, effects, and proprieties of things, may truly be esteemed as a species of philosophy.

But here it should be noted, that this art is usually distinguished into a twofold kind †.

1. RATIONAL.
2. CHIRURGICAL.

The rational is that which treats of those principles and fundamental notions, which may concern these mechanical practices.

The chirurgical or manual doth refer to the making of these instruments, and the exercising of such particular experiments. As in the works of architecture, fortifications, and the like.

The first of these is the subject of this discourse, and may properly be styled liberal, as justly deserving the pro-

* Lypsius Poliorcet. l. 2. Dial. 3. That's a senseless absurd etymology, imposed by some, *Quia intellectus in eis mæchatur,* as if these arts did prostitute and adulterate the understanding.

† Pappus Proœm. in Collect. Mathem. l. 8.

secution of an ingenious mind.   For if we consider it according to its birth and original, we shall find it to spring
from honourable parentage, being produced by geometry
on the one side, and natural philosophy on the other.   If
according to its use and benefit, we may then discern that
to this should be referred all those arts and professions, so
necessary for human society, whereby nature is not only
directed in her usual course, but sometimes also com-
manded against her own law.   The particulars that concern architecture, navigation, husbandry, military affairs,
&c. are most of them reducible to this art, both for their
invention and use.

Those other disciplines of logic, rhetoric, &c. do not
more protect and adorn the mind, than these mechanical
powers do the body.

And therefore are they well worthy to be entertained
with greater industry and respect, than they commonly
meet with in these times ; wherein there be very many
that pretend to be masters in all the liberal arts, who scarce
understand any thing in these particulars.

The subject of this art is concerning the heaviness of
several bodies, or the proportion that is required betwixt
any weight, in relation to the power which may be able to
move it.   And so it refers likewise to violent and artificial
motion, as philosophy doth to that which is natural.

The proper end for which this art is intended, is to teach
how by understanding the true difference betwixt the
weight and the power, a man may add such a fitting sup-
plement to the strength of the power, that it shall be able
to move any conceiveable weight, though it should never
so much exceed that force which the power is naturally
endowed with.

The art itself may be thus described to be a mathematical discipline, which by the help of geometrical principles
doth teach to contrive several weights and powers unto
any kind, either of motion, or rest, according as the artificer shall determine.

If it be doubted how this may be esteemed a species of mathematics, when as it treats of weights, and not of quantity * : for satisfaction to this, there are two particulars considerable.

1. Mathematics in its latitude is usually divided into pure and mixed: and though the pure do handle only abstract quantity in general, as geometry, arithmetic: yet that which is mixed, doth consider the quantity of some particular determinate subject. So astronomy handles the quantity of heavenly motions; music of sounds, and mechanics of weights and powers.

2. Heaviness or weight is not here considered, as being such a natural quality, whereby condensed bodies do of themselves tend downwards; but rather, as being an affection, whereby they may be measured. And in this sense, Aristotle himself refers it amongst the other species of quantity †, as having the same proper essence, which is to be compounded of integral parts. So a pound doth consist of ounces, drams, scruples. Whence it is evident, that there is not any such repugnancy in the subject of this art, as may hinder it from being a true species of mathematics.

* Dav. Rivaltus præf. in l. Archim. de centro gravitatis.
† Metaph. l. 10. c. 2.

CHAP. III.

Of the first mechanical faculty, the Balance.

THE mechanical faculties by which the experiments of this nature must be contrived, are usually reckoned to be these six.

1. *Libra.*	1. *The Balance.*
2. *Vectis.*	2. *The Leaver.*
3. *Axis in Peritrochio.*	3. *The Wheel.*
4. *Trochlea.*	4. *The Pulley.*
5. *Cuneus.*	5. *The Wedge.*
6. *Cochlea.*	6. *The Screw.*

Unto some of which, the force of all mechanical inventions must necessarily be reduced. I shall speak of them severally, and in this order.

First, concerning the balance: this and the leaver are usually confounded together, as being but one faculty; because the general grounds and proportions of either's force is so exactly the same. But for better distinction, and more clear discovery of their natures, I shall treat of them severally.

The first invention of the balance is commonly attributed to Astrea, who is therefore deified for the goddess of Justice; and that instrument itself advanced amongst the celestial signs.

The particulars concerning it are so commonly known, and of such easy experiment, that they will not need any large explication. The chief end and purpose of it, is for the distinction of several ponderosities: for the understanding of which, we must note, that if the length of the sides in the balance, and the weights at the ends of them, be both mutually equal, then the beam will be in a horizontal situation. But on the contrary, if either the weights alone be equal, and not their distances, or the distances alone, and not the weights, then the beam will accordingly decline.

As in this following diagram.

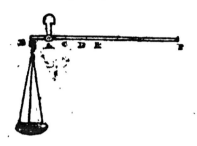

Suppose an equal weight at C, unto that at B; (which points are both equally distant from the centre A) it is evident that then the beam B F will hang horizontally. But if the weight supposed at C, be unequal to that at B, or if there be an equal weight at D E, or any of the other unequal distances; the beam must then necessarily decline.

With this kind of balance, it is usual, by the help only of one weight, to measure sundry different gravities, whether more or less, than that by which they are measured*. As by the example here described, a man may with one pound alone, weigh any other body within ten pounds; because the heaviness of any weight doth increase proportionably to its distance from the centre. Thus one pound at D, will equiponderate unto two pounds at B; because the distance A D is double unto A B. And for the same reason, one pound at *E*, will equiponderate to three pound at B; and one pound at F, unto ten at B; because there is still the same disproportion betwixt their several distances.

This kind of balance is usually stiled *Romana statera*. It seems to be of ancient use, and is mentioned by Aristotle † under the name of *Φαλαγξ*.

Hence it is easy to apprehend how that false balance may be composed, so often condemned by the wise men,

---

*Cardan. Subtil. l. 1.   † Mechan. c. 21.

as being an abomination to the Lord*. If the sides of the beam be not equally divided, as suppose one have 10 parts and the other 11 ; then any two weights that differ according to this proportion, (the heavier being placed on the shorter side, and the lighter on the longer) will equiponderate ; and yet both the scales being empty, will hang in *æquilibrio*, as if they were exactly just and true†: as in this description.

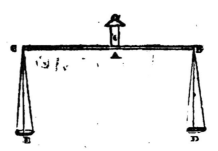

Suppose A C to have 11 such parts, whereof A B has but 10, and yet both of them to be in themselves of equal weight ; it is certain, that whether the scales be empty, or whether in the scale D we put 11 pound, and at E 10 pound ; yet both of them shall equiponderate, because there is just such a disproportion in the length of the sides A C, being unto A B, as 11 to 10.

The frequency of such cozenages in these days, may be evident from common experience ; and that they were used also in former ages, may appear from Aristotle's testimony concerning the merchants in his time‡. For the remedying of such abuses, the ancients did appoint divers officers, stiled ζυγοστάται ‖, who were to overlook the common measures.

So great care was there amongst the Jews, for the preservation of commutative justice from all abuse and falsification in this kind, that the public standards and originals,

---

* Prov. xi. 1. xvi. 11. item xx. 10. 23.
† Pappus Collect. Math. l. 8.   ‡ Quæstion. Mechan. c. 2. Budæus.
‖ Hence the proverb, Zygostatica fides.

by which all other measures were to be tried and allowed, were with much religion preserved in the sanctuary; the care of them being committed to the priests and levites, whose office it was to look unto all manner of measures and size. Hence is that frequent expression, according to the shekel of the sanctuary; and that law, all thy estimations shall be according to the shekel of the sanctuary * : which doth not refer to any weight, or coin, distinct from, and more than the vulgar, (as some fondly conceive), but doth only oblige men in their dealing and traffic, to make use of such just measures, as were agreeable unto the public standards that were kept in the sanctuary.

The manner how such deceitful balances may be discovered is, by changing the weights into each other scale, and then the inequality will be manifest.

From the former grounds rightly apprehended, it is easy to conceive how a man may find out the just proportion of a weight, which in any point given, shall equiponderate to several weights given, hanging in several places of the beam.

Some of these balances are made so exact, (those especially which the refiners use) as to be sensibly turned with the eightieth part of a grain : which (though it may seem very strange) is nothing to what Capellus † relates of one at Sedan, that would turn with the four hundredth part of a grain.

There are several contrivances to make use of these, in measuring the weight of blows, the force of powder, the strength of strings, or other oblong substances; condensed air : the distinct proportion of several metals mixed together; the different gravity of divers bodies in the water, from what they have in the open air; with divers the like ingenious inquiries.

* 1 Chron. xxiii. 29. Exod. xxx. 13, Lev. xxvii. 25.

† De ponderibus & nummis, l. 1.

CHAP. IV.

Concerning the second mechanic faculty, the Leaver.

THE second mechanical faculty is the leaver: the first invention of it is usually ascribed to Neptune, and represented by his trident, which in the Greek are both called by one name *, and are not very unlike in form, being both of them somewhat broader at one end, than in the other parts.

There is one main principle concerning it, which is (as it were) the very sum and epitome of this whole art. The meaning of it is thus expressed by Aristotle: Ὁ τὸ κινεμενον βαρος προς το κινεν, το μηκος προς το μηκος αντιπεπονθεν. That is, as the weight is to an equivalent power, so is the distance betwixt the weight and the centre unto the distance betwixt the centre and the power, and so reciprocally. Or thus, the power that doth equiponderate with any weight, must have the same proportion unto it, as there is betwixt their several distances from the centre or fulciment; as in this following figure.

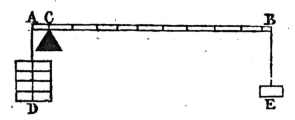

Where suppose the leaver to be represented by the length AB, the centre or prop † at the point C, the weight to be sustained D, the power that doth uphold it E.

---

* μοχλος. Aristotle Quæst. Mechan. cap. 4. Archimedes, de Æquiponderant. l. 1. prop. 7. Vitruvius Architect. l. 10. c. 8.

† This Aristotle calls υπομοχλιον; Vitruvius, pressio; Whaldus, fulcimentum; Dan. Barbarus, scabellum.

Now the meaning of the foresaid principle doth import thus much; that the power at E, must bear the same proportion to the weight D, as the distance C A doth to the other C B; which, because it is octuple in the present example, therefore it will follow that one pound at B, or E, will equiponderate to eight pounds at A, or D; as is expressed in the figure. The ground of which maxim is this, because the point C is supposed to be the centre of gravity, on either side of which, the parts are of equal weight.

And this kind of proportion is not only to be observed when the power doth press downwards, (as in the former example) but also in the other species of violent motion; as lifting, drawing, and the like. Thus if the prop or fulciment were supposed to be at the extremity of the leaver,

as in this diagram at A, then the weight B would require such a difference in the strengths or powers that did sustain it, as there is betwixt the several distances A C, and B C. For as the distance A B is unto A C, so is the power at C to the weight at B; that is the power at A must be double to that at C, because the distance B C is twice as much as B A*. From whence it is easy to conceive, how any burthen carried betwixt two persons, may be proportioned according to their different strengths. If the weight were imagined to hang at the number 2, then the power at C would sustain but two of those parts, whereof that at A did uphold 16. If it be supposed at the figure 3, then the strength at C, to that at A, would be but as three to fifteen. But if it were situated at the figure 9, then each of the extremities would participate of it alike; because that being the middle, both the distances are equal. If at the number 12, then the strength at C is required to be double unto that at A. And in the like manner are we to conceive of the other intermediate divisions.

* The right understanding of this doth much conduce to the explication of the pulley.

Thus also must it be, if we suppose the power to be placed betwixt the fulciment and the weight, as in this example.

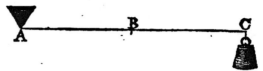

Where, as A C is to A B so is the power at B, to the weight at C.

Hence likewise may we conceive the reason why it is much harder to carry any long substance, either on the shoulders, or in the hand, if it be held by either of the extremes, than if it be sustained by the middle of it. The strength that must equiponderate at the nearer end, sometimes increasing the weight almost double to what it is in itself.

Imagine the point A to be the place where any long substance (as suppose a pike) is sustained; it is evident from the former principle, that the strength at B (which makes it lie level) must be equal to all the length A C, which is almost the whole pike.

And as it is in the depressing, or elevating, so likewise is it in the drawing of any weight, as a coach, plough, or the like.

Let the line D B represent the pole or carriage on which the burthen is sustained, and the line A C the cross-bar; at each of its extremities, there is a several spring-tree G H, and I K, to which either horses or oxen may be fastened. Now because A and C are equally distant from the middle B, therefore in this case the strength must be equal on both sides; but if we suppose one of these spring-trees to be fastened unto the points E or F, then the strength required to draw on that side, will be so much more, as the distance E B or F B is less than that of A B; that is, either as three to four, as E B to B A, or as one to two, as F B to B A. So that the beast fastened at A, will not draw so much by a quarter as the other at E, but half as much as one at F.

Whence it is easy to conceive how a husbandman *(cum inæquales veniunt ad aratra juvenci)* may proportion the labour of drawing, according to the several strength of his oxen.

Unto this mechanical faculty should be reduced sundry other instruments in common use. Thus the oars, stern, masts, &c. according to their force whereby they give motion to the ship, are to be conceived under this head *.

Thus likewise for that engine, whereby brewers and dyers do commonly draw water, which Aristotle calls κηλονειον, and others tollenon. This being the same kind of instrument by which Archimedes drew up the ships of Marcellus †.

CHAP. V.

How the natural motion of living creatures is conformable to these artificial rules.

THE former principle being already explained, concerning artificial and dead motions, it will not be altogether impertinent, if in the next place we apply it unto those that

---

* Arist. Mechan. c. 5, 6, 7. Vide Guevar. Comment.

† Mechan. c. 29. Pet. Crinitus, de honesta disciplina, l. 19. c. 2. calls it corruptly Tellenon.

are natural in living bodies, and examine whether these also are not governed by the same kind of proportions.

In all perfect living creatures, there is a twofold kind of motive instruments :

1. Primary, the muscles.

2. Secondary, the members.

The muscles are naturally fitted to be instruments of motion, by the manner of their frame and composure; consisting of flesh as their chief material, and besides of nerves, ligatures, veins, arteries, and membranes.

The nerves serve for the conveyance of the motive faculty from the brain. The ligatures for the strengthening of them, that they may not flag and languish in their motions. The veins for their nourishment. The arteries for the supplying of them with spirit and natural vigour. The membranes for the comprehension or inclosure of all these together, and for the distinction of one muscle from another. There are besides divers fibræ, or hairy substances, which nature hath bestowed for the farther corroborating of their motions ; these being dispersed through every muscle, do so join together in the end of them, as to make entire nervous bodies, which are called tendons, almost like the gristles. Now this (saith *Galen* *) may fitly be compared to the broader part of the leaver, that is put under the weight; which, as it ought to be so much the stronger, by how much it is put to a greater force, so likewise by this, doth nature enable the muscles and nerves for those motions, which otherwise would be too difficult for them.

Whence it may evidently appear, that according to the opinion of that eminent physician, these natural motions are regulated by the like grounds with the artificial.

2. Thus also is it in those secondary instruments of motion, the members: amongst which, the hand is οργανον οργανων, the instrument of instruments, (as Galen † stiles it;) and as the soul of man doth bear in it the image of the

---

* De Placit. Hippoc. & Platon. L 1. cap. 10.

† De usu part. l. 1. c. 2.

divine wisdom and providence, so this part of the body seems in some sort to represent the omnipotency of God, whilst it is able to perform such various and wonderful effects by the help of this art. But now for its own proper natural strength, in the lifting any great weight, this is always proportioned according to its extension from the body, being of least force when it is fully stretched out, or at arms-end, (as we say) because then the shoulder-joint is as the centre of its motion, from which the hand in that posture being very remote, the weight of any thing it holds must be accordingly augmented. Whereas the arm being drawn in, the elbow-joint doth then become its centre, which will diminish the weight proportionably, as that part is nearer unto it than the other.

To this purpose also, there is another subtle problem proposed by Aristotle *, concerning the postures of sitting and rising up. The quære is this : why a man cannot rise up from his seat, unless he first either bend his body forward, or thrust his feet backward ?

In the posture of sitting, our legs are supposed to make a right angle with our thighs, and they with our backs, as in this figure.

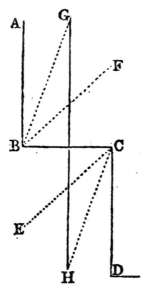

* Mechan. c. 31.

Where let A B represent the back, BC the thighs, C D the legs. Now it is evident, that a man cannot rise from this posture, unless either the back AB do first incline unto F, to make an acute angle with the thighs BC; or else that the legs CD do incline towards E, which may also make an acute angle with the thighs BC; or lastly, unless both of them do incline to the points GH, where they may be included in the same perpendicular.

For the resolution of which, the philosopher proposes these two particulars.

1. A right angle (saith he) is a kind of equality, and that being naturally the cause of rest, must needs be an impediment to the motion of rising.

2. Because when either of the parts are brought into an acute angle, the head being removed over the feet, or they under the head; in such a posture the whole man is much nearer disposed to the form of standing, wherein all these parts are in one strait perpendicular line, than he is by the other of right angles, in which the back and legs are two parallels; or that of turning these strait angles into obtuse, which would not make an erect posture, but declining.

But neither of these particulars (as I conceive) do fully satisfy the present quære; neither do the commentators, Monantholius, or Guevara, better resolve it. Rather suppose BC to be a vectis or leaver, towards the middle of which is the place of the fulciment, A B as the weight, C D the power that is to raise it.

Now the body being situate in this rectangular form, the weight A B must needs be augmented proportionably to its distance from the fulciment, which is about half the thighs: whereas, if we suppose either the weight to be inclined unto F, or the power to E, or both of them to G H; then there is nothing to be lifted up, but the bare weight itself; which in this situation, is not at all increased with any addition by distance.

For in these conclusions concerning the leaver, we must always imagine that point which is touched by a perpendicular from the centre of gravity, to be one of the terms.

So that the diverse elevation or depression of the instrument, will infer a great alteration in the weight itself; as may more clearly be discerned by this following diagram.

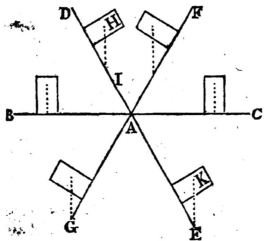

Where A is supposed to be the place of the prop, or fulciment; BC, a leaver which stands horizontally; the power and the weight belonging unto it being equal, both in themselves, and also in their distances from the prop.

But now suppose this instrument to be altered according to the situation D E; then the weight D will be diminished by so much, as the perpendicular from its centre of gravity H I, doth fall nearer to the prop or fulciment at A: and the power at E will be so much augmented, as the perpendicular from its centre K E does fall farther from the point at A. And so on the contrary, in that other situation of the leaver, F G: whence it is easy to conceive the true reason, why the inclining of the body, or the putting back of the leg, should so much conduce to the facility of rising.

From these grounds likewise may we understand, why the knees should be most weary in ascending, and the thighs in descending; which is, because the weight of the body doth bear most upon the knee-joints, in raising itself up; and most upon the muscles of the thighs, when it stays itself in coming down *

* Sir Francis Bacon's Natural History. Experiment 731.

There are divers other natural problems to this purpose, which I forbear to recite. We do not so much as go, or sit, or rise, without the use of this mechanical geometry.

CHAP. VI.

Concerning the Wheel.

THE third mechanical faculty is commonly stiled *axis in peritrochio* *. It consists of an axis, or cylinder, having a rundle about it, wherein there are fastened divers spokes, by which the whole may be turned round; according to this figure.

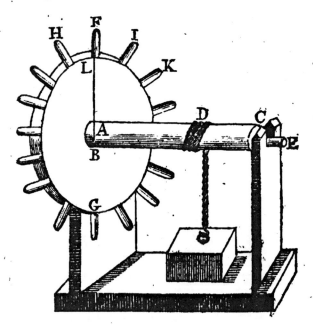

Where BC does represent the cylinder, which is supposed to move upon a smaller axis at E; (this being all one, in comparison to the several proportions, as if it were

* Called likewise *τ*⊕·. Arist. Mechan. c. 14.

a mere mathematical line;) L G is the rundle, or wheel;
H F I K, several spokes or handles that are fastened in it;
D, the place where the cord is fastened, for the drawing or
lifting up of any weight.

The force of this instrument doth consist in that disproportion of distance which there is betwixt the semidiameter of the cylinder A B, and the semidiameter of the rundle
with the spokes, F A.   For let us conceive the line F B to
be as a leaver, wherein A is the centre or fulciment, B the
place of the weight, and F of the power.   Now it is evident from the former principles, that by how much the
distance F A is greater than A B, by so much less need the
power be at F, in respect of the weight at B.   Suppose A B
to be as the tenth part of A F, then that power or strength,
which is but as a hundred pound at F, will be equal to a
thousand pound at B.

For the clearer explication of this faculty, it will not be
amiss to consider the form of it, as it will appear, being
more fully exposed to the view: as in this other diagram.

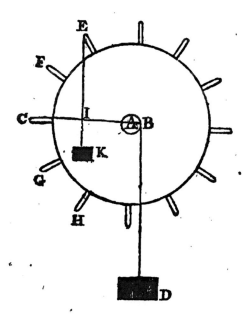

Suppose A B for the semidiameter of the axis or cylinder, and A C for the semidiameter of the rundle with

the spokes; then the power at C, which will be able to support the weight D, must bear the same proportion unto it, as A B doth to A C: so that by how much shorter the distance A B is, in comparison to the distance A C, by so much less need the power be at C, which may be able to support the weight D hanging at B.

And so likewise is it for the other spokes or handles, E F G H; at either of which, if we conceive any power, which shall move according to the same circumference wherein these handles are placed; then the strength of this power will be all one, as if it were at C. But now, supposing a dead weight hanging at any of them, (as at E) then the disproportion will vary: the power being so much less than that at C, by how much the line A C is longer than A I; the weight K being of the same force at E, as if it were hung at I, in which point the perpendicular of its gravity doth cut the diameter.

The chief advantage which this instrument doth bestow above that of the leaver, doth consist in this particular: in a leaver, the motion can be continued only for so short a space, as may be answerable to that little distance betwixt the fulciment and the weight; which is always by so much lesser, as the disproportion betwixt the weight and the power is greater, and the motion itself more easy: but now in this invention, that inconvenience is remedied; for by a frequent rotation of the axis, the weight may be moved for any height, or length, as occasion shall require.

Unto this faculty may we refer the force of all those engines, which consist of wheels with teeth in them.

Hence also may we discern the reason, why sundry instruments in common use, are framed after the like form with these following figures.

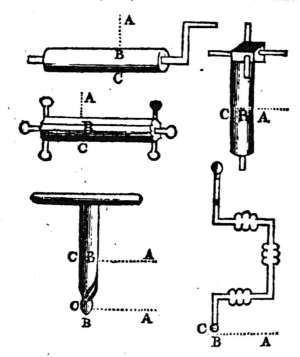

All which are but several kinds of this third mechanical faculty, in which the points A B C do represent the places of the power, the fulciment, and the weight; the power being in the same proportion unto the weight, as B C is unto B A.

CHAP. VII.

Concerning the Pulley.

THAT which is reckoned for the fourth faculty, is the pulley; which is of such ordinary use, that it needs not any particular description. The chief parts of it are divers little rundles, that are moveable about their proper axes *. These are usually divided, according to their several situations, into the upper and lower. If an engine

* Arist. Mechan. c. 19.

have two of these rundles above, and two below, it is usually called διπλαστος, if three, τριπλαστος, if many, πολυπλαστος.

The lower pullies only do give force to the motion. If we suppose a weight to hang upon any of the upper rundles, it will then require a power that in itself shall be fully equal for the sustaining of it.

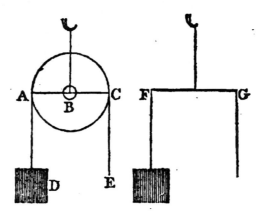

The diameter A C being as the beam of a balance, of which B is the prop or centre; now the parts A and C being equally distant from this centre, therefore the power at E must be equal to the weight at D; it being all one, as if the power and the weight were fastened by two several strings, at the ends of the balance F G.

Now all the upper pullies being of the same nature, it must necessarily follow, that none of them do in themselves conduce to the easing of the power, or lightening the weight, but only for the greater conveniency of the motion; the cords by this means running more easily moved, than otherwise they would.

But now, suppose the weight to be sustained above the pulley, as it is in all those of the lower sort; and then the power which supports it, need be but half as much as the weight itself.

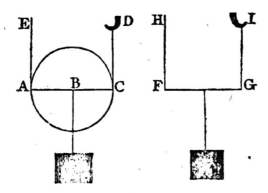

Let A C represent the diameter of a lower pulley, on whose centre at B the weight is fastened, one end of the cord being tied to a hook at D. Now it is evident, that half the weight is sustained at D, so that there is but the other half left to be sustained by the power at E : it being all one, as if the weight were tied unto the middle of the balance F G, whose ends were upheld by two several strings, F H, and G I.

And this same subduple proportion will still remain, though we suppose an upper pulley joined to the power ; as in these two other figures.

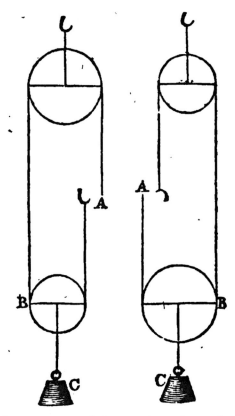

Where the power at A is equal to the weight at B: now the weight at B being but half the ponderosity C, therefore the power at A, notwithstanding the addition of the upper rundle, must be equivalent to half the weight; and as the upper pulley alone doth not abate any thing of the weight, so neither being joined with the lower; and the same sub-duple difference betwixt the power and the weight, which is caused by the lower pulley alone, doth still remain unaltered, though there be an upper pulley added unto it.

Now, as one of these under-pullies doth abate half of that heaviness which the weight hath in itself, and cause the power to be in a subduple proportion unto it; so two of them do abate half of that which remains, and cause a sub-quadruple proportion betwixt the weight and the power; three of them a subsextuple, four a suboctuple: and so for five, six, or as many as shall be required; they will all of them diminish the weight, according to this proportion.

Suppose the weight in itself to be 1200 pound, the applying unto it one of these lower pulleys, will make it but as 600; two of them, as 300; three of them, as 150, &c.

But now, if we conceive the first part of the string to be fastened unto the lower pulley, as in this other figure at F;

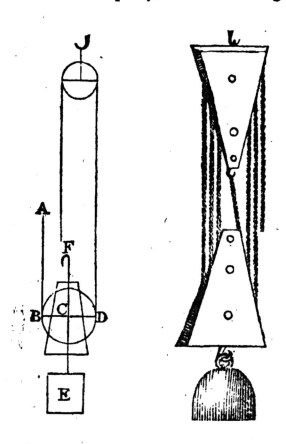

then the power at A, will be in a subtriple proportion to the weight E, because the heaviness would be then equally divided unto the three points of the lower diameter B, C, D, each of them supporting a like share of the burthen. If unto this lower pulley there were added another, then the power would be unto the weight in a subquintuple proportion. If a third, a subsextuple, and so of the rest. For we must note, that the cords in this instrument are as so many powers, and the rundles as so many leavers, or balances.

Hence it is easy to conceive, how the strength of the power may be proportioned according to any such degree, as shall be required; and how any weight given may be moved by any power given.

It is not material to the force of this instrument, whether the rundles of it be big or little, if they be made equal to one another in their several orders: but it is most convenient, that the upper should each of them increase as they are higher, and the other as they are lower; because by this means the cords will be kept from tangling.

These pulleys may be multiplied according to sundry different situations, not only when they are subordinate, as in the former examples, but also when they are placed collaterally.

From the former grounds it it easy to contrive a ladder, by which a man may pull himself up unto any height. For the performance of this, there is required only an upper and a lower rundle,

To the uppermost of these at A, there should be fastened a sharp grapple or cramp of iron, which may be apt to take

hold of any place where it lights. This part being first cast up and fastened, and the staff D E, at the nether end, being put betwixt the legs, so that a man may sit upon the other B C, and take hold of the cord at F, it is evident that the weight of the person at E, will be but equal to half so much strength at F; so that a man may easily pull himself up to the place required, by leaning but little more than half of his own weight on the string F. Or if the pulleys be multiplied, this experiment may then be wrought with less labour.

CHAP. VIII.

Of the Wedge.

THE fifth mechanical faculty is the wedge, which is a known instrument, commonly used in the cleaving of wood. The efficacy and great strength of it may be resolved unto these two particulars:

1. The form of it.

2. The manner whereby the power is impressed upon it, which is by the force of blows.

1. The form of it represents (as it were) two leavers,

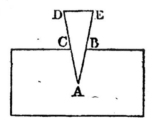

Each side A D, and A E, being one, the points B C, being instead of several props or fulciments; the weight to be moved at A, and the power that should move it, being applied to the top D E, by the force of some stroke or blow: as Aristotle * hath explained the several parts of this faculty.

* Mechan. c. 18.

But now, because this instrument may be so used that the point of it shall not touch the body to be moved, as in these other figures:

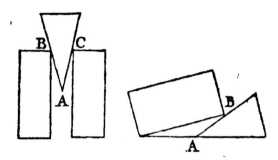

Therefore Ubaldus hath more exactly applied the several parts of it according to this form, that the point A, should be as the common fulciment, in which both the sides do meet, and (as it were) uphold one another; the points B, and C, representing that part of the leavers where the weight is placed.

It is a general rule, that the more acute the angles of these wedges are, by so much more easy will their motion be; the force being more easily impressed, and the space wherein the body is moved, being so much the less.

The second particular whereby this faculty hath its force, is the manner whereby the power is imprest upon it, which is by a stroke or blow; the efficacy of which doth much exceed any other strength.   For though we suppose a wedge being laid on a piece of timber, to be pressed down with never so great a weight; nay, though we should apply unto it the power of those other mechanical engines, the pulley, screw, &c. yet the effect would be scarce considerable in comparison to that of a blow.   The true reason of which, is one of the greatest subtilties in nature, nor is it fully rendered by any of those who have undertaken the resolution of it.   Aristotle, Cardan, and Scaliger*, do generally ascribe it unto the swiftness of that motion: but there seems to be something more in the matter than so;

* Mechan. c. 10. Subtil. 1. 17. Exercit. 331.

for otherwise it would follow that the quick stroke of a light hammer should be of greater efficacy than any softer and more gentle striking of a great sledge.   Or according to this, how should it come to pass, that the force of an arrow or bullet discharged near at hand (when the impression of that violence whereby they are carried, is most fresh, and so in probability the motion at its swiftest) is yet notwithstanding much less than it would be at a greater distance. There is therefore further considerable, the quality of that instrument by which this motion is given, and also the conveniency of distance through which it passes.

Unto this faculty is usually reduced the force of files, saws, hatchets, &c. which are as it were but so many wedges fastened unto a vectis or leaver.

CHAP. IX.

Of the Screw.

THAT which is usually recited for the sixth and last mechanic faculty, is the screw, which is described to be a kind of wedge that is multiplied, or continued by a helical revolution about a cylinder, receiving its motion not from any stroke, but from a vectis at one end of it*.   It is usually distinguished into two several kinds: the male which is meant in the former description, and the female which is of a concave superficies.

* Pappus Collect. Mathemat. l. 8.

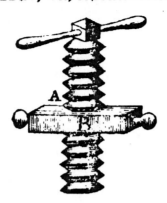

The former is noted in the figure with the letter A, the other with B.

Aristotle himself doth not so much as mention this instrument, which yet notwithstanding is of greater force and subtilty than any of the rest. It is chiefly applied to the squeezing or pressing of things downwards, as in the presses for printing; for wine, oil, and extracting the juice from other fruits. In the performance of which, the strength of one man, may be of greater force than the weight of a heavy mountain. It is likewise used for the elevating or lifting up of weights.

The advantage of this faculty above the rest, doth mainly consist in this: the other instruments do require so much strength for the supporting of the weight to be moved, as may be equal unto it, besides that other superadded power whereby it is out-weighed and moved; so that in the operations by these, a man does always spend himself in a continued labour.

Thus (for example) a weight that is lifted up by a wheel or pulley, will of itself descend, if there be not an equal power to sustain it. But now in the composure of a screw, this inconvenience is perfectly remedied; for so much force as is communicated unto this faculty from the power that is applied unto it, is still retained by the very frame and nature of the instrument itself; since the motion of it cannot possibly return, but from the very same place where it first began. Whence it comes to pass, that any weight lifted up with the assistance of this engine, may likewise be sustained by it without the help of any external power; and cannot again descend unto its former place, unless the handle of the screw (where the motion first began) be turned back: so that all the strength of the power may be employed in the motion of the weight, and none spent in the sustaining of it.

The chief inconvenience of this instrument is, that in a short space it will be screwed unto its full length, and then it cannot be of any further use for the continuance of the motion, unless it be returned back, and undone again as at the first. But this is usually remedied by another invention, commonly styled a perpetual screw, which hath the motion of a wheel, and the force of a screw, being both infinite.

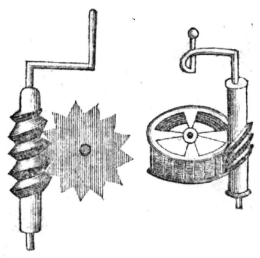

. For the composure of which, instead of the female, or concave screw, there must be a little wheel with some notches in it, equivalent to teeth*, by which the other may take hold of it, and turn it round, as in these other figures.

This latter engine does so far exceed all other contrivances to this purpose, that it may justly seem a wonder why it is not of as common use in these times and places, as any of the rest.

* It is used in some watches.

CHAP. X.

An enquiry into the magnificent works of the ancients, which much exceeding our latter times, may seem to infer a decay in these mechanical arts.

THUS have I briefly treated concerning the general principles of mechanics, together with the distinct proportions betwixt the weight and the power in each several faculty of it : whence it is easy to conceive the truth and ground of those famous ancient monuments, which seem almost incredible to these following ages. And because many of them recorded by antiquity, were of such vast labour and magnificence, and so mightily disproportionable to human strength, it shall not therefore be impertinent unto the purpose I aim at, for to specify some of the most remarkable amongst them, and to enquire into the means and occasion upon which they were first attempted.

Amongst the Egyptians we read of divers pyramids of so vast a magnitude, as time itself in the space of so many hundred years hath not yet devoured. Herodotus * mentions one of them, erected by Cleopes an Egyptian king, wherein there was not any one stone less than 30 foot long, all of them being fetched from Arabia. And not much after, the same author relates, how Amasis, another Egyptian, made himself a house of one entire stone, which was 21 cubits long, 14 broad, and 8 cubits high. The same Amasis is reported to have made the statue of a sphink, or Egyptian cat, all of one single stone; whose length was 143 foot, its height 62 foot, the compass of this statue's head containing 102 foot †. In one of the Egyptian temples consecrated to Jupiter, there is related to be an obelisk, consisting of 4 smaragds or emeralds; the whole is 40 cubits high, 4 cubits broad at the bottom, and two at the top ‡. Sesostris the king of Egypt, in a temple at Mem-

---

* Lib. 2. c. 175.   † Plin. l. 36. c. 12.   ‡ Plin. l. 37. cap. 5.

phis, dedicated to Vulcan, is reported to have erected two statues; one for himself, the other for his wife, both consisting of two several stones, each of which were 30 cubits high *.

Amongst the Jews we read in sacred writ of Solomon's temple, which for its state and magnificence, might have been justly reckoned amongst the other wonders of the world; wherein besides the great riches of the materials, there were works too of as great labour. Pillars of brass 18 cubits high, and 12 cubits round; great and costly stones for the foundation of it †: Josephus ‡ tells us that some of them were 40 cubits, others 45 cubits long. And in the same chapter he mentions the three famous towers built by Herod; wherein every stone being of white marble, was 20 cubits long, 10 broad, and 5 high. And which was the greatest wonder, the old wall itself was situated on a steep rising ground, and yet the hills upon it, on the tops of which these towers were placed, were about 30 cubits high, that it is scarce imaginable by what strength so many stones of such great magnitude should be conveyed to so high a place.

Amongst the Grecians we read of the Ephesian temple dedicated to Diana; wherein there were 127 columns made of so many several stones, each of them 60 foot high, being all taken out of the quarries in Asia ‖. It is storied also of the brazen colossus, or great statue in the island of Rhodes, that it was 70 cubits high. The thumbs of it being so big that no man could grasp one of them about with both his arms; when it stood upright, a ship might have passed betwixt the legs of it, with all its sails fully displayed; being thrown down by an earthquake, the brass of it did load 900 camels §. But above all ancient designs to this purpose, that would have been most wonderful, which a Grecian architect ¶ did propound unto

---

* Diodor. Sicul. Biblioth. l. 1. sect. 2.

† 1 King. vii. 15. v. 17.   ‡ De Bello Jud. l. 6. cap. 6.

‖ Plin. l. 36. cap. 14. Pancirol. Deperd. Tit. 32.

§ Plin. l. 34. cap. 3.   ¶ Vitruv. Archit. l. 2.

Alexander, to cut the mountain Athos into the form of a statue, which in his right hand should hold a town capable of ten thousand men, and in his left a vessel to receive all the water that flowed from the several springs in the mountain. But whether Alexander in his ambition did fear that such an idol should have more honour than he himself, or whether in his good husbandry, he thought that such a microcosm (if I may so style it) would have cost him almost as much as the conquering of this great world, or whatever else was the reason, he refused to attempt it.

Amongst the Romans we read of a brazen colossus, made at the command and charges of Nero *, which was 120 foot high; Martial calls it sydereus, or starry.

Hic ubi sydereus propius videt astra colossus.

And it is storied of M. Curio † that he erected two theatres sufficiently capacious of people, contrived moveable upon certain hinges; sometimes there were several plays and shows in each of them, neither being any disturbance to the other; and sometimes they were both turned about, with the people in them, and the ends meeting together, did make a perfect amphitheatre; so that the spectators which were in either of them, might jointly behold the same spectacles.

There were besides at Rome sundry obelisks ‡, made of so many entire stones, some of them 40, some 80, and others 90 cubits high. The chief of them were brought out of Egypt, where they were dug out of divers quarries, and being wrought into form, were afterwards (not without incredible labour, and infinite charges) conveyed unto Rome. In the year 1586, there was erected an old obelisk which had been formerly dedicated unto the memory of Julius Cæsar. It was one solid stone, being an ophite or kind of spotted marble. The height of it was 107 foot, the breadth of it at the bottom was 12 foot, at the top 8. Its whole weight is reckoned to be 956148 pounds; besides the hea-

---

* Suet. Ner.   † Pancirol. Deperd. Tit. 28.   ‡ Idem Tit. 31.

viness of all those instruments that were used about it, which (as it is thought) could not amount to less than 1042824 pounds. It was transplaced at the charges of pope Sixtus the fifth, from the left side of the Vatican unto a more eminent place about a hundred foot off, where now it stands. The moving of this obelisk is celebrated by the writings of above 56 several authors, (saith Monantholius [*],) all of them mentioning it, not without much wonder and praise. Now if it seem so strange and glorious an attempt to move this obelisk for so little a space, what then may we think of the carriage of it out of Egypt, and divers other far greater works performed by antiquity? This may seem to infer that these mechanical arts are now lost, and decayed amongst the many other ruins of time: which yet notwithstanding cannot be granted, without much ingratitude to those learned men, whose labours in this kind we enjoy, and may justly boast of. And therefore for our better understanding of these particulars, it will not be amiss to enquire both why, and how such works should be performed in those former and ruder ages, which are not, and (as it should seem) cannot be effected in these later and more learned times. In the examination of which, we shall find that it is not the want of art that disables us for them, since these mechanical discoveries are altogether as perfect, and (I think) much more exact now, than they were heretofore; but it is, because we have not either the same motives to attempt such works, or the same means to effect them as the ancients had.

CHAP. XI.

That the ancients had divers motives and means for such vast magnificent works, which we have not.

THE motives by which they were excited to such magnificent attempts, we may conceive to be chiefly three:

[*] Comment. in Mechan. Arist. c. 19.

$\left\{\begin{array}{l}\text{Religion.}\\\text{Policy.}\\\text{Ambition.}\end{array}\right.$

1. Religion. Hence was it that most of these stately buildings were intended for some sacred use, being either temples or tombs *, all of them dedicated to some of their deities. It was an inbred principle in those ancient heathen, that they could not chuse but merit very much by being liberal in their outward services. And therefore we read of Crœsus †, that being overcome in a battle, and taken by Cyrus, he did revile the gods of ingratitude, because they had no better care of him, who had so frequently adored them with costly oblations. And as they did conceive themselves bound to part with their lives in defence of their religion, so likewise to employ their utmost power and estate about any such design which might promote or advance it. Whereas now, the generality of men, especially the wisest sort amongst them, are in this respect of another opinion, counting such great and immense labours, to be at the best but glorious vanities. The temple of Solomon indeed was to be a type, and therefore it was necessary that it should be so extraordinarily magnificent, otherwise perhaps a much cheaper structure might have been as commendable and serviceable.

2. Policy. That by this means they might find out employment for the people, who of themselves being not much civilized, might by idleness quickly grow to such a rudeness and barbarism, as not to be bounded within any laws of government. Again, by this means the riches of the kingdom did not lie idly in their kings treasuries, but was always in motion; which could not but be a great advantage and improvement to the commonwealth ‡. And perhaps some of them feared lest if they should leave too much money unto their successors, it might be an occasion to ensnare them in such idle and vain courses, as would ruin their kingdoms: whereas in these latter ages, none of

* As Pyramids, Obelisks.   † Herodot. l. 1.
‡ Plin. l. 6. c. 12.

all these politic incitements can be of any force, because now there is employment enough for all, and money little enough for every one.

3. Ambition to be known unto posterity; and hence likewise arose that incredible labour and care they bestowed, to leave such monuments behind them as might continue for ever *, and make them famous unto all after-ages. This was the reason of Absalom's pillar, spoken of in scripture, to keep his name in remembrance †. And doubtless this too was the end which many other of the ancients have aimed at, in those (as they thought) everlasting buildings.

But now these later ages are much more active and stirring; so that every ambitious man may find so much business for the present, that he shall scarce have any leisure to trouble-himself about the future. And therefore in all these respects, there is a great disproportion betwixt the incitements of those former and these later times unto such magnificent attempts.

Again, as they differ much in their motives unto them, so likewise in the means of effecting them.

There was formerly more leisure and opportunity, both for the great men to undertake such works, and for the people to perfect them. Those past ages were more quiet and peaceable, the princes rather wanting employment, than being overpressed with it, and therefore were willing to make choice of such great designs, about which to busy themselves. Whereas now the world is grown more politic, and therefore more troublesome; every great man having other private and necessary business about which to employ both his time and means. And so likewise for the common people, who then living more wildly, without being confined to particular trades and professions, might be more easily collected about such famous employments; whereas now, if a prince have any occasion for an army, it is very hard for him to raise so great a multitude as were

* Psal. iv. 11. † 2 Sam. i. 18.

usually employed about these magnificent buildings. We
read of 360000 men that were busied for twenty years in
making one of the Egyptian pyramids. And Herodotus *
tells us of 1000000 men who were as long in building another of them. About the carriage of one stone for Amasis
the distance of twenty days journey, there was for three
years together employed 2000 chosen men, governors, besides many other under-labourers. It was the opinion of
Josephus † and Nazianzen, that these pyramids were built
by Joseph for granaries against the years of famine. Others
think that the brick made by the children of Israel was
employed about the framing of them, because we read that
the tower of Babel did consist of brick or artificial stone,
Gen. xi. 3. And if these were the labourers that were busied about them, it is no wonder though they were of so
vast a magnitude; for we read that the children of Israel
at their coming out of Egypt, were numbered to be six
hundred thousand, and three thousand, and five hundred
and fifty men, Numb. i. 46. So many handfuls of earth
would almost make a mountain, and therefore we may easily believe that so great a multitude in so long a space as
their bondage lasted, for above four hundred years, might
well enough accomplish such vast designs.

In the building of Solomon's temple, there were threescore and ten thousand that bare burthens, and fourscore
thousand hewers in the mountains, 1 Kings v. 15.

The Ephesian temple was built by all Asia joining together; the 127 pillars were made by so many kings, according to their several successions, the whole work being not
finished under the space of two hundred and fifteen years.
Whereas the transplacing of that obelisk at Rome by Sixtus
the Vth, (spoken of before) was done in some few days by
five or six hundred men; and as the work was much less
than many other recorded by antiquity, so the means by
which it was wrought, was yet far less in this respect than
what is related of them.

* Lib. 2.   † Antiq. l. 2. c. 5.

2. The abundance of wealth, which was then ingrossed in the possession of some few particular persons, being now diffused amongst a far greater number. There is now a greater equality amongst mankind, and the flourishing of arts and sciences hath so stirred up the sparks of men's natural nobility, and made them of such active and industrious spirits, as to free themselves in a great measure from that slavery, which those former and wilder nations were subjected unto.

In building one of the pyramids, there was expended for the maintenance of the labourers with radish and onions, no less than eighteen hundred talents, which is reckoned to amount unto 1880000 crowns, or thereabouts. And considering the cheapness of these things in those times and places, so much money might go farther than a sum ten times greater could do in the maintenance of so many now.

In Solomon's temple we know how the extraordinary riches of that king, the general flourishing of the whole state, and the liberality of the people did jointly concur to the building of the temple. *Pecuniarum copia et populi largitas, majora dictu conabatur,* (saith Josephus[*].) The Rhodian colossus is reported to have cost three hundred talents the making; and so were all those other famous monuments of proportionable expence.

Pancirollus[†] speaking of those theatres that were erected at the charges of some private Roman citizens, saith thus: *nostro hoc sæculo vel rex satis haberet quod ageret ædificio ejusmodi erigendo;* and a little after upon the like occasion, *res mehercule miraculosa, quæ nostris temporibus vix à potentissimo aliquo rege possit exhiberi.*

3. Add unto the two former considerations, that exact care and indefatigable industry which they bestowed in the raising of those structures; these being the chief and only designs on which many of them did employ all their best thoughts and utmost endeavours. Cleopes an Egyptian

---

[*] De Bell. Jud. l. 6. cap. 6.   [†] Deperd. Tit. 18.

king is reported to have been so desirous to finish one of the pyramids, that having spent all about it he was worth, or could possibly procure, he was forced at last to prostitute his own daughter for necessary maintenance.   And we read of Ramises * another king of Egypt, how that he was so careful to erect an obelisk, about which he had employed 20000 men, that when he feared lest through the negligence of the artificers, or weakness of the engine, the stone might fall and break, he tied his own son to the top of it, that so the care of his safety might make the workmen more circumspect in their business.   And what strange matters may be effected by the mere diligence and labour of great multitudes, we may easily discern from the wild Indians, who having not the art or advantage of engines, did yet by their unwearied industry remove stones of an incredible greatness.   Acosta † relates that he himself measured one at Tiaguanaco, which was thirty-eight foot long, eighteen broad, and six thick; and he affirms, that in their stateliest edifices there were many other of much vaster magnitude.

From all which considerations, it may appear, that the strangeness of those ancient monuments above any that are now effected, does not necessarily infer any defect of art in these later ages.   And I conceive, it were as easy to demonstrate the mechanical arts in these times to be so far beyond the knowledge of former ages, that had we but the same means as the ancients had, we might effect far greater matters than any they attempted, and that too in a shorter space, and with less labour.

* Plin. l. 36. c. 9.   † Histor. Ind. l. 6. c. 14.

CHAP. XII.

Concerning the force of the mechanic faculties; particularly the Balance and Leaver. How they may be contrived to move the whole world, or any conceivable weight.

ALL these magnificent works of the ancients before specified, are scarce considerable in respect of art, if we compare them with the famous speeches and acts of Archimedes: of whom it is reported, that he was frequently wont to say, how that he could move *datum pondus, cum data potentiá;* the greatest conceivable weight, with the least conceivable power: and that if he did but know where to stand and fasten his instrument, he could move the world, all this great globe of sea and land. Which promises, though they were altogether above the vulgar apprehension or belief, yet because his acts were somewhat answerable thereunto, therefore the king of Syracuse did enact a law, whereby every man was bound to believe whatever Archimedes would affirm.

It is easy to demonstrate the geometrical truth of those strange assertions, by examining them according to each of the forenamed mechanic faculties, every one of which is of infinite power.

To begin with the two first of them, the balance and the leaver, (which I here join together, because the proportions of both are wholly alike;) it is certain, though there should be the greatest imaginable weight, and the least imaginable power, (suppose the whole world, and the strength of one man, or infant;) yet if we conceive the same disproportion betwixt their several distances in the former faculties, from the fulciment, or centre of gravity, they would both equipondcrate. And if the distance of the power from the centre, in comparison to the distance of the weight, were but any thing more than the heaviness of the weight is in respect of the power, it may then be evident from the former principles, that the power would be of greater force than the weight, and consequently able to move it.

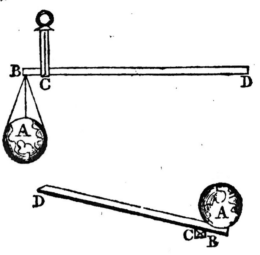

Thus, if we suppose this great globe at A to contain 24000000000000000000000000 pounds, allowing a hundred pounds for each cubical foot in it, (as Stevinius * hath calculated) yet a man or child at D, whose strength perhaps is but equivalent to one hundred, or ten pounds weight, may be able to outweigh and move it; if there be but a little greater disproportion betwixt the two distances C D and C B, than there is betwixt the heaviness of the weight, and the strength of the power; that is, if the distance C D, unto the other distance C B, be any thing more than 24000000000000000000000000 unto 100 or 10, every ordinary instrument doth include all these parts really, though not sensibly distinguished.

Under this latter faculty, I did before mention that engine, by which Archimedes drew up the Roman ships at the siege of Syracuse †. This is usually stiled Tollenon, being of the same form with that which is commonly used by brewers and dyers, for the drawing of water. It consists of two posts; the one fastened perpendicularly in the

---

* Static. l. 3. prop. 10.   † Lipsius Poliorcet. l. 1. Dialog. 6.

ground, the other being jointed on cross to the top of it.
At the end he fastened a strong hook or grapple of iron,
which being let over the wall to the river, he would thereby
take hold of the ships, as they passed under; and afterwards, by applying some weight, or perhaps the force of
screws to the other end, he would thereby lift them into the
open air; where having swinged them up and down till he
had shaken out the men and goods that were in them, he
would then dash the vessels against the rocks, or drown
them in their sudden fall: insomuch that Marcellus, the
Roman general, was wont to say, τον μεν ναυσιν αυτε κυαδιζειν
εκ θαλατίης Αρχιμηδη *.   That Archimedes made use of
his ships instead of buckets to draw water with.

This faculty will be of the same force, not only when it
is continued in one, but also when it is multiplied in divers
instruments; as may be conceived in this other form;
which I do not mention, as if it could be serviceable for any
other motion, (since the space by which the weight would
be moved, will be so little as not to fall under sense) but
only for the better explication of this mechanic principle,
and for the right understanding of that force arising from
multiplication in the other faculties, which do all depend
upon this.   The wheel, and pulley, and screw, being but
as so many leavers of a circular form and motion, whose
strength may be therefore continued to a greater space.

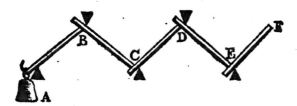

Imagine the weight A to be a hundred thousand pounds,
and the distance of that point, wherein every leaver touches
either the weight, or one another from the point where
they touch the prop, to be but one such part, whereof the

* Plutarch in his life.

remainder contains ten; then according to the former grounds, 10000 at B will equiponderate to A, which is 100000; so that the second leaver hath but 10000 pounds to move. Now, because this observes the same proportions with the other, in the distances of its several points, therefore 1000 pounds at C will be of equal weight to the former: and the weight at C being but as a thousand pound, that which is but as a hundred at D, will be answerable unto it; and so still in the same proportion, that which is but 10 at E, will be equal to 100 at D; and that which is but one pound at F, will also be equal to ten at E. Whence it is manifest, that one pound at F is equal to 100000 at A; and the weight must always be diminished in the same proportion as ten to one, because in the multiplication of these leavers, the distance of the point where the instrument touches the weight, from that where it touches the prop, is but as one such part, whereof the remainder contains ten. But now if we imagine it to be as the thousandth part, then must the weight be diminished according to this proportion; and then in the same multiplication of leavers, 1 pound will be equal to 1000 000 000 000 000 pounds : so that though we suppose the weight to be never so heavy, yet let the disproportion of distances be greater, or the leavers more, and any little power may move it.

* See the figures, c. 6.

CHAP. XIII.

Of the Wheel: by multiplication of which, it is easy to move any imaginable weight.

THE wheel, or axis in peritrochio, was before demonstrated to be of equivalent force with the former faculties *. If we conceive the same difference betwixt the semidiameter of the wheels, or spokes A C, and the semidiameter of the axis A B, as there is betwixt the weight of the world, and the strength of a man; it may then be evident, that this strength of one man, by the help of such an instrument, will equiponderate to the weight of the whole world. And if the semidiameter of the wheel A C, be but any thing more in respect of the semidiameter of the axis A B, than the weight of the world supposed at D, is in comparison to the strength of a man at C; it may then be manifest from the same grounds, that this strength will be of so much greater force than the weight, and consequently able to move it.

The force of this faculty may be more conveniently understood and used by the multiplication of several wheels *, together with nuts belonging unto each of them; as it may be easily experimented in the ordinary jacks that are used for the roasting of meat, which commonly consist but of three wheels; and yet if we suppose a man tied in the place of the weight, it were easy by a single hair fastened unto the fly or balance of the jack, to draw him up from the ground: as will be evident from this following figure.

* An engine of many wheels is commonly called glossocomus.

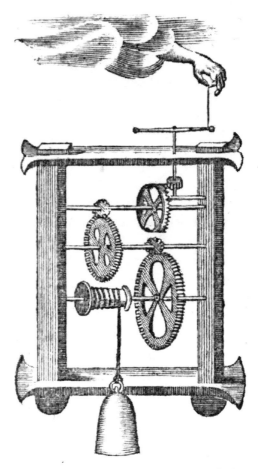

Where suppose the length of the fly or balance in comparison to the breadth of its axis, to be as 10 to one, and so for the three other wheels in respect of the nuts that belong unto them; (though this difference be oftentimes less, as we may well allow it to be); withal suppose the weight (or a man tied in the place of it) to be a hundred pounds: I say according to this supposition, it is evident that the power at the balance which shall be equal to the weight, need be but as 1 to 10000. For the first axis is conceived to be but as the tenth part of its wheel; and therefore though the weight in itself be as 10000, yet unto a power that hath this advantage, it is but as 1000, and therefore this thousand unto the like power at the second wheel, will be but as 100, and this 100 at the third but as 10; and lastly, this ten at the balance but as one. But the weight was before supposed to be 100, which to the first wheel will be but 10, to the second as one, to the third as a decimal, or one tenth to the sails as one hundredth part · so that if the hair be but strong enough to lift $\frac{1}{10000}$, that is, one ten thousandth part of a man, or (which is all one) one hundredth part of a pound, it may as well serve by the help of this instrument for the drawing of him up. And though there be not altogether so great a disproportion betwixt the several parts of a jack (as in many perhaps there is not ;) and though a man may be heavier than is here supposed, yet it is withal considerable, that the strength of a hair is able to bear much more than the hundredth part of a pound.

Upon this ground Mersennus * tells us out of Solomon de Cavet, that if there were an engine of twelve wheels, each of them with teeth, as also the axes or nuts that belong unto them ; if the diameter of these wheels were unto each axis as a hundred to one ; and if we suppose these wheels to be so placed, that the teeth of the one might take hold of the axis that belongs unto the next, and that the axis of the handle may turn the first wheel, and the weight be tied unto the axis of the last ; with such an engine as this, saith he, a child (if he could stand anywhere without this earth) might with much ease move it towards him.

For according to the former supposition, that this globe of sea and land did contain as many hundred pounds as it doth cubical feet, viz. 24000000000000000000000000, it may be evident that any strength, whose force is but equivalent to three pounds, will by such an engine be able to move it,

Of this kind was that engine so highly extolled by Stevinus †, which he calls pancration, or omnipotent, preferring it before the inventions of Archimedes. It consisted

* Comment in Gen. c. 1. v. 10. art. 6. De viribus motricibus, Theor. 16.
† De Static. praxi.

of wheels and nuts, as that before specified is supposed. Hither also should be referred the force of racks, which serve for bending of the strongest bows *, as also that little pocket engine, wherewith a man may break or wrench open any door, together with divers the like instruments in common use.

CHAP. XIV.

Concerning the infinite strength of Wheels, Pullies, and Screws. That it is possible by the multiplication of these, to pull up any oak by the roots with a hair, lift it up with a straw, or blow it up with one's breath, or to perform the greatest labour with the least power.

FROM what hath been before delivered concerning the nature of the pulley, it is easy to understand how this faculty also may be proportioned betwixt any weight, and any power, as being likewise of infinite strength.

It is reported of Archimedes, that with an engine of pullies, to which he applied only his left hand, he lifted up 5000 bushels of corn at once †, and drew a ship with all its lading upon dry land. This engine Zetzes calls trispatum, or trispastum, which signifies only a threefold pulley: but herein he doth evidently mistake, for it is not possible that this alone should serve for the motion of so great a weight; because such an engine can but make a subsextuple, or at most a subseptuple proportion betwixt the weight and power; which is much too little to reconcile the strength of a man unto so much heaviness. Therefore Ubaldus ‡ doth more properly style it, polyspaston; or an instrument of many pullies. How many, were easy to find out, if we

---

* Ramelli, fig. 160.   † 7000 saith Zetzes, Chiliad. 2. Hist. 35.
‡ Præf. ad. Mechan.

did exactly know the weight of those ancient measures; supposing them to be the same with our bushel in England, which contains 64 pints or pounds, the whole would amount to 320000 pounds; half of which would be lightened, by the help of one pulley, three quarters by two pullies, and so onward, according to this subduple, subquadruple, and subsextuple proportion. So that if we conceive the strength of the left hand to be equivalent unto twenty or forty pounds, it is easy to find out how many pullies are required to enable it for the motion of so great a weight.

Upon this ground Mersennus * tells us, that any little child with an engine of an hundred double pullies, might easily move this great globe of earth, though it were much heavier than it is. And in reference to this kind of engine (saith Monantholius †) are we to understand that assertion of Archimedes, (as he more immediately intended it) concerning the possibility of moving the world.

The wedge was before demonstrated to be as a double vectis or leaver, and therefore it would be needless to explain particularly how this likewise may be contrived of infinite force.

The screw is capable of multiplication, as well as any of the other faculties, and may perhaps be more serviceable for such great weights, than any of the rest. Archimedes his engine of greatest strength, called caristion, is by some thought to consist of these. *Axes habebat cum infinitis cochleis* ‡. And that other engine of his called helix, (mentioned by ‖ Athenæus) wherewith he lifted Hiero's great ship into the sea, without any other help, is most likely to be framed of perpetual screws, saith Rivaltus.

Whence it may evidently appear, that each of these mechanic faculties are of infinite power, and may be contrived proportionable unto any conceivable weight. And that no natural strength is anyway comparable unto these artificial inventions.

* Comment in Gen. c. i. v. 10. art. 6.
† Præf ad. Mechan Aristotle.
‡ Stevin. de Static. prax. See Besson.
‖ Deipnosophist. l. 5. Oper. exter. Archimed.

It is reported of Sampson *, that he could carry the gates of a city upon his shoulders; and that the strongest bonds were unto him but as flax burnt with fire, and yet his hair being shaved off, all his strength departed from him. We read of Milo † that he could carry an ox upon his back, and yet when he tried to tear an oak asunder that was somewhat riven before, having drawn it to its utmost, it suddenly joined together again, catching his hands in the cleft, and so strongly manacled him, that he became a prey to the wild beasts.

But now by these mechanical contrivances, it were easy to have made one of Sampson's hairs that was shaved off, to have been of more strength than all of them when they were on. By the help of these arts it is possible (as I shall demonstrate) for any man to lift up the greatest oak by the roots with a straw, to pull it up with a hair, or to blow it up with his breath.

Suppose the roots of an oak to extend a thousand foot square, (which is almost a quarter of a mile) and forty foot deep, each cubical foot being an hundred pound weight; which though it be much beyond the extension of any tree, or the weight of earth; the compass of the roots in the ground (according to common opinion) not extending further than the branches of it in the air, and the depth of it not above ten foot, beyond which the greatest rain doth not penetrate (saith Seneca ‡.) *Ego vinearum diligens fossor affirmo nullam pluviam esse tam magnam, quæ terram ultra decem pedes in altitudinem madefaciat.* And because the root must receive its nourishment from the help of showers, therefore it is probable that it doth not go below them. So that (I say) though the proportions supposed do much exceed the real truth, yet it is considerable that some great overplus must be allowed for that labour which there will be in the forcible divulsion or separation of the parts of the earth which are continued.

---

* Judges xv.   † A. Gell. Noct. Att. l. 15. c. 16.
‡ Nat. Qu. L. 3. c. 7.

According to this supposition, the work of forcing up the oak by the roots will be equivalent to the lifting up of 4000000000 pound weight, which by the advantage of such an engine, as is here described, may be easily performed with the least conceivable power.

The whole force of this engine doth consist in two double pullies, twelve wheels, and a sail. One of these pullies at the bottom will diminish half of the weight, so that it shall be but as 2000000000, and the other pulley will abate ¼ three quarters of it; so that it shall be but as 1000000000. And because the beginning of the string being fastened unto the lower pulley, makes the power to be in a subquintuple proportion unto the weight, therefore a power that shall be as 1000000000, that is, a subquadruple, will be so much stronger than the weight, and consequently able to move it *. Now suppose the breadth of all the axes and nuts to be unto the diameters of the wheel as ten to one; and it will then be evident that to a power at the

First wheel, the weight is but as 100000000:
To the second as 10000000:
To the third as 1000000:
To the fourth as 100000:
To the fifth as 10000:
To the sixth as 1000:
To the seventh as 100:
To the eighth as 10:
To the ninth as 1:
To the tenth as $\frac{1}{10}$, one decimal:
To the eleventh as $\frac{1}{1000}$:
To the twelfth as $\frac{1}{10000}$:
And to the sails yet less:

So that if the strength of the straw, or hair, or breath, be but equal to the weight of one thousandth part of a pound, it may be of sufficient force to pull up the oak.

If in this engine we suppose the disproportion betwixt the wheels and nuts to be as a hundred to one, then it is very evident that the same strength of breath, or a hair, or a straw, would be able to move the whole world, as will be easily found by calculation Let this great globe of sea and land be imagined (as before) to weigh so many hundred pounds as it contains cubical feet; namely, 2400000000000000000000000 pounds. This will be to the first pulley, 12000000000000000000000000. To the second less than 6000000000000000000000000. But for

---

* See chap. viii.

more easy and convenient reckoning, let it be supposed to be somewhat more, viz. 1000000000000000000000000. This

To the first wheel will be but as 10000000000000000000000.
To the second as . . . . 10000000000000000000000 .
To the third as . . . . 100000000000000000000.
To the fourth as . . . . 10000000000000000.
To the fifth as . . . . 100000000000000.
To the sixth as . . . . 1000000000000.
To the seventh as . . . . 10000000000.
To the eighth as . . . . 100000000.
To the ninth as . . . . 1000000.
To the tenth as . . . . 10000.
To the eleventh as . . . 100.
To the twelfth as . . . . 1.
To the sails as . . . . . $\frac{1}{100}$.

So that a power which is much less than the hundredth part of a pound will be able to move the world.

It were needless to set down any particular explication, how such mechanical strength may be applied unto all the kinds of local motion; since this is in itself so facil and obvious, that every ordinary artificer doth sufficiently understand it.

The species of local violent motion are by Aristotle * reckoned to be these four: pulsio, tractio, vectio, vertigo ; thrusting, drawing, carrying, turning; unto some of which all these artificial operations must necessarily be reduced, the strength of any power being equally appliable unto all of them : so that there is no work impossible to these contrivances ; but there may be as much acted by this art, as can be fancied by imagination.

* Phys. l. 7. c. 3.

CHAP. XV.

Concerning the proportion of slowness and swiftness in mechanical motions.

HAVING already discoursed concerning the strength of these mechanical faculties; it remains, for the more perfect discovery of their natures, that we treat somewhat concerning those two differences of artificial motion : slowness, and swiftness : without the right understanding of which, a man shall be exposed to many absurd mistakes, in attempting of those things which are either in themselves impossible, or else not to be performed with such means as are applied unto them. I may safely affirm, that many, if not most mistakes in these mechanical designs, do arise from a misapprehension of that difference which there will be betwixt the slowness or swiftness of the weight and power, in comparison to the proportion of their several strengths.

Hence it is, that so many engines invented for mines and waterworks, do so often fail in the performance of that for which they were intended ; because the artificers many times do forget to allow so much time for the working of their engine, as may be proportionable to the difference betwixt the weight and power that belong unto them : whereas, he that rightly understands the grounds of this art, may as easily find out the difference of space and time required to the motion of the weight and power, as he may their different strengths ; and not only tell how any power may move any weight, but also in what a space of time it may move it any space or distance.

If it were possible to contrive such an invention, whereby any conceivable weight may be moved by any conceivable power, both with the same quickness and speed, (as it is in those things which are immediately stirred by the hand, without the help of any other instrument ;) the works of nature would be then too much subjected to the power of art, and men might be thereby encouraged (with the builders of Babel, or the rebel giants) to such bold designs as would not become a created being. And therefore the wisdom of providence hath so confined these human arts, that what any invention hath in the strength of its motion, is abated in the slowness of it; and what it hath in the extraordinary quickness of its motion, must be allowed for in the great strength that is required unto it.

For it is to be observed as a general rule, that the space of time or place, in which the weight is moved, in comparison to that in which the power doth move, is in the same proportion as they themselves are unto one another.

So that if there be any great difference betwixt the strength of the weight and the power, the same kind of differences will there be in the spaces of their motion.

To illustrate this by an example :

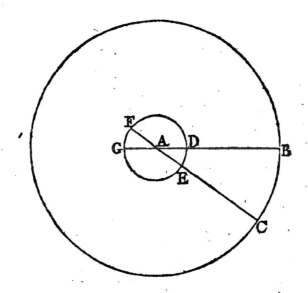

Let the line G A B represent a balance, or leaver; the weight being supposed at the point G, the fulciment at A, and the power sustaining the weight at B. Suppose the point G, unto which the weight is fastened, to be elevated unto F, and the opposite point B to be depressed unto C;

it is evident that the arch, F G, or (which is all one) D E, doth shew the space of the weight, and the arch B C the motion of the power. Now both these arches have the same proportion unto one another, as there is betwixt the weight and the power, or (which is all one) as there is betwixt their several distances from the fulciment. Suppose A G unto A B to be as one unto four; it may then be evident, that F G, or D E, will be in the same proportion unto B C: for as any two semidiameters are unto one another, so are the several circumferences described by them, as also any proportional parts of the same circumferences.

And as the weight and power do thus differ in the spaces of their motions, so likewise in the slowness of it; the one moving the whole distance B C, in the same time wherein the other passes only G F. So that the motion of the power from B to C, is four times swifter than that of the weight from G to F. And thus will it be, if we suppose the disproportions to be far greater; whether or no we conceive it, either by a continuation of the same instrument and faculty, as in the former example; or by a multiplication of divers, as in pullies, wheels, &c. By how much the power is in itself less than the weight, by so much will the motion of the weight be slower than that of the power.

To this purpose, I shall briefly touch at one of the diagrams expressed before in the twelfth chapter, concerning the multiplication of leavers.

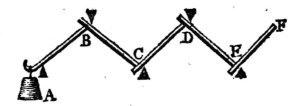

In which, as each instrument doth diminish the weight according to a decuple proportion, so also do they diminish the space and slowness of its motion. For if we should conceive the first leaver B to be depressed unto its lowest, suppose ten foot, yet the weight A would not be raised above one foot : but now the second leaver, at its utmost, could move but a tenth part of the first, and the third leaver but a tenth part of the second ; and so of the rest. So that the last leaver F being depressed, will pass a space 100000 greater, and by a motion, 100000 swifter than the weight at A.

Thus are we to conceive of all the other faculties, wherein there is constantly the same disproportion betwixt the weight and power, in respect of the spaces and slowness of their motions, as there is betwixt their several gravities. If the power be unto the weight but as one unto a hundred, then the space through which the weight moves, will be a hundred times less, and consequently the motion of the weight a hundred times slower than that of the power.

So that it is but a vain and impossible fancy for any one to think that he can move a great weight with a little power, in a little space ; but in all these mechanical attempts, that advantage which is gotten in the strength of the motion, must be still allowed for the slowness of it.

Though these contrivances do so extremely increase the power, yet they do proportionably protract the time. That which by such helps one man may do in a hundred days, may be done by the immediate strength of a hundred men in one day.

CHAP. XVI.

That it is possible to contrive such an artificial motion, as shall be of a slowness proportionable to the swiftness of the heavens.

IT were a pretty subtilty to inquire after, whether or no it be not possible to contrive such an artificial motion, that should be in such a proportion slow, as the heavens are supposed to be swift.

For the exact resolution of which, it would be requisite that we should first pitch upon some medium, or indifferent motion, by the distance from which, we may judge of the proportions on either side, whether slowness, or swiftness. Now, because there is not any such natural medium, which may be absolutely stiled an indifferent motion, but that the swiftness and slowness of every thing is still proportioned either to the quantity of bodies in which they are, or some other particular end for which they are designed; therefore we must take liberty to suppose such a motion; and this we may conceive to be about 1000 paces, or a mile in an hour.

The starry heaven, or 8th sphere, is thought to move 42398437 miles in the same space: so that if it may be demonstrated that it is possible to contrive such a motion, which going on in a constant direct course, shall pass but the 42398437 part of a mile in an hour; it will then be evident, that an artificial motion may be slow, in the same proportion as the heavens are swift.

Now it was before manifested, that according to the difference betwixt the weight and power, so will the difference be betwixt the slownesss or swiftness of their motions; whence it will follow, that in such an engine, wherein the weight shall be 42398437 pounds, and the power that doth equiponderate it, but the 42398437 part of a pound (which is easy to contrive) in this engine the power being supposed to move with such a swiftness as may be answerable to a mile an hour, the weight will pass but the 42398437 part of a mile in the same space, and so consequently will be proportionably slow unto the swiftness of the heavens.

It is related by our countryman I. Dee *, that he and Cardan being both together in their travels, did see an instrument which was at first sold for twenty talents of gold, wherein there was one wheel, which constantly moving

---

* Preface to Euclid.

round amongst the rest, did not finish one revolution under the space of seven thousand years.

But if we farther consider such an instrument of wheels as was mentioned before in the fourteenth chapter, with which the whole world might be easily moved, we shall then find that the motion of the weight by that, must be much more slow, than the heavens are swift. For though we suppose (saith Stevinus *) the handle of such an engine with twelve wheels to be turned about 4000 times in an hour (which is as often as a man's pulse doth beat) yet in ten years space the weight by this would not be moved above $\frac{10512}{2400}$ 0000000000000000 parts of one foot, which is nothing near so much as a hair's breadth. And it could not pass an inch in 1000000 years, saith Mersennus †.

The truth of which we may more easily conceive, if we consider the frame and manner of this twelve wheeled engine. Suppose that in each axis or nut, there were ten teeth, and on each wheel a thousand : then the sails of this engine must be turned a hundred times, before the first wheel, (reckoning downward) could be moved round once, and ten thousand times before the second wheel can finish one revolution, and so through the twelve wheels, according to this multiplied proportion.

So that besides the wonder which there is in the force of these mechanical motions, the extreme slowness of them is no less admirable. If a man considers that a body should remain in such a constant direct motion, that there could not be one minute of time, wherein it did not rid some space and pass on further, and yet that this body in many years together should not move so far as a hair's breadth.

Which notwithstanding may evidently appear from the former instance. For since it is a natural principle, that there can be no penetration of bodies ; and since it is supposed, that each of the parts in this engine do touch one

* De stat. pract.   † Phænom. Mechan. Prop. 11.

another in their superficies; therefore it must necessarily follow, that the weight does begin and continue to move with the power; and (however it is insensible) yet it is certain there must be such a motion so extremely slow as is here specified. So full is this art of rare and incredible subtilties.

I know it is the assertion of Cardan *, *Motus valde tardi, necessario quietes habent intermedias.* Extreme slow motions have necessarily some intermediate stops and rests. But this is only said, not proved, and he speaks it from sensible experiments, which in this case are fallible: our senses being very incompetent judges of the several proportions, whether greatness or littleness, slowness or swiftness, which there may be amongst things in nature. For, ought we know, there may be some organical bodies as much less than ours, as the earth is bigger. We see what strange discoveries of extreme minute bodies, (as lice, wheal-worms, mites, and the like) are made by the microscope, wherein their several parts (which are altogether invisible to the bare eye) will distinctly appear: and perhaps there may be other insects that live upon them as they do upon us. It is certain that our senses are extremely disproportioned for comprehending the whole compass and latitude of things. And because there may be such difference in the motion as well as in the magnitude of bodies; therefore, though such extreme slowness may seem altogether impossible to sense and common apprehension, yet this can be no sufficient argument against the reality of it.

* De Varietate Rerum, l. 9. c. 47.

CHAP. XVII.

Of Swiftness: how it may be increased to any kind of
proportion. Concerning the great force of Archimedes
his engines. Of the Ballista.

BY that which hath been already explained concerning
the slowness of motion, we may the better understand
the nature of swiftness, both of them (as is the nature of
opposites) being produced by contrary causes. As the
greatness of the weight in respect of the power, and the
great distance of the power from the fulciment in comparison to that of the weight, does cause a slow motion; so
the greatness of the power above the weight, and the greater
distance of the weight from the centre, in comparison to
that of the power, does cause a swift motion.

And as it is possible to contrive a motion unto any kind
of slowness, by finding out an answerable disproportion
betwixt the weight and power, so likewise unto any kind of
swiftness: for so much as the weight does exceed the
power, by so much will the motion of the weight be slower,
and so much as the power does exceed the weight, by so
much will the motion of the weight be swifter.

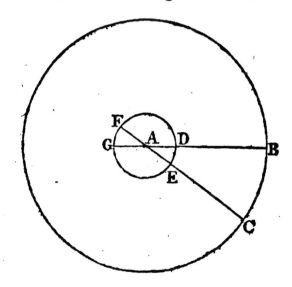

In the diagram set down before, if we suppose F to be the place of the power, and C of the weight, the point A being the fulciment or centre, then in the same space of time wherein the power does move from F to G, the weight will pass from C to B. These distances having the same disproportion unto one another, as there is betwixt AF and A C, which is supposed to be quadruple. So that in this example, the weight will move four times swifter than the power; and according as the power does exceed the weight in any greater disproportion, so will the swift-ness of the weight be augmented.

Hence may we conceive the reason of that great force which there is in slings, which have so much a greater swiftness than a stone thrown from the hand, by how much the end of the sling is farther off from the shoulder-joint, which is the centre of motion. The sacred history concerning David's victory over Goliath * may sufficiently evidence the force of these. Vegetius † relates that it was usual this way to strike a man dead, and beat the soul out of his body, without so much as breaking his armour, or fetching blood. *Membris integris læthale tamen vulnus important, & sine invidia sanguinis, hostis lapidis ictu intereat.*

In the use of these, many of the ancients have been of very exquisite and admirable skill. We read of seven hundred Benjamites left-handed, that could sling a stone at a hair's breadth, and not miss ‡. And there is the like storied of a whole nation amongst the Indians, who from their excellency in this art, were stiled Baleares ‖. They were so strict in teaching this art unto their young ones, *ut cibum puer à matre non accipit, nisi quem ipsa monstrante percussit*; that the mother would not give any meat to her child, till (being set at some distance) he could hit it with slinging.

* 1 Sam. xvii. 49.   † Lipsius Polior. l. 4. Dialogue 21.
‡ Judges xx. 16.
‖ Απο τυ ϐαλλειν, Diodor. Sicul. Biblioth. l. 5. L. Florus Hist. l. 3. cap. 8. Io. Boemus Aubanus de moribus gentium, l. 3. c. 26.

For the farther illustration of this subject, concerning the swiftness of motion, I shall briefly specify some particulars concerning the engines of war used by the ancients. Amongst these, the most famous and admirable were those invented by Archimedes; by which he did perform such strange exploits, as (were they not related by so many and such judicious authors) would scarce seem credible even to these more learned ages. The acts of that most famous engineer, are largely set down by Polybius*, Tzetzes†, Proclus‡, Plutarch||, Livy§, and divers others. From the first of whom alone, we may have sufficient evidence for the truth of those relations: for besides that he is an author noted to be very grave and serious in his discourse, and does solemnly promise in one place¶ that he will relate nothing, but what either he himself was an eye-witness of, or else what he had received from those that were so: I say, besides all this, it is considerable, that he himself was born not above thirty years after the siege of Syracuse. And afterwards having occasion to tarry some weeks in that city, when he travelled with Scipio, he might there perhaps see those engines himself, or at least take his information from such as were eye-witnesses of their force: so that there can be no colourable pretence for any to distrust the particulars related of them.

In brief, the sum of their reports is this. When the Roman forces under the conduct of Marcellus, had laid siege unto that famous city, (of which, both by their former successes, and their present strength, they could not chuse but promise themselves a speedy victory;) yet the arts of this one mathematician, notwithstanding all their policies and resolutions, did still beat them back to their great disadvantage. Whether they were near the wall, or farther from it, they were still exposed to the force of his engines, και μακραν αφεστωτας και συνεγγυς οντας, ε μονον απρακτες παρεσ-

---

* Histor. l. 4.　　　† Histor. Chilios 2. Histor. 35.
‡ Lib. 2. c. 3.　　　|| Marcellus.　　　§ Histor. l. 24.
¶ Histor. l. 4. juxta initium.

κευαζε προς τας ιδιας επιβολας, αλλα και διεφθειρε τας πλειστας αυτων. From the multitude of those stones and arrows which he shot against them, was he stiled εκατογχειρ or Briareus *. Those defensive engines that were made by the Romans in the form of pent-houses †, for to cover the assailants from the weapons of the besieged, these would he presently batter in pieces with great stones and blocks. Those high towers erected in some of the ships, out of which the Romans might more conveniently fight with the defendants on the wall, these also were so broken by his engines, that no cannon, or other instrument of gunpowder, (saith a learned man ‡) had they been then in use, could have done greater mischief. In brief, he did so molest them with his frequent and prodigious batteries, that the common soldiers were utterly discouraged from any hopes of success.

What was the particular frame and manner of these engines, cannot certainly be determined; but to contrive such as may perform the like strange effects, were not very difficult to any one who is thoroughly versed in the grounds of this art. Though perhaps those of Archimedes, in respect of divers circumstances, were much more exact and proper for the purposes to which they were intended, than the invention of others could be; he himself being so extraordinarily subtle and ingenious above the common sort of men.

It is probable that the general kind of these engines were the same with those that were used afterwards, amongst the Romans and other nations. These were commonly divided into two sorts; stiled ballistæ, catapultæ, both which names are sometimes used promiscuously ‖; but according to their propriety, ballista § does signify an engine

---

* Cæl. Rhod. Ant. lect. l. 2. c. 16.   † Pluteus Testudo.
‡ Sir Walt. Raleigh, Histor. l. 5. c. 3. § 16.
‖ Vid. Naudæum de Stud. Militar. l. 2.
§ Απο τ8 βαλλειν, called also λιθοβολος, πετροβολος. Fundibalus, Petraria. lib. 3.

for the shooting of stones, and catapulta for darts or arrows.

The former of these was fitted either to carry divers lesser stones, or else one greatest one. Some of these engines made for great stones, have been proportioned to so vast and immense a weight, as may seem almost incredible; which occasioned that in Lucan,

At saxum quoties ingenti verberis ictu
Excutitur, qualis rupes quam vertice montis
Abscidit impulsu ventorum adjuta vetustas,
Frangit cuncta ruines; nec tantum corpora pressa
Exanimat, totos cum sanguine dissipat artus.

With these they could easily batter down the walls and towers of any fort. So Ovid.

Quam grave ballistæ mœnia pulsat onus.

And Statius

Quo turbine bellica quondam,
Librati saliunt portarum in claustra molares.

The stones that were cast from these, were of any form, *enormes et sepulchrales*, mill-stones or tomb-stones[*]. Sometimes for the farther annoyance and terror of any besieged place, they would by these throw into it dead bodies, either of men or horses, and sometimes only parts of them, as men's heads.

Athenæus[†] mentions one of these ballistæ that was proportioned unto a stone of three talents weight, each talent being 120 pounds (saith Vitruvius[‡],) so that the whole will amount to 360 pounds. But it is storied of Archimedes[||], that he cast a stone into one of Marcellus his ships, which was found to weigh ten talents. There is some difference amongst authors[§], concerning what kind of talent this should be understood, but it is certain that in Plutarch's time, (from whom we have this relation) one talent did amount to 120 pounds (saith Suidas:) according

---

[*] Lipsius Poliorcet. l. 3. Dial. 3.   [†] Deipnosoph. l. 5.
[‡] Archit. l. 10. c. ult. λιθον δικαταλαιτον.   [||] Plut. Marcell.
[§] Dav. Rivaltus Comment. in Archim. Oper. Ext.

to which account, the stone itself was of no less than twelve hundred pounds weight. A weapon (one would think) big enough for those rebel giants that fought against the gods. Now the greatest cannon in use, does not carry above 64 pound weight, which is far short of the strength in these mathematical contrivances *. Amongst the Turks indeed, there have been sometimes used such powder instruments, as may equal the force of those invented by Archimedes. Gab. Naudæus † tells us of one bullet shot from them at the siege of Constantinople, which was of above 1200 pound weight; this he affirms from the relation of an archbishop, who was then present, and did see it; the piece could not be drawn by less than a hundred and fifty yoke of oxen, which might almost have served to draw away the town itself. But though there hath been perhaps some one or two cannons of such a prodigious magnitude, yet it is certain that the biggest in common use, does come far short of that strength which was ordinarily in these mechanical engines.

There are divers figures of these ballistæ, set out by Vegetius, Lipsius, and others ‡; but being without any explication, it is not very facil to discover in what their forces did consist.

I have here expressed one of them most easy to be apprehended; from the understanding of which, you may the better guess at the nature of the rest.

* Naudæus de Studio Milit. l. 2.   † De Stud. Mil. l. 2.
‡ See Rob. Valteurius de Re Milit. l. 10. c. 4.

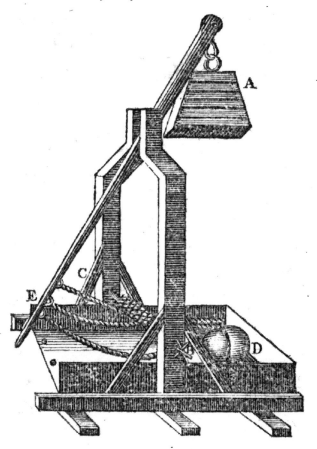

That great box or cavity at A, is supposed to he full of some heavy weight, and is forced up by the turning of the axis and spokes B C. The stone or bullet to be discharged, being in a kind of sling at D; which when the greater weight A descends, will be violently whirled upwards, till that end of the sling at E, coming to the top will fly off, and discharge the stone as the skilful artist should direct it.

CHAP. XVIII.

Concerning the Catapultæ, or engines for arrows.

THE other kind of engine was called catapulta *, απο της πελτης, which signifies a spear or dart, because it was used for the shooting off such weapons†: some of these were proportioned unto spears of twelve cubits long; they did carry with so great a force, *ut interdum nimio ardore scintillant,* (saith Ammianus ‡) that the weapons discharged from them were sometimes (if you can believe it) set on fire by the swiftness of their motion.

The first invention of these is commonly ascribed to Dionysius the younger ‖, who is said to have made them amongst his other preparations against Carthage. But we have good reason to think them of more ancient use, because we read in scripture, that Uzziah made in Jerusalem engines invented by cunning men to shoot arrows and great stones withal §: though it is likely these inventions were much bettered by the experience of after ages.

The usual form of these catapultæ, was much after the manner of great bows placed on carriages, and wound up by the strength of several persons. And from that great force which we find in lesser bows, we may easily guess at the greater power of these other engines ¶. It is related of the Turkish bow, that it can strike an arrow through a piece of steel or brass two inches thick, and being headed only with wood, it pierces timber of eight inches. Which though it may seem incredible, yet it is attested by the experience of divers unquestionable witnesses: Barclay in his *Icon Animorum,* a man of sufficient credit, affirms that he

---

* In Greek καταπιλτης.   † Athenæus. Deipnos. l. 5.
‡ Lib. 23. Lipsius Poliorcet. l. 3. Dial 2.
‖ Diod. Sicul. Biblioth. l. 14. Sardus de Invent. Rerum, l. 2.
§ 2 Chron. xxvi. 15.   ¶ Sir Fran. Bacon, Nat. Hist. Exp. 704.

was an eye-witness, how one of these bows with a little arrow did pierce through a piece of steel three fingers thick. And yet these bows being somewhat like the long bows in use amongst us, were bent only by a man's immediate strength, without the help of any bender or rack that are used to others.

Some Turkish bows are of that strength, as to pierce a plank of six inches in thickness, (I speak what I have seen) saith M. Jo. Greaves in his pyramodographia. How much greater force then may we conceive to be impressed by the catapultæ?

These were sometimes framed for the discharging of two or three arrows together, so that each of them might be directed unto a several aim. But it were as easy to contrive them after the like manner for the carriage of twenty arrows, or more; as in this figure.

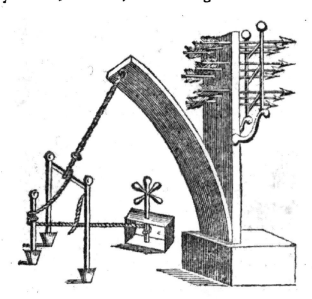

Both these kinds of engines, when they were used at the siege of any city, were commonly carried in a great wooden turret (first invented by Demetrius*.) It was

---

* Who was therefore stiled Poliorcetes. This kind of turret was first used at the siege of Cyprus, and is thus described by Diodorus Sicul. Biblioth. l. 20.

driven upon four wheels at the bottom, each of its sides being forty-five cubits, its height ninety. The whole was divided in nine several partitions, every one of which did contain divers engines for battery: from its use in the battering and taking of cities it is stiled by the name of helepolis.

He that would be informed in the nature of bows, let him consult *Mersennus de Ballistica et Acontismologia*, where there are divers subtile enquiries and demonstrations, concerning the strength required to the bending of them to any distance, the force they have in the discharge, according to several bents, the strength required to be in the string of them, the several proportions of swiftness and distance in an arrow shot vertically, or horizontally, or transversally.

Those strange effects of the Turkish bow (mentioned before) so much exceeding the force of others, which yet require far greater strength for the bending of them, may probably be ascribed either to the natural cause of attraction by similitude of substance (as the Lord Bacon conjectures:) for in these experiments the head of the arrow should be of the same substance (whether steel or wood) with that which it pierces: or else to that just proportion betwixt the weight of the arrow, and the strength of the bow, which must needs much conduce to the force of it, and may perhaps be more exactly discovered in these, than it is commonly in others.

CHAP. XIX.

A Comparison betwixt these ancient Engines, and the Gunpowder Instruments now in use.

IT shall not be altogether impertinent to enquire somewhat concerning the advantages and disadvantages betwixt those military offensive engines used amongst the ancients, and those of these later ages.

In which enquiry there are two particulars to be chiefly examined.

1. The force of these several contrivances, or the utmost that may be done by them.

2. Their price, or the greatness of the charges required unto them.

1. As for the force of these ancient inventions, it may sufficiently appear from those many credible relations mentioned before; to which may be added that in Josephus *, which he sets down from his own eye-sight, being himself a chief captain at the siege of Jotapata, where these events happened. He tells us that besides the multitude of persons, who were slain by these Roman engines, being not able to avoid their force, by reason they were placed so far off, and out of sight; besides this, they did also carry such great stones, with so great a violence, that they did therewith batter down their walls and towers. A great bellied woman walking about the city in the day-time, had her child struck out of her womb, and carried half a furlong from her. A soldier standing by his captain Josephus, on the wall, had his head struck off by another stone sent from these Roman engines, and his brains carried three furlongs off.

To this purpose Cardan † relates out of Ammianus Marcellinus. *Tanto impetu fertur lapis ut uno viso lapide, quamvis intacti barbari fuerint ab eo, destiterunt à pugnâ et abierunt.* Many foreign people being so amazed at the strange force of these engines, that they durst not contest with those who were masters of such inventions. It is frequently asserted, that bullets have been melted in the air, by that extremity of violent motion imprest from these slings.

> *Fundaque contorto transverberat aëra plumbo,*
> *Et mediis liquidæ glandes in nubibus errant.*

---

* De Bello Judaico, l. 3. c. 9.   † De Variet. l. 12. c. 58.

So Lucan, speaking of the same engines.

Inde faces et saxa volant, spatioque solutæ
Aeris et calidæ liquefactæ pondere glandes.

Which relations, though they may seem somewhat poetical and improbable, yet Aristotle himself (*de Cælo, lib.* 2. c. 7.) doth suppose them as unquestionable. From whence it may be inferred, that the force of these engines does rather exceed than come short of our gunpowder inventions.

Add to this that opinion of a learned man * (which I cited before) that Archimedes in the siege of Syracuse † did more mischief with his engines, than could have been wrought by any cannons, had they been then in use.

In this perhaps there may be some disadvantage, because these mathematical engines cannot be so easily and speedily wound up, and so certainly levelled as the other may.

2. As for the price or charges of both these, it may be considered under three particulars:

1. Their making.
2. Their carriage or conveyance.
3. Their charge and discharging.

In all which respects, the cannons now in use, are of much greater cost than these other inventions.

1. The making or price of these gun-powder instruments is extremely expensive, as may be easily judged by the weight of their materials. A whole cannon weighing commonly 8000 pounds, a half cannon 5000, a culverin 4500, a demiculverin 3000; which whether it be in iron or brass, must needs be very costly, only for the matter of them; besides the farther charges required for the form and making of them, which in the whole must needs amount to several hundred pounds. Whereas these mathematical inventions consisting chiefly of timber, and

* Sir Walt. Raleigh. Hist. l. 5. c. 3. sect. 16.
† See Lipsius de Militiâ Romanâ, l. 5.

cords, may be much more cheaply made; the several degrees of them which shall answer in proportion to the strength of those other, being at the least ten times cheaper; that is, ten engines that shall be of equal force either to a cannon or demicannon, culverin or demiculverin, may be framed at the same price that one of these will amount to: so that in this respect there is a great inequality.

2. As for their carriage or conveyance; a whole cannon does require at the least 90 men, or 16 horses, for the draught of it; a half cannon 56 men, or 9 horses; a culverin 50 men, or 8 horses; a demiculverin 36 men, or 7 horses; supposing the way to be hard and plain, in which notwithstanding the motion will be very slow. But if the passage prove rising and steep, or rotten and dirty, then they will require a much greater strength and charge for the conveyance of them. Whereas these other inventions are in themselves more light (if there be occasion for the draught of them) being easily taken asunder into several parts. And besides, their materials are to be found every where, so that they need not be carried up and down at all, but may be easily made in the place where they are to be used.

3. The materials required to the charging of these gunpowder instruments, are very costly. A whole cannon requiring for every charge 40 pounds of powder, and a bullet of 64 pounds; a half cannon 18 pounds of powder, and a bullet of 24 pounds; a culverin 16 pounds of powder, and a bullet of 19 pounds; a demiculverin 9 pounds of powder, and a bullet of 12 pounds: whereas those other engines may be charged only with stones, or (which may serve for terror) with dead bodies, or any such materials as every place will afford without any cost.

So then, put all these together: if it be so that those ancient inventions did not come short of these other in regard of force, and if they do so much excel them in divers other respects; it should seem then, that they are much more commodious than these latter inventions, and should be preferred before them. But this enquiry cannot be fully determined without particular experience of both.

CHAP. XX.

That it is possible to contrive such an artificial motion, as may be equally swift with the supposed motion of the heavens.

FOR the conclusion of this discourse, I shall briefly examine (as before concerning slowness) whether it be possible to contrive such an artificial motion, as may be equal unto the supposed swiftness of the heavens. This question hath been formerly proposed and answered by Cardan *, where he applies it unto the swiftness of the moon's orb; but that orb being the lowest of all, and consequently of a dull and sluggish motion, in comparison to the rest; therefore it will perhaps be more convenient to understand the question concerning the eighth sphere, or starry heaven.

For the true resolution of this, it should be first observed, that a material substance is altogether incapable of so great a celerity, as is usually ascribed to the celestial orbs, (as I have proved elsewhere †,) and therefore the quære is not to be understood of any real and experimental, but only notional, and geometrical contrivance.

Now that the swiftness of motion may be thus increased according to any conceivable proportion, will be manifest from what hath been formerly delivered concerning the grounds and nature of slowness and swiftness. For ac-

---

* De Variet. Rerum. l. 9. c. 47.   † Prop. 9.

cording as we shall suppose the power to exceed the weight: so may the motion of the weight be swifter than that of the power.

But to answer more particularly: let us imagine every wheel in this following figure to have a hundred teeth in it, and every nut ten:

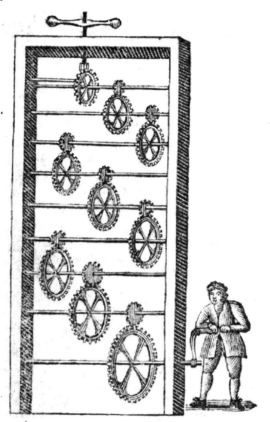

It may then be evident, that one revolution of the first wheel, will turn the nut, and consequently the second wheel on the same axis ten times, the third wheel a hundred times, the fourth a thousand times, the fifth 10000, the sixth a hundred thousand times, the seventh 1000000 times, the eighth 10000000 times, the ninth 100000000 times, the sails 1000000000 times: so that if we suppose the compass of these sails to be five foot, or one pace: and that the first wheel is turned about after the rate of one thousand times in an hour: it will then be evident, that the sails shall be turned 1000000000000 times, and consequently shall pass 100000000 miles in the same space. Whereas a star in the equator (according to common hypothesis) does move but 42398437 miles in an hour: and therefore it is evident that it is possible geometrically to contrive such an artificial motion, as shall be of greater swiftness then the supposed revolutions of the heavens,

DÆDALUS;

OR,

MECHANICAL MOTIONS,

BOOK II.

CHAP. I.

The divers kinds of Automata, or Self-movers. Of Mills,
and the contrivance of several motions by rarified air.
A brief digression concerning Wind-guns.

AMONGST the variety of artificial motions, those are
of most use and pleasure, in which, by the application
of some continued strength, there is bestowed a regular
and lasting motion.

These we call the αυτοματα, or self-movers: which name,
in its utmost latitude, is sometimes ascribed unto those motions, that are contrived from the strength of living creatures, as chariots, carts, &c. But in its strictness and propriety, it is only appliable unto such inventions, wherein
the motion is caused either by something that belongs unto
its own frame, or else by some external inanimate agent.

Whence these αυτοματα are easily distinguishable into
two sorts:

1. Those that are moved by something which is extrin-
sical unto their own frame; as mills, by water or wind.

2. Those that receive their motion from something that does belong to the frame itself; as clocks, watches, by weights, springs, or the like.

Of both which sorts, there have been many excellent inventions: in the recital of them, I shall insist chiefly on such as are most eminent for their rarity and subtilty.

Amongst the αυτοματα that receive their motion from some external agent, those of more common use are mills.

And first, the water-mills; which are thought to be before the other, though neither the first author, nor so much as the time wherein they were invented is fully known. And therefore Polydore Virgil * refers them amongst other fatherless inventions. Pliny † indeed doth mention them, as being commonly used in his time; and yet others affirm, that Belisarius, in the reign of Justinian, did first invent them: whence Pancirollus ‡ concludes, that it is likely their use was for some space intermitted, and being afterwards renewed again, they were then thought to be first discovered.

However, it is certain that this invention hath much abridged and advantaged the labours of men, who were before condemned unto this slavery ||, as now unto the galleys. And as the force of waters hath been useful for this, so likewise may it be contrived to divers other purposes. Herein doth the skill of an artificer chiefly consist, in the application of these common motions unto various and beneficial ends; making them serviceable, not only for the grinding of corn, but for the preparing of iron, or other ore; the making of paper, the elevating of water, or the like.

To this purpose also are the mills that are driven by wind, which are so much more convenient than the other, by how much their situations may be more easy and common. The motions of these may likewise be accommodated to as various uses as the other; there being scarce

---

* De Invent. Rerum, l. 3. c. 18.   † Nat. Hist. l. 18. c. 10.
‡ De Repert. Tit. 22. || Ad pistrinum.

any labour, to the performance of which, an ingenious artificer cannot apply them.   To the sawing of timber, the ploughing of land, or any other the like service, which cannot be dispatched the ordinary way, without much toil and tediousness.   And it is a wonderful thing to consider, how much men's labours might be eased and contracted in sundry particulars, if such as were well skilled in the principles and practices of these mechanical experiments, would but thoroughly apply their studies unto the enlargement of such inventions.

There are some other motions by wind or air, which (though they are not so common as the other, yet) may prove of excellent curiosity, and singular use.   Such was that musical instrument invented by Cornelius Dreble; which being set in the sunshine, would of itself render a soft and pleasant harmony; but being removed into the shade, would presently become silent.   The reason of it was this: the warmth of the sun working upon some moisture within it, and rarifying the inward air unto so great an extension that it must needs seek for vent or issue, did thereby give several motions unto the instrument *.

Somewhat of this nature are the æolipiles, which are concave vessels, consisting of some such material as may endure the fire, having a small hole, at which they are filled with water, and out of which (when the vessels are heated) the air doth issue forth with a strong and lasting violence. These are frequently used for the exciting and contracting of heat in the melting of glasses, or metals: they may also be contrived to be serviceable for sundry other pleasant uses; as for the moving of sails in a chimney-corner; the motion of which sails may be applied to the turning of a spit, or the like.

* Marcell. Vrankhein. Epist. ad Joh. Ernestum.   Like that statue of Memnon, in Egypt, which makes a strange noise whenever the sun begins to shine upon it.   Tacit. Annal. 2.   Strabo affirms, that he had both seen and heard it.

But there is a better invention to this purpose, mentioned in Cardan *, whereby a spit may be turned (without the help of weights) by the motion of the air that ascends the chimney; and it may be useful for the roasting of many, or great joints: for as the fire must be increased according to the quantity of meat, so the force of the instrument will be augmented proportionably to the fire.   In which contrivance, there are these conveniences above the jacks of ordinary use:

1. It makes little or no noise in the motion.

2. It needs no winding up, but will constantly move of itself, while there is any fire to rarify the air.

3. It is much cheaper than the other instruments that are commonly used to this purpose; there being required unto it only a pair of sails, which must be placed in that part of the chimney where it begins to be straitened; and one wheel, to the axis of which the spit-line must be fastened, according to this following diagram.

* De Variet. Rerum, l. 12. c. 58.

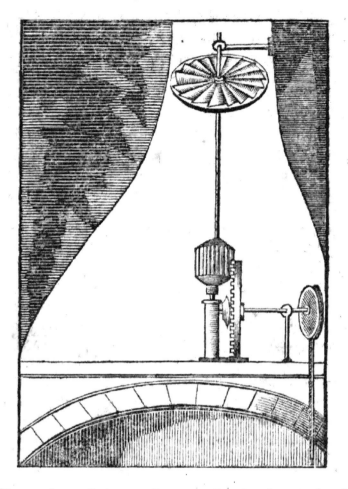

The motion of these sails may likewise be serviceable for sundry other purposes, besides the turning of a spit; for the chiming of bells, or other musical devices; and there cannot be any more pleasant contrivance for continual and cheap music. It may be useful also for the reeling of yarn, the rocking of a cradle, with divers the like domestic occasions. For (as was said before) any constant motion being given, it is easy for an ingenious artificer to apply it unto various services.

These sails will always move both day and night, if there is but any fire under them, and sometimes though there be none. For, if the air without be much colder than that within the room, then must this which is more warm and rarified, naturally ascend through the chimney, to give place unto the more condensed and heavy, which does usually blow in at every chink or cranny, as experience shews.

Unto this kind of motion may be reduced all those representations of living creatures, whether birds, or beasts, invented by Ctesibius, which were for the most part performed by the motion of air, being forced up either by rarefaction, with fire, or else by compression, through the fall of some heavier body, as water, which by possessing the place of the air, did thereby drive it to seek for some other vent.

I cannot here omit (though it be not altogether so pertinent) to mention that late ingenious invention of the windgun, which is charged by the forcible compression of air, being injected through a syringe; the strife and distention of the imprisoned air, serving by the help of little falls or shuts within; to stop and keep close the vents by which it was admitted. The force of it in the discharge is almost equal to our powder-guns. I have found upon frequent trials (saith Mersennus*) that a leaden bullet shot from one of these guns against a stone wall, the space of 24 paces from it, will be beaten into a thin plate. It would be a considerable addition to this experiment, which the same author mentions a little after, whereby he will make the same charge of air to serve for the discharge of several arrows or bullets after one another, by giving the air only so much room, as may immediately serve to impress a violence in sending away the arrow or bullet, and then screwing it down again to its former confinement, to fit it for another shooting. But against this there may be many considerable doubts, which I cannot stand to discuss.

* Phænomena pneumatica, prop. 32.

CHAP. II.

Of a Sailing Chariot, that may without horses be driven on the land by the wind, as ships are on the sea.

THE force of wind in the motion of sails may be applied also to the driving of a chariot, by which a man may sail on the land, as well as by a ship on the water. The labour of horses or other beasts, which are usually applied to this purpose, being artificially supplied by the strength of winds.

That such chariots are commonly used in the champion plains of China, is frequently affirmed by divers credible authors. Boterus mentions that they have been tried also in Spain *, though with what success he doth not specify. But above all other experiments to this purpose, that sailing chariot at Sceveling in Holland, is more eminently remarkable. It was made by the direction of Stephinus, and is celebrated by many authors. Walceius † affirms it to be of so great a swiftness for its motion, and yet of so great a capacity for its burthen: *ut in medio freto secundis ventis commissas naves, velocitate multis parasangis post se relinquat, et paucarum horarum spatio, viginti aut triginta milliaria germanica continuo cursu emetiatur, concreditosque sibi plus minus vectores sex aut decem, in petitum locum transferat, facillimo illius ad clavum qui sedet nutu, quaqua versum minimo labore velis commissum, mirabile hoc continenti currus navigium dirigentis.* That it did far exceed the speed of any ship, though we should suppose it to be carried in the open sea with never so prosperous wind: and that in some few hours space it would convey six or ten persons, 20 or 30 German miles, and all this with very little labour of him that sitteth at the stern, who may easily guide the course of it as he pleaseth.

---

* De Incremento Urbium, l. 1. c. 10.
† Fabularum Decas, Fab. 9.

That eminent inquisitive man Peireskius, having travelled to Sceveling for the sight and experience of this chariot, would frequently after with much wonder mention the extreme swiftness of its motion. *Commemorare solebat stuporem quo correptus fuerat cum vento translatus citatissimo non persentiscere tamen, nempe tam citus erat quam ventus**. Though the wind were in itself very swift and strong, yet to passengers in this chariot it would not be at all discernible, because they did go with an equal swiftness to the wind itself: men that ran before it seeming to go backwards, things which seem at a great distance being presently overtaken and left behind. In two hours space it would pass from Sceveling to Putten, which are distant from one another above 14 *horaria milliaria*, (saith the same author,) that is, more than two and forty miles.

Grotius is very copious and elegant in the celebrating of this invention, and the author of it, in divers epigrams.

Ventivolum Tiphys deduxit in æquora navim,
  Jupiter in stellas, æthereamque domum.
In terrestre solum virtus Stevinia, nam nec
  Tiphy tuum fuerat, nec Jovis istud opus †.

And in another place ‡:

Imposuit plaustro vectantem carbasa, malum
  An potius navi, subdidit ille rotas ?
——— *Scandit aquas navis currus ruit aere prono,*
  Et merito dicas hic volat, illa natat.

These relations did at the first seem unto me, (and perhaps they will so to others) somewhat strange and incredible. But upon farther enquiry, I have heard them frequently attested from the particular eye-sight and experience of such eminent persons, whose names I dare not cite in a business of this nature, which in those parts is so very common, and little observed.

I have not met with any author who doth treat particu-

* Pet. Gassendus, Vita Peireskii, l. 2.
† Grotii Poemata, Ep. 19.   ‡ Ep. 5.

larly concerning the manner of framing this chariot, though
Grotius mentions an elegant description of it in copper by
one Geynius *: and Hondius in one of his large maps of
Asia, does give another conjectural description of the like
chariots used in China.

The form of it is related to be very simple and plain,
after this manner.

The body of it being somewhat like a boat, moving upon
four wheels of an equal bigness, with two sails like those in a
ship; there being some contrivance to turn and steer it, by
moving a rudder which is placed beyond the two hindmost
wheels; and for the stopping of it, this must be done,
either by letting down the sail, or turning it from the wind.

* Epig. 20. et 21.

Of this kind they have frequently in Holland other little vessels for one or two persons to go upon the ice, having sledges instead of wheels, being driven with a sail; the bodies of them like little boats, that if the ice should break, they might yet safely carry a man upon the water, where the sail would be still useful for the motion of it.

I have often thought that it would be worth the experiment to enquire, whether or no such a sailing chariot might not be more conveniently framed with moveable sails, whose force may be imprest from their motion, equivalent to those in a wind-mill. Their foremost wheels (as in other chariots) for the greater facility, being somewhat lower than the other, answerable to this figure.

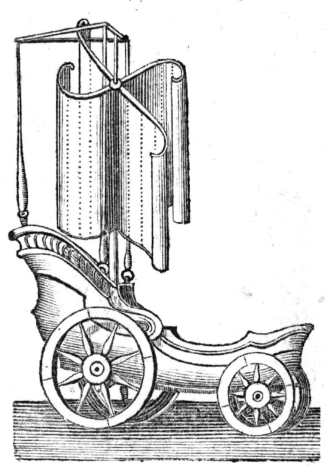

In which the sails are so contrived, that the wind from any coast will have a force upon them to turn them about; and the motion of these sails must needs turn the wheels, and consequently carry on the chariot itself to any place (though fully against the wind) whither it shall be directed.

The chief doubt will be, whether in such a contrivance, every little ruggedness or unevenness of the ground, will not cause such a jolting of the chariot, as to hinder the motion of its sails. But this perhaps (if it should prove so) is capable of several remedies.

I have often wondered, why none of our gentry who live near great plains, and smooth champions, have attempted any thing to this purpose. The experiments of this kind being very pleasant, and not costly: what could be more delightful, or better husbandry, than to make use of the wind (which costs nothing, and eats nothing) instead of horses? This being very easy to be effected by those, the convenience of whose habitations doth accommodate them for such experiments.

CHAP. III.

Concerning the fixed automata, clocks, spheres, representing the heavenly motions: the several excellencies that are most commendable in such kind of contrivances.

THE second kind of αυτοματα were described to be such engines, as did receive a regular and lasting motion from something belonging to their own frame, whether weights, or springs, &c.

They are usually distinguished into αυτοματα στατα, fixed and stationary; υπαγοντα, moveable and transient.

1. The fixed are such as move only according to their several parts, and not according to their whole frame; in

which, though each wheel hath a distinct rotation, yet the whole doth still remain unmoved. The chiefest kind of these are the clocks and watches in ordinary use; the framing of which is so commonly known by every mechanic, that I shall not trouble the reader with any explication of it. He that desires fuller satisfaction, may see them particularly described by Cardan *, D. Flood †, and others.

The first invention of these (saith Pancirollus ‡) was taken from that experiment in the multiplication of wheels, mentioned in Vitruvius ‖, where he speaks of an instrument, whereby a man may know how many miles or paces he doth go in any space of time, whether or no he do pass by water in a boat, or ship, or by land in a chariot, or coach: they have been contrived also into little pocket-instruments, by which, after a man hath walked a whole day together, he may easily know how many steps he hath taken. I forbear to enter upon a larger explication of these kind of engines, because they are impertinent unto the chief business that I have proposed for this discourse. The reader may see them more particularly described in the above-cited place of Vitruvius, in Cardan §, Bessonius ¶, and others; I have here only mentioned them, as being the first occasion of the chiefest αυτοματα, that are now in use.

Of the same kind with our clocks and watches (though perhaps more elaborate, and subtle) was that sphere invented by Archimedes, which did represent the heavenly motions: the diurnal, and annual courses of the sun, the changes, and aspects of the moon, &c. ** This is frequently celebrated in the writings of the ancients, particularly in that known epigram of Claudian:

---

* De Variet. Rer. l. 9. c. 47.   † Tract. 2. part. 7. l. 1. cap. 4.
‡ Repert. Tit. 10.   ‖ Architect. l. 10. c. 14.   § Subtil. l. 18.
¶ Theatrum Instrumentorum. Wecker de Secretis, l. 15. c. 32.
** Mentioned by Cicero, Tuscul. Quæst. l. 1. item De Nat. Deorum, l. 2.

Jupiter in parvo cum cerneret æthera vitro,
Risit, et ad superos talia dicta dedit;
Huccine mortalis progressa potentia curæ?
Jam meus in fragili luditur orbe labor.
Jura poli, rerumque fidem, legesque deorum,
Ecce Syracusius transtulit arte senex.
Inclusus variis famulatur * spiritus astris,
Et vivum certis motibus urget opus.
Percurrit proprium mentitus signifer annum;
Et simulata novo Cynthia mense redit.
Jamque suum volvens audax industria mundum
Gaudet, et humana sidera mente regit.
Quid falso insontem tonitru Salmonea miror?
Æmula naturæ parva reperta manus.

Excellently translated by T. Randolph:

Jove saw the heavens fram'd in a little glass,
And laughing, to the gods these words did pass;
Comes then the power of mortal cares so far?
In brittle orbs my labours acted are.
The statutes of the poles, the faith of things,
The laws of gods, this Syracusian brings
Hither by art: spirits inclos'd attend
Their several spheres, and with set motions bend
The living work: each year the feigned sun,
Each month returns the counterfeited moon.
And viewing now her world, bold industry
Grows proud, to know the heavens his subjects be,
Believe, Salmoneus hath false thunders thrown,
For a poor hand is nature's rival grown.

But, that this engine should be made of glass, is scarce credible. Lactantius † mentioning the relation of it, affirms it to consist of brass, which is more likely. It may be the outside or case was glass, and the frame itself of brass. Cœlius Rhodoginus ‡ speaking of the wonderous art in the contrivance of this sphere, breaks out into this quære. *Nonne igitur miraculorum omnium, maximum miraculum est homo?* He might have said *mathematicus:*

---

* The secret force from which the motion was impressed.
† Instit. l. 2. c. 5.   ‡ Antiq. lect. L 2. c. 16.

and another to this purpose *. *Sic manus ejus naturam, ut natura ipsa manum imitata putetur.* Pappus † tells us, that Archimedes writ a book *de sphæropæia*, concerning the manner of framing such engines; and after him, Possidonius composed another discourse on the same subject; though now either the ignorance, or the envy of time hath deprived us of both those works. And yet the art itself is not quite perished, for we read of divers the like contrivances in these latter times. Agrippa affirms ‡ that he himself had seen such a sphere; and Ramus tells us how he beheld two of them in Paris, the one brought thither amongst other spoils from Sicily, and the other out of Germany. And it is commonly reported, that there is yet such a sphere at Strasburg in Germany. Rivaltus ‖ relates how Marinus Burgesius a Norman made two of them in France for the king. And perhaps these latter (saith he) were more exact than the former, because the heavenly revolutions are now much better understood than before. And besides it is questionable, whether the use of steel-springs was known in those ancient times; the application of which unto these kind of spheres, must needs be much more convenient than weights.

It is related also of the consul Boethius §, that amongst other mathematical contrivances, (for which he was famous) he made a sphere to represent the sun's motion; which was so much admired, and talked of in those times, that Gundibaldus, king of Burgundy, did purposely send over ambassadors to Theodoricus the emperor, with intreaties that he would be a means to procure one of these spheres from Boethius; the emperor thinking hereby to make his kingdom more famous and terrible unto foreign nations, doth write an epistle to Boethius, persuading him

* Guid, Ubaldus Præf. ad Mechan.
† Collect. Mathem. Procem. ad l. 8.
‡ De Vanit. Scient. c. 22. Schol. Mathem. l. 1. So Cardan too, l. 17. Monanth. in Mecha. Arist. Com. c. 1. Dr. Hackwell, Apol. l. 3. c. 10. sect. 1.   ‖ De Vita Archimedis.
§ Cassiodor. Chron. Pet. Bertius Præf. ad Consolat. Philos.

to send this instrument. *Quoties non sunt credituri quod viderint? Quoties hanc veritatem lusoria somnia putabunt? Et quanto fuerint à stupore conversi, non audebunt se æquales nobis dicere, apud quos sciunt sapientes talia cogitasse.* So much were all these kind of inventions admired in those ruder and darker times: whereas the instruments that are now in use amongst us (though not so much extolled) yet do altogether equal (if not exceed) the other, both in usefulness and subtilty. The chiefest of these former engines receiving their motion from weights, and not from springs, (which as I said before) are of later and more excellent invention *.

The particular circumstances, for which the automata of this kind are most eminent, may be reduced to these four.

1. The lastingness of their motion, without needing of any new supply; for which purpose there have been some watches contrived to continue without winding up for a week together, or longer.

2. The easiness and simplicity of their composition; art itself being but the facilitating and contracting of ordinary operations; therefore the more easy and compendious such inventions are, the more artificial should they be esteemed. And the addition of any such unnecessary parts, as may be supplied some other way, is a sure sign of unskilfulness and ignorance. Those antiquated engines that did consist of such a needless multitude of wheels, and springs, and screws, (like the old hypothesis of the heavens) may be compared to the notions of a confused knowledge, which are always full of perplexity and complications, and seldom in order; whereas the inventions of art are more regular, simple, and perspicuous, like the apprehensions of a distinct and thoroughly-informed judgment. In this respect the manner of framing the ordinary automata hath been much bettered in these later times above the former, and shall hereafter perhaps be yet more advantaged. These kind of

* Polyd. Virgil de Invent. Rerum, l. 2. c. 5. Cardan Subtil.

experiments (like all other human arts) receiving additions from every day's experiment.

To this purpose there is an invention consisting only of one hollow orb or wheel, whereby the hours may be as truly distinguished, as by any ordinary clock or watch. This wheel should be divided into several cavities, through each of which successively either sand or water must be contrived to pass; the heaviness of these bodies (being always in the ascending side of the wheel) must be counterpoised by a plummet that may be fastened about the pulley on the axis: this plummet will leisurely descend, according as the sand by running out of one cavity into the next, doth make the several parts of the wheel lighter or heavier, and so consequently there will be produced an equal and lasting motion, which may be easily applied to the distinction of hours.

3. The multitude and variety of those services for which they may be useful. Unto this kind may we refer those watches by which a man may tell not only the hour of the day, but the minute of the hour, the day of the month, the age and aspects of the moon, &c. Of this nature likewise was that larum mentioned by Walchius *, which though it were but two or three inches big, yet would both wake a man, and of itself light a candle for him at any set hour of the night. And those weights or springs which are of so great force as to turn a mill †, (as some have been contrived) may be easily applied to more various and difficult labours.

4. The littleness of their frame. *Nunquam ars magis quam in minimis nota est* (saith Aquinas.) The smallness of the engine doth much commend the skill of the artificer; to this purpose there have been watches contrived in the form and quantity of a jewel for the ear, where the striking of the minutes may constantly whisper unto us, how our lives do slide away by a swift succession. Cardan ‡ tells

---

* Fab. 9.   † Ramel. fig. 130.
‡ De Subtil. l. 2. item 1. 17.

us of a smith who made a watch in the jewel of a ring, to be worn on the finger, which did shew the hours, *(non solum sagitta, sed ictu)* not only by the hand, but by the finger too (as I may say) by pricking it every hour.

CHAP. IV.

Of the moveable and gradient automata, representing the motions of living creatures, various sounds, of birds, or beasts, and some of them articulate.

THUS much of those automata, which were said to be fixed and stationary.

The other kind to be enquired after, are those that are moveable and transient, which are described to be such engines as move not only according to their several parts, but also according to their whole frames. These are again distinguishable into two sorts:

1. Gradient.
2. Volant.

1. The gradient or ambulatory, are such as require some basis or bottom to uphold them in their motions*. Such were those strange inventions (commonly attributed to Dædalus) of self-moving statues, which (unless they were violently detained) would of themselves run away. Aristotle† affirms that Dædalus did this by putting quicksilver into them. But this would have been too gross a way for so excellent an artificer; it is more likely that he did it with wheels and weights. Of this kind likewise were Vulcan's Tripodes, celebrated by Homer‡, that were made to move up and down the house, and fight with one another ‖.

* Plato in Menone. Arist. Polit. l. 1. c. 3.
† De Anima, l. 1. c. 3.   ‡ Iliad. 18.
‖ There have been also chariots driven by the force of a spring contrived within them.

He might as well have contrived them into journeymen statues, each of which with a hammer in his hand should have worked at the forge.

But amongst these fighting images, that in Cardan * may deserve a mention, which holding in its hand a golden apple, beautified with many costly jewels; if any man offered to take it, the statue presently shot him to death. The touching of this apple serving to discharge several short bows, or other the like instruments that were secretly couched within the body of the image. By such a treachery was king Chennettus murdered (as Boetius relates.)

It is so common an experiment in these times to represent the persons and actions of any story by such self-moving images, that I shall not need to explain the manner how the wheels and springs are contrived within them.

Amongst these gradient automata, that iron spider mentioned in Walchius †, is more especially remarkable, which being but of an ordinary bigness, besides the outward similitude, (which was very exact) had the same kind of motions with a living spider, and did creep up and down as if it had been alive. It must needs argue a wonderful art and accurateness, to contrive all the instruments requisite for such a motion in so small a frame.

There have been also other motions contrived from magnetical qualities, which will shew the more wonderful, because there is no apparent reason of their motion, there being not the least contiguity or dependance upon any other body that may occasion it; but it is all one as if they should move up and down in the open air. Get a glass sphere, fill it with such liquors as may be clear of the same colour, immixable, such as are oil of tartar, and spirit of wine: in which it is easy so to poise a little globe or other statue, that it shall swim in the centre. Under this glass sphere, there should be a loadstone concealed, by the mo-

---

* De Variet. Rerum, l. 12. c. 58.

† Fab. 9. There have been other inventions to move on the water, Navigium sponte mobile, ac sui remigii autorem, faciam nullo negotio, saith Scaliger, Exerc. 326.

tion of which, this statue (having a needle touched within it) will move up and down, and may be contrived to shew the hour or sign. See several inventions of this kind in *Kircher de Arte Magnetica*, l. 2.

There have been some artificial images, which besides their several postures in walking up and down, have been made also to give several sounds, whether of birds, as larks, cuckoos, &c. or beasts, as hares, foxes. The voices of which creatures shall be rendered as clearly and distinctly by these artificial images, as they are by those natural living bodies, which they represent.

There have been some inventions also which have been able for the utterance of articulate sounds, as the speaking of certain words. Such are some of the Egyptian idols related to be. Such was the brazen head made by Friar Bacon *, and that statue, in the framing of which Albertus Magnus bestowed thirty years, broken by Aquinas, who came to see it, purposely that he might boast, how in one minute he had ruined the labour of so many years.

Now the ground and reason how these sounds were con-trived, may be worth our inquiry.

First then, for those of birds or beasts, they were made from such pipes or calls, as may express the several tones of those creatures which are represented : these calls are so commonly known and used, that they need not any fur-ther explication.

But now, about articulate sounds there is much greater difficulty. Walchius † thinks it possible entirely to pre-serve the voice, or any words spoken, in a hollow trunk, or pipe, and that this pipe being rightly opened, the words will come out of it in the same order wherein they were spoken. Somewhat like that cold country, where the peo-ple's discourse doth freeze in the air all winter, and may be heard the next summer, or at a great thaw. But this con-jecture will need no refutation.

* Cœl Rhod. Lect. Ant. l. 2, c. 17, Maiolus Colloq.   † Fab. 9.

The more substantial way for such a discovery, is by marking how nature herself doth employ the several instruments of speech, the tongue, lips, throat, teeth, &c. To this purpose the Hebrews have assigned each letter unto its proper instrument. And besides, we should observe what inarticulate sounds do resemble any of the particular letters *. Thus we may note the trembling of water to be like the letter L, the quenching of hot things to the letter Z, the sound of strings, unto the letters N g, the jirking of a switch the letter Q, &c. By an exact observation of these particulars, it is (perhaps) possible to make a statue speak some words.

CHAP. V.

Concerning the possibility of framing an Ark for submarine navigations. The difficulties and conveniencies of such a contrivance. c

IT will not be altogether impertinent unto the discourse of these gradient automata, to mention what Mersennus † doth so largely and pleasantly descant upon, concerning the making of a ship, wherein men may safely swim under the water.

That such a contrivance is feasible and may be effected, is beyond all question, because it hath been already experimented here in England by Cornelius Dreble; but how to improve it unto public use and advantage, so as to be serviceable for remote voyages, the carrying of any considerable number of men, with provisions and commodities, would be of such excellent use, as may deserve some further inquiry.

* Bacon Nat. Hist. Exper. 139. 200.
† Tract. de Magnetis Proprietatibus.

Concerning which there are two things chiefly considerable.

The many difficulties, with their remedies.
The great conveniences.

1. The difficulties are generally reducible to these three heads :

1. The letting out, or receiving in any thing, as there shall be occasion, without the admission of water. If it have not such a convenience, these kind of voyages must needs be very dangerous and uncomfortable, both by reason of many noisome, offensive things, which should be thrust out, and many other needful things which should be received in. Now herein will consist the difficulty, how to contrive the opening of this vessel so, that any thing may be put in or out, and yet the water not rush into it with much violence, as it doth usually in the leak of a ship.

In which case, this may be a proper remedy ; let there be certain leather bags made of several bignesses, which for the matter of them should be both tractable for the use and managing of them, and strong to keep out the water ; for the figure of them, being long and open at both ends. Answerable to these, let there be divers windows, or open places in the frame of the ship, round the sides of which one end of these bags may be fixed, the other end coming within the ship, being to open and shut as a purse. Now if we suppose this bag thus fastened, to be tied close about towards the window, then any thing that is to be sent out, may be safely put into that end within the ship, which being again close shut, and the other end loosened, the thing may be safely sent out without the admission of any water.

So again, when any thing is to be taken in, it must be first received into that part of the bag towards the window, which being (after the thing is within it) close tied about, the other end may then be safely opened. It is easy to conceive, how by this means any thing or person may be sent out, or received in, as there shall be occasion ; how the water, which will perhaps by degrees leak into several

parts, may be emptied out again, with divers the like advantages. Though if there should be any leak at the bottom of this vessel, yet very little water would get in, because no air could get out.

2. The second difficulty in such an ark will be the motion or fixing of it according to occasion: the directing of
it to several places, as the voyage shall be designed, without which, it would be very useless, if it were to remain
only in one place, or were to remove only blindfold, without
any certain direction: and the contrivance of this may
seem very difficult, because these submarine navigators will
want the usual advantages of winds and tides for motion,
and the sight of the heavens for direction.

But these difficulties may be thus remedied; as for the
progressive motion of it, this may be effected by the help
of several oars, which in the outward ends of them, shall
be like the fins of a fish to contract and dilate. The passage where they are admitted into the ship being tied about
with such leather bags (as were mentioned before) to keep
out the water. It will not be convenient perhaps that the
motion in these voyages should be very swift, because of
those observations and discoveries to be made at the bottom of the sea, which in a little space may abundantly re-
compence the slowness of its progress.

If this ark be so ballast as to be of equal weight with
the like magnitude of water, it will then be easily moveable
in any part of it.

As for the ascent of it, this may be easily contrived, if
there be some great weight at the bottom of the ship (being
part of its ballast) which by some cord within may be
loosened from it: as this weight is let lower, so will the
ship ascend from it (if need be) to the very surface of the
water; and again, as it is pulled close to the ship, so will it
descend.

For direction of this ark, the mariner's needle may be
useful in respect of the latitude of places; and the course
of this ship being more regular than others, by reason it is
not subject to tempests or unequal winds, may more certainly guide them in judging of the longitude of places.

3. But the greatest difficulty of all will be this, how the air may be supplied for respiration : how constant fires may be kept in it for light and the dressing of food, how those vicissitudes of rarefaction and condensation may be maintained.

It is observed, that a barrel or cap, whose cavity will contain eight cubical feet of air, will not serve a urinator or diver for respiration, above one quarter of an hour; the breath which is often sucked in and out, being so corrupted by the mixture of vapours, that nature rejects it as unserviceable. Now in an hour a man will need at least three hundred and sixty respirations, betwixt every one of which there shall be ten second minutes, and consequently a great change and supply of air will be necessary for many persons, and any long space.

And so likewise for the keeping of fire ; a close vessel containing ten cubical feet of air, will not suffer a wax candle of an ounce to burn in it above an hour before it be suffocated ; though this proportion (saith Mersennus) doth not equally increase for several lights, because four flames of an equal magnitude will be kept alive the space of sixteen second minutes, though one of these flames alone in the same vessel will not last above thirty-five, or at most thirty seconds ; which may be easily tried in large glass bottles, having wax candles lighted in them, and with their mouths inverted in water.

For the resolution of this difficulty, though I will not say that a man may, by custom (which in other things doth produce such strange incredible effects) be enabled to live in the open water, as the fishes do, the inspiration and expiration of water serving instead of air, this being usual with many fishes that have lungs ; yet it is certain, that long use and custom may strengthen men against many such inconveniencies of this kind, which to unexperienced persons may prove very hazardous : and so it will not perhaps be unto these so necessary, to have the air for breathing so pure and defecated, as is required for others.

But further, there are in this case these three things considerable :

1. That the vessel in itself should be of a large capacity, that as the air in it is corrupted in one part, so it may be purified and renewed in the other: or if the mere refrigeration of the air would fit it for breathing, this might be somewhat helped with bellows, which would cool it by motion.

2. It is not altogether improbable, that the lamps or fires in the middle of it, like the reflected beams in the first region, rarefying the air, and the circumambient coldness towards the sides of the vessel, like the second region, cooling and condensing of it, would make such a vicissitude and change of air, as might fit it for all its proper uses.

3. Or if neither of these conjectures will help, yet Mersennus tells us in another place *, that there is in France one Barrieus a diver, who hath lately found out another art, whereby a man might easily continue under water for six hours together ; and whereas ten cubical feet of air will not serve another diver to breathe in for half an hour, he by the help of a cavity, not above one or two foot at most, will have breath enough for six hours, and a lantern scarce above the usual size to keep a candle burning as long as a man please, which (if it be true, and were commonly known) might be a sufficient help against this greatest difficulty.

As for the many advantages and conveniencies of such a contrivance, it is not easy to recite them.

1. It is private ; a man may thus go to any coast of the world invisibly, without being discovered or prevented in his journey.

2. It is safe ; from the uncertainty of tides, and the violence of tempests, which do never move the sea above five or six paces deep. From pirates and robbers which do so infest other voyages. From ice and great frosts, which do so much endanger the passages towards the poles.

* Harmon. l. 4, prop. 6. Monit. 5.

3. It may be of very great advantage against a navy of enemies, who by this means may be undermined in the water, and blown up.

4. It may be of special use for the relief of any place that is besieged by water, to convey unto them invisible supplies; and so likewise for the surprisal of any place that is accessible by water.

5. It may be of unspeakable benefit for submarine experiments and discoveries; as,

The several proportions of swiftness betwixt the ascent of a bladder, cork, or any other light substance, in comparison to the descent of stones or lead. The deep caverns, and subterraneous passages, where the sea-water, in the course of its circulation, doth vent itself into other places, and the like. The nature and kinds of fishes, the several arts of catching them, by alluring them with lights, by placing divers nets about the sides of this vessel, shooting the greater sort of them with guns, which may be put out of the ship by the help of such bags as were mentioned before, with divers the like artifices and treacheries, which may be more successfully practised by such who live so familiarly together. These fish may serve not only for food, but for fewel likewise, in respect of that oil which may be extracted from them; the way of dressing meat by lamps, being in many respects the most convenient for such a voyage.

The many fresh springs that may probably be met with in the bottom of the sea, will serve for the supply of drink, and other occasions.

But above all, the discovery of submarine treasures is more especially considerable; not only in regard of what hath been drowned by wrecks, but the several precious things that grow there; as pearl, coral, mines; with innumerable other things of great value, which may be much more easily found out, and fetched up by the help of this, than by any other usual way of the urinators.

To which purpose, this great vessel may have some lesser cabins tied about it, at various distances; wherein several persons, as scouts, may be lodged for the taking of observations, according as the admiral shall direct them: some of them being frequently sent up to the surface of the water, as there shall be occasion.

All kind of arts and manufactures may be exercised in this vessel. The observations made by it, may be both written, and (if need were) printed here likewise. Several colonies may thus inhabit, having their children born, and bred up without the knowledge of land, who could not chuse but be amazed with strange conceits upon the discovery of this upper world.

I am not able to judge what other advantages there may be suggested, or whether experiment would fully answer to these national conjectures. But however, because the invention did unto me seem ingenious and new, being not impertinent to the present inquiry, therefore I thought it might be worth the mentioning.

CHAP. VI.

Of the volant Automata, Archytas his Dove, and Regiomontanus his Eagle. The possibility, and great usefulness of such inventions.

THE volant, or flying automata, are such mechanical contrivances as have a self-motion, whereby they are carried aloft in the open air like the flight of birds. Such was that wooden dove made by Archytas, a citizen of Tarentum, and one of Plato's acquaintance: and that wooden eagle framed by Regiomontanus at Noremberg, which, by way of triumph, did fly out of the city to meet Charles the

Fifth. This latter author is also reported to have made an iron fly, *Quæ ex artificis manu egressa, convivas circumvolitavit, tandemque veluti defessa in domini manus reversa est;* which, when he invited any of his friends, would fly to each of them round the table, and at length (as being weary) return unto its master *.

Cardan † seems to doubt the possibility of any such contrivance: his reason is, because the instruments of it must be firm and strong, and consequently they will be too heavy to be carried by their own force; but yct (saith he) if it be a little helped in the first rising, and if there be any wind to assist it in the flight, then there is nothing to hinder, but that such motions may be possible. So that he doth in effect grant as much as may be sufficient for the truth and credit of those ancient relations; and to distrust them without a stronger argument, must needs argue a blind and perverse incredibility. As for his objection concerning the heaviness of the materials in such an invention, it may be answered, that it is easy to contrive such springs, and other instruments, whose strength shall much exceed their heaviness. Nor can he shew any cause why these mechanical motions may not be as strong, (though not so lasting) as the natural strength of living creatures.

Scaliger ‡ conceives the framing of such volant automata to be very easy. *Volantis columbæ machinulam, cujus autorem Archytam tradunt, vel facillime profiteri audeo.* Those ancient motions were thought to be contrived by the force of some included air: so Gellius ∥,

---

* Diog. Laer. l. 8. Pet. Crinitus de honest. discip. l. 17. c. 12. Ramus Schol. Mathem. l. 2. Dubartas 6 days, 1 W. I. Dee Preface to Euclid.

† De Variet. Rerum, lib. 12. c. 58.   ‡ Subtil. Exercit. 326.

∥ Noct. Attic. l. 10. cap. 12. where he thinks it so strange an invention, that he styles it res abhorrens a fide. Athan. Kircher de Magnete. l. 2. par. 4. Proem. doth promise a large discourse concerning these kind of inventions in another treatise, which he styles Œdipus Ægyptiacus.

ita erat scilicet libramentis suspensum, et aurá spiritus inclusa, atque occulta consitum, &c. As if there had been some lamp, or other fire within it, which might produce such a forcible rarefaction, as should give a motion to the whole frame.

But this may be better performed by the strength of some such spring, as is commonly used in watches. This spring may be applied unto one wheel, which shall give an equal motion to both the wings; these wings having unto each of them another smaller spring, by which they may be contracted and lifted up: so that being forcibly depressed by the strength of the great and stronger spring, and lifted up again by the other two; according to this supposition, it is easy to conceive how the motion of flight may be performed and continued.

The wings may be made either of several substances joined, like the feathers in ordinary fowl, as Dædalus is feigned to contrive them, according to that in the poet,

> ——*Ignotas animum dimittit in artes,*
> *Naturamque novat, nam ponit in ordine pennas*
> *A minimo cœptas longam breviore sequente,*
> *Ut clivo crevisse putes, &c *.*

Or else of one continuate substance, like those of bats. In framing of both which, the best guidance is to follow (as near as may be) the direction of nature, this being but an imitation of a natural work. Now in both these, the strength of each part is proportioned to the force of its employment. But nothing in this kind can be perfectly determined without a particular trial.

Though the composing of such motions may be a sufficient reward to any one's industry in the searching after them, as being in themselves of excellent curiosity, yet there are some other inventions depend upon them of more general benefit, and greater importance. For, if there be any such artificial contrivances that can fly in the air, (as is evident from the former relations, together with the grounds

* Ovid. Metam. l. 8.

here specified, and, I doubt not, may be easily effected by a diligent and ingenious artificer) then it will clearly follow, that it is possible also for a man to fly himself; it being easy from the same grounds, to frame an instrument wherein any one may sit, and give such a motion unto it, as shall convey him aloft through the air; than which there is not any imaginable invention, that could prove of greater benefit to the world, or glory to the author; and therefore it may justly deserve their inquiry, who have both leisure and means for such experiments.

But in these practical studies, unless a man be able to go the trial of things, he will perform but little. In such matters,

> —— *Studium sine divite venâ,*

(as the poet saith *) a general speculation, without particular experiment, may conjecture at many things, but can certainly effect nothing; and therefore I shall only propose unto the world, the theory and general grounds that may conduce to the easy and more perfect discovery of the subject in question, for the encouragement of those that have both minds and means for such experiments. This same scholar's fate,

> *Res angusta domi,* and
> —— *Curta suppellex,*

is that which hinders the promoting of learning in sundry particulars, and robs the world of many excellent inventions. We read of Aristotle, that he was allowed by his pupil Alexander eight hundred talents a year, for the payment of fishers, fowlers, and hunters, who were to bring him in several creatures, that so by his particular experience of their parts and dispositions, he might be more fitly prepared to write of their natures. The reason why the world hath not many Aristotles, is because it hath so few Alexanders.

Amongst other impediments of any strange invention, or attempts, it is none of the meanest discouragements, that

---

* Horace.

they are so generally derided by common opinion; being esteemed only as the dreams of a melancholy and distempered fancy. Eusebius * speaking, with what necessity every thing is confined by the laws of nature, and the decrees of providence, so that nothing can go out of that way unto which naturally it is designed; as a fish cannot reside on the land, nor a man in the water, or aloft in the air; infers, that therefore none will venture upon any such vain attempt, as passing in the air, η μελαγχολιας νοσηματα αν περιπεσοι, unless his brain be a little crazed with the humour of melancholy; whereupon he advises that we should not in any particular, endeavour to transgress the bounds of nature, ὑδε απτερον εχοντα το σωμα, τα των πτηνων επι τη δευειν, and since we are destitute of wings, not to imitate the flight of birds. That saying of the poet,

> Demens, qui nimbos, et non imitabile, fulmen, &c †.

hath been an old censure, applied unto such as ventured upon any strange or incredible attempt.

Hence may we conceive the reason, why there is so little intimation in the writings of antiquity, concerning the possibility of any such invention. The ancients durst not so much as mention the art of flying, but in a fable.

> Dædalus, ut fama est, fugiens Minoïa regna,
> Præpetibus pennis ausus se credere cælo,
> Insuetum per iter gelidas enavit ad arctos, &c.

It was the custom of those former ages, in their overmuch gratitude, to advance the first authors of any useful discovery amongst the number of their gods. And Dædalus, being so famous amongst them for sundry mechanical inventions (especially the sails of ships) though they did not for these place him in the heavens, yet they have promoted him as near as they could, feigning him to fly aloft in the air, when as he did but fly in a swift ship, as Diodorus relates the historical truth on which that fiction is grounded ‡.

---

* Contra. Hierocl. Confut. l, 1.   † Virgil's Æneid, l. 6.

‡ So Eusebius too.

CHAP. VII.

Concerning the art of Flying. The several ways whereby this hath been, or may be attempted.

I HAVE formerly in two other discourses * mentioned the possibility of this art of flying, and intimated a farther inquiry into it, which is a kind of engagement to some fuller disquisitions and conjectures to that purpose,

There are four several ways whereby this flying in the air hath been, or may be attempted. Two of them by the strength of other things, and two of them by our own strength.

1. By spirits, or angels.
2. By the help of fowls.
3. By wings fastened immediately to the body,
4. By a flying chariot.

1. For the first, we read of divers that have passed swiftly in the air, by the help of spirits and angels †; whether good angels, as Elias ‡ was carried unto heaven in a fiery chariot, as Philip ‖ was conveyed to Azotus, and Habakkuk from Jewry to Babylon, and back again immediately §: or by evil angels, as our Saviour was carried by the devil to the top of a high mountain, and to the pinnacle of the temple ¶. Thus witches are commonly related to pass unto their usual meetings, in some remote place; and, as they do sell winds unto mariners **, so likewise are they sometimes hired to carry men speedily through the open air. Acosta †† affirms, that such kind of passages are usual amongst divers sorcerers with the Indians at this day.

---

* World in the Moon, cap. 14. Mercury; or, the Secret and Swift Messenger, c. 4.

† Zanch. de Oper. part 1. l. 4. ‡ 2 Kings, ii. 11.

‖ Acts viii. 39. § Dan. Apoc. 39. ¶ Luke iv.

** Erastus de Lamus. †† Hist. Ind. l. 5. c. 26.

So Kepler, in his astronomical dream, doth fancy a witch to be conveyed unto the moon by her familiar.

Simon Magus was so eminent for miraculous sorceries, that all the people in Samaria, from the least to the greatest, did esteem him as the great power of God *. And so famous was he at Rome, that the emperor erected a statue to him with this inscription, Simoni Deo sancto †. It is storied of this magician, that having challenged Saint Peter to do miracles with him, he attempted to fly from the Capitol to the Aventine Hill; but when he was in the midst of the way, Saint Peter's prayers did overcome his sorceries, and violently bring him to the ground; in which fall having broke his thigh, within a while after he died ‡.

But none of all these relations may conduce to the discovery of this experiment, as it is here inquired after, upon natural and artificial grounds.

2 There are others, who have conjectured a possibility of being conveyed through the air by the help of fowls, to which purpose, that fiction of the ganzas is the most pleasant and probable. They are supposed to be great fowl, of a strong lasting flight, and easily tameable : divers of which may be so brought up, as to join together in the carrying the weight of a man, so as each of them shall partake his proportionable share of the burthen, and the person that is carried may by certain reins, direct and steer them in their courses. However this may seem a strange proposal, yet it is not certainly more improbable than many other arts, wherein the industry of ingenious men hath instructed these brute creatures. And I am very confident, that one whose genius doth enable him for such kind of experiments upon leisure, and the advantage of such helps as are requisite for various and frequent trials, might effect some strange things by this kind of inquiry.

---

* Acts viii. 10.   † Hegesip. l. 3. c. 2.

‡ Pol. Virgil. de Inven. Rerum, l. 8. c. 3.   Pet. Crinitus de Honestâ Disciplin. l. 8. c. 1. mistrusts this relation as fabulous.   Non enim Lucas hoc omisisset.

It is reported as a custom amongst the Leucatians, that they were wont upon a superstition, to precipitate a man from some high cliff into the sea, tying about him with strings at some distance, many great fowls, and fixing upon his body divers feathers, spread to break the fall; which (saith the learned Bacon *, if it were diligently and exactly contrived) would be able to hold up, and carry any proportionable weight; and therefore he advises others to think further upon this experiment, as giving some light to the invention of the art of flying.

3. It is the more obvious and common opinion, that this may be effected by wings fastened immediately to the body, this coming nearest to the imitation of nature, which should be observed in such attempts as these. This is that way which Fredericus Hermannus, in his little discourse *de arte volandi*, doth only mention and insist upon; and if we may trust credible story, it hath been frequently attempted not without some success †. It is related of a certain English monk, called Elmerus, about the Confessor's time, that he did by such wings fly from a tower above a furlong; and so another from Saint Mark's steeple in Venice; another at Norinberg; and Busbequius speaks of a Turk in Constantinople, who attempted something this way ‡. M. Burton mentioning this quotation, doth believe that some new-fangled wit (it is his cynical phrase) will some time or other find out this art. Though the truth is, most of these artists did unfortunately miscarry by falling down, and breaking their arms or legs, yet that may be imputed to their want of experience, and too much fear, which must needs possess men in such dangerous and strange attempts ‖. Those things that seem very difficult and fearful at the first, may grow very facil after frequent trial and exercise: and therefore he that would effect any thing in this kind, must be brought up to the constant practice of it from his youth;

* Nat. Hist. experim. 886   † So the ancient British Bladuds.
‡ Ernestus Burgravus in Panoplia Physico-Vulcania. Sturmius in Lat. Linguæ Resolut.
‖ Melancholy, part 2. sect. 1. mem. 3.

trying first only to use his wings, in running on the ground, as an ostrich or tame goose will do, touching the earth with his toes; and so by degrees learn to rise higher, till he shall attain unto skill and confidence. I have heard it from credible testimony, that one of our own nation hath proceeded so far in this experiment, that he was able by the help of wings, in such a running pace, to step constantly ten yards at a time.

It is not more incredible, that frequent practice and custom should enable a man for this, than for many other things which we see confirmed by experience. What strange agility and activeness do our common tumblers and dancers on the rope attain to by continual exercise? It is related of certain Indians *, that they are able, when a horse is running in his full career, to stand upright on his back, to turn themselves round, to leap down, gathering up any thing from the ground, and immediately to leap up again, to shoot exactly at any mark, the horse not intermitting his course: and so upon two horses together, the man setting one of his feet upon each of them. These things may seem impossible to others, and it would be very dangerous for any one to attempt them, who hath not first gradually attained to these arts by long practice and trial; and why may not such practice enable him as well for this other experiment, as for these things?

There are others, who have invented ways to walk upon the water as regularly and firmly as upon the land. There are some so accustomed to this element, that it hath been almost as natural to them as to the fish; men that could remain for above an hour together under water. Pontanus mentions one, who could swim above a hundred miles together, from one shore to another, with great speed, and at all times of the year. And it is storied of a certain young man, a Sicilian by birth, and a diver by profession, who had so continually used himself to the water, that he could not enjoy his health out of it. If at any time he staid with

* Maffæus Hist. Ind. l. 1.

his friends on the land, he should be so tormented with a pain in his stomach, that he was forced for his health to return back again to sea; wherein he kept his usual residence, and when he saw any ships, his custom was to swim to them for relief; which kind of life he continued till he was an old man, and died *.

I mention these things, to shew the great power of practice and custom, which might more probably succeed in this experiment of flying (if it were but regularly attempted) than in such strange effects as these.

It is a usual practice in these times, for our funambulones, or dancers on the rope, to attempt somewhat like to flying, when they will, with their heads forwards, slide down a long cord extended; being fastened at one end to the top of some high tower, and the other at some distance on the ground, with wings fixed to their shoulders, by the shaking of which they will break the force of their descent. It would seem that some attempts of this kind were usual amongst the Romans. To which that expression in Salvian † may refer; where, amongst other public shews of the theatre, he mentions the Petaminaria; which word (saith Jo. Brassicanus ‡) is scarce to be found in any other author, being not mentioned either in Julius Pollux, or Politian. It is probably derived from the Greek word πεταϭϑαι, which signifies to fly, and may refer to such kind of rope dancers.

But now, because the arms extended are but weak, and easily wearied, therefore the motions by them are like to be but short and slow, answerable it may be to the flight of such domestic fowl as are most conversant on the ground, which of themselves we see are quickly weary; and therefore much more would the arm of a man, as being not naturally designed to such a motion.

It were therefore worth the inquiry, to consider whether this might not be more probably effected by the labour of the feet, which are naturally more strong and indefatigable:

* Treatise of Custom.   † De Guber. Dei, l. 6.
‡ Annot. in Salvi

in which contrivance the wings should come down from the shoulders on each side, as in the other, but the motion of them should be from the legs being thrust out, and drawn in again one after another, so as each leg should move both wings; by which means a man should (as it were) walk or climb up into the air; and then the hands and arms might be at leisure to help and direct the motion, or for any other service proportionable to their strength. Which conjecture is not without good probability, and some special advantages above the other.

4. But the fourth and last way seems unto me altogether as probable, and much more useful than any of the rest. And that is by a flying chariot, which may be so contrived as to carry a man within it; and though the strength of a spring might perhaps be serviceable for the motion of this engine, yet it were better to have it assisted by the labour of some intelligent mover, as the heavenly orbs are supposed to be turned. And therefore if it were made big enough to carry sundry persons together, then each of them in their several turns might successively labour in the causing of this motion; which thereby would be much more constant and lasting, than it could otherwise be, if it did wholly depend on the strength of the same person. This contrivance being as much to be preferred before any of the other, as swimming in a ship before swimming in the water.

CHAP VIII.

A resolution of the two chief difficulties that seem to oppose the possibility of a flying chariot.

THE chief difficulties against the possibility of any such contrivance may be fully removed in the resolution of these two queries.

1. Whether an engine of such capacity and weight, may be supported by so thin and light a body as the air?

2. Whether the strength of the persons within it may be sufficient for the motion of it?

1. Concerning the first; when Callias * was required by the men of Rhodes, to take up that great helepolis, brought against them by Demetrius, (as he had done before unto some less which he himself had made) he answered that it could not be done. *Nonnulla enim sunt quæ in exemplaribus videntur similia, cum autem crescere cœperunt, dilabuntur* †. Because those things that appear probable in lesser models, when they are increased to a greater proportion, do thereby exceed the power of art. For example, though a man may make an instrument to bore a hole, an inch wide, or half an inch, and so less; yet to bore a hole of a foot wide, or two foot, is not so much as to be thought of. Thus, though the air may be able to uphold some lesser bodies, as those of birds, yet when the quantity of them is increased to any great extension, it may justly be doubted, whether they will not exceed the proportion that is naturally required unto such kind of bodies.

To this I answer, that the engine can never be too big or too heavy, if the space which it possesses in the air, and the motive-faculty in the instrument be answerable to its weight. That saying of Callias was but a groundless shift and evasion, whereby he did endeavour to palliate his own ignorance and disability. The utmost truth which seems to be implied in it, is this: that there may be some bodies of so great a bigness, and gravity, that it is very difficult to apply so much force unto any particular instrument, as shall be able to move them.

Against the example it may be affirmed and easily proved, that it is equally possible to bore a hole of any bigness, as well great as little, if we suppose the instrument, and the strength, and the application of this strength to be proportionable; but because of the difficulty of these concurrent circumstances in those greater and more unusual operations, therefore do they falsely seem to be absolutely impossible.

---

* Vitruvius Archit. l. 10. c. 22.   † So Ramus, Schol. Mathem. l. 1.

So that the chief inference from this argument and ex-ample, doth imply only thus much, that it is very difficult to contrive any such motive power, as shall be answerable to the greatness and weight of such an instrument as is here discoursed of; which doth not at all impair the truth to be maintained: for if the possibility of such a motion be yielded, we need not make any scruple of granting the difficulty of it; it is this must add a glory to the invention; and yet this will not perhaps seem so very difficult to any one who hath but diligently observed the flight of some other birds, particularly of a kite, how he will swim up and down in the air, sometimes at a great height, and presently again lower, guiding himself by his train, with his wings extended without any sensible motion of them; and all this, when there is only some gentle breath of air stirring, without the help of any strong forcible wind. Now I say, if that very fowl (which is none of the lightest) can so easily move itself up and down in the air, without so much as stirring the wings of it, certainly then it is not improbable, but that when all the due proportions in such an engine are found out, and when men by long practice have arrived to any skill and experience, they will be able in this (as well as in many other things) to come very near unto the imitation of nature.

As it is in those bodies which are carried on the water, though they be never so big or so ponderous, (suppose equal to a city or a whole island) yet they will always swim on the top, if they be but any thing lighter than so much water as is equal to them in bigness *. So likewise is it in the bodies that are carried in the air. It is not their greatness (though never so immense) that can hinder their being supported in that light element, if we suppose them to be extended unto a proportionable space of air. And as from the former experiments, Archimedes hath composed a subtle science in his book *De insidentibus humido*, concerning the weight of any heavy body, in reference to the water

* Sen. Nat. Qu. l. 1. c. 25.

wherein it is; so from the particular trial of these other experiments, that are here inquired after, it is possible to raise a new science, concerning the extension of bodies, in comparison to the air, and motive faculties by which they are to be carried.

We see a great difference betwixt the several quantities of such bodies as are commonly upheld by the air; not only little gnats, and flies, but also the eagle and other fowl of vaster magnitude. Cardan and Scaliger * do unanimously affirm, that there is a bird amongst the Indians of so great a bigness, that his beak is often used to make a sheath or scabbard for a sword. And Acosta † tells us of a fowl in Peru called candores, which will of themselves kill and eat up a whole calf at a time. Nor is there any reason why any other body may not be supported and carried by the air, though it should as much exceed the quantity of these fowl, as they do the quantity of a fly.

Marcus Polus mentions a fowl in Madagascar, which he calls a ruck, the feathers of whose wings are twelve paces, or threescore foot long, which can with as much ease scoop up an elephant, as our kites do a mouse. If this relation were any thing credible, it might serve as an abundant proof for the present query. But I conceive this to be already so evident, that it needs not any fable for its further confirmation.

2. The other doubt was, whether the strength of the other persons within it, will be sufficient for the moving of this engine? I answer, the main difficulty and labour of it will be in the raising of it from the ground; near unto which, the earth's attractive vigour is of greatest efficacy. But for the better effecting of this, it may be helped by the strength of winds, and by taking its first rise from some mountain or other high place. When once it is aloft in the air, the motion of it will be easy, as it is in the flight of all kind of birds, which being at any great distance from the

---

* Subtil. l. 10. Exercit. 231.   † Histor. Nov. Orb. l. 4. c. 37.

earth, are able to continue their motion for a long time and way, with little labour or weariness.

It is certain from common relation and experience that many birds do cross the seas for divers hundred miles together *. Sundry of them amongst us, which are of a short wing and flight, as blackbirds, nightingales, &c. do fly from us into Germany, and other remoter countries. And mariners do commonly affirm that they have found some fowl above six hundred miles from any land. Now if we should suppose these birds to labour so much in those long journies, as they do when they fly in our sight and near the earth, it were impossible for any of them to pass so far without resting. And therefore it is probable, that they do mount unto so high a place in the air, where the natural heaviness of their bodies does prove but little or no impediment to their flight : though perhaps either hunger, or the sight of ships, or the like accident, may sometimes occasion their descending lower ; as we may guess of those birds which mariners have thus beheld, and divers others that have been drowned and cast up by the sea.

Whence it may appear, that the motion of this chariot (though it may be difficult at the first) yet will still be easier as it ascends higher, till at length it shall become utterly devoid of gravity, when the least strength will be able to bestow upon it a swift motion : as I have proved more at large in another discourse †.

But then, (may some object) if it be supposed that a man, in the æthereal air does lose his own heaviness, how shall he contribute any force towards the motion of this instrument ?

I answer, the strength of any living creature in these external motions, is something really distinct from, and superadded unto its natural gravity : as common experience may shew, not only in the impression of blows or violent motions, as a river hawk will strike a fowl with a far greater force, than the mere descent or heaviness of his body could

* Plin. l. 10. c. 23.   † World in the Moon, cap. 14.

possibly perform : but also in those actions which are done without such help, as the pinching of the finger, the biting of the teeth, &c. all which are of much greater strength than can proceed from the mere heaviness of those parts.

As for the other particular doubts, concerning the extreme thinness and coldness of this æthereal air, by reason of which, it may seem to be altogether impassible, I have already resolved them in the above-cited discourse.

The uses of such a chariot may be various : besides the discoveries which might be thereby made in the lunary world, it would be serviceable also for the conveyance of a man to any remote place of this earth : as suppose to the Indies or antipodes. For when once it was elevated for some few miles, so as to be above that orb of magnetic virtue, which is carried about by the earth's diurnal revolution, it might then be very easily and speedily directed to any particular place of this great globe.

If the place which we intended were under the same parallel, why then the earth's revolution once in twenty-four hours, would bring it to be under us ; so that it would be but descending in a straight line, and we might presently be there. If it were under any other parallel, it would then only require that we should direct it in the same meridian, till we did come to that parallel ; and then (as before) a man might easily descend unto it.

It would be one great advantage in this kind of travelling, that one should be perfectly freed from all inconveniencies of ways or weather, not having any extremity of heat or cold, or tempests to molest him. This æthereal air being perpetually in an equal temper and calmness. *Pars superior mundi ordinatior est, nec in nubem cogitur, nec in tempestatem impellitur, nec versatur in turbinem, omni tumultu caret, inferiora fulminant* *. The upper parts of the world are always quiet and serene, no winds and blustering there, they are these lower cloudy regions that are so full of tempests and combustion.

* Sen de Ira, l. 3. c. 6. Pacem summa tenent. Lucan.

As for the manner how the force of a spring, or (instead of that) the strength of any living person, may be applied to the motion of these wings of the chariot, it may easily be apprehended from what was formerly delivered.

There are divers other particulars to be more fully inquired after, for the perfecting of such a flying chariot; as concerning the proportion of the wings both for the length and breadth, in comparison to the weight which is to be carried by them *; as also concerning those special contrivances, whereby the strength of these wings may be severally applied, either to ascent, descent, progressive, or a turning motion; all which, and divers the like inquiries can only be resolved by particular experiments. We know the invention of sailing in ships does continually receive some new addition from the experience of every age, and hath been a long while growing up to that perfection unto which it is now arrived. And so must it be expected for this likewise, which may at first perhaps seem perplexed with many difficulties and inconveniencies, and yet upon the experience of frequent trials, many things may be suggested to make it more facil and commodious.

He that would regularly attempt any thing to this purpose, should observe this progress in his experiments; he should first make inquiry what kind of wings would be most useful to this end; those of a bat being most easily imitable, and perhaps nature did by them purposely intend some intimation to direct us in such experiments; that creature being not properly a bird, because not amongst the *ovipara*, to imply that other kind of creatures are capable of flying as well as birds; and if any should attempt it, that would be the best pattern for imitation.

After this he may try what may be effected by the force of springs in lower models, answerable unto Archytas his dove, and Regiomontanus his eagle: in which he must be careful to observe the various proportions betwixt the

* As well too long as too short, too broad as too narrow, may be an impediment to the motion, by making it more difficult, slow, and flagging.

strength of the spring, the heaviness of the body, the breadth of the wings, the swiftness of the motion, &c.

From these he may by degrees ascend to some larger essays.

CHAP. IX.

Of a perpetual motion.   The seeming facility and real difficulty of any such contrivance.   The several ways whereby it hath been attempted, particularly by chymistry.

IT is the chief inconvenience of all the automata beforementioned, that they need a frequent repair of new strength, the causes whence their motion does proceed being subject to fail, and come to a period; and therefore it would be worth our inquiry, to examine whether or no there may be made any such artificial contrivance, which might have the principle of moving from itself; so that the present motion should constantly be the cause of that which succeeds.

This is that great secret in art, which, like the philosopher's stone in nature, hath been the business and study of many more refined wits, for divers ages together; and it may well be questioned, whether either of them as yet hath ever been found out; though if this have, yet, like the other, it is not plainly treated of by any author.

Not but that there are sundry discourses concerning this subject, but they are rather conjectures than experiments. And though many inventions in this kind, may at first view bear a great shew of probability, yet they will fail, being brought to trial, and will not answer in practice what they promised in speculation.   Any one who hath been versed in these experiments must needs acknowledge that he hath been often deceived in his strongest confidence; when the imagination hath contrived the whole frame of such an instrument, and conceives that the event must infallibly answer its hopes, yet then does it strangely deceive in the proof, and discovers to us some defect which we did not before take notice of.

Hence it is, that you shall scarce talk with any one who hath never so little smattering in these arts, but he will instantly promise such a motion, as being but an easy atchievement, till further trial and experience hath taught him the difficulty of it. There being no inquiry that does more entice with the probability, and deceive with the subtilty. What one speaks wittily concerning the philosopher's stone, may be justly applied to this, that it is *casta meretrix*, a chaste whore; *quia multos invitat, neminem admittit*, because it allures many, but admits none.

I shall briefly recite the several ways whereby this hath been attempted, or seems most likely to be effected; thereby to contract and facilitate the inquiries of those who are addicted to these kind of experiments; for when they know the defects of other inventions, they may the more easily avoid the same, or the like in their own.

The ways whereby this hath been attempted, may be generally reduced to these three kinds:

1. By chymical extractions.
2. By magnetical virtues.
3. By the natural affection of gravity.

1. The discovery of this hath been attempted by chymistry. Paracelsus and his followers have bragged, that by their separations and extractions, they can make a little world which shall have the same perpetual motions with this microcosm, with the representation of all meteors, thunder, snow, rain, the courses of the sea in its ebbs and flows, and the like; but these miraculous promises would require as great a faith to believe them, as a power to perform them: and though they often talk of such great matters,

At nusquam totos inter qui talia curant,
Apparet ullus, qui re miracula tanta
Comprobet ———

yet we can never see them confirmed by any real experiment; and then besides, every particular author in that art hath such a distinct language of his own, (all of them being so full of allegories and affected obscurities) that it is very hard for any one (unless he be thoroughly versed amongst them) to find out what they mean, much more to try it.

One of these ways (as I find it set down *) is this. Mix five ounces of ☿, with an equal weight of ♃, grind them together with ten ounces of sublimate, dissolve them in a cellar upon some marble for the space of four days, till they become like oil olive; distil this with fire of chaff, or driving fire, and it will sublime into a dry substance: and so by repeating of these dissolvings and distillings, there will be at length produced divers small atoms, which being put into a glass well luted, and kept dry, will have a perpetual motion.

I cannot say any thing from experience against this; but methinks it does not seem very probable, because things that are forced up to such a vigorousness and activity as these ingredients seem to be by their frequent sublimatings and distillings, are not likely to be of any duration; the more any thing is stretched beyond its usual nature, the less does it last; violence and perpetuity being no companions. And then besides, suppose it true, yet such a motion could not well be applied to any use, which must needs take much from the delight of it.

Amongst the chymical experiments to this purpose, may be reckoned up that famous motion invented by Cornelius Dreble, and made for king James †; wherein was represented the constant revolutions of the sun and moon, and that without the help either of springs or weights. Marcellus Vranckhein ‡, speaking of the means whereby it was performed, he calls it, *scintillula animæ magneticæ mundi, seu astralis et insensibilis spiritus;* being that grand

---

* Etten. Mathem. Recreat. prob. 118.
† Celebrated in an epigram by Hugo Grotius, l. 1.
‡ Epist. ad Ernestum de Lamp. Vitæ.

secret, for the discovery of which, those dictators of philosophy, Democritus, Pythagoras, Plato, did travel unto the gymnosophists, and Indian priests. The author himself in his discourse upon it, does not at all reveal the way how it was performed. But there is one Thomas Tymme *, who was a familiar acquaintance of his, and did often pry into his works, (as he professes himself) who affirms it to be done thus; by extracting a fiery spirit out of the mineral matter, joining the same with his proper air, which included in the axletree (of the first moving wheel) being hollow, carrieth the other wheels, making a continual rotation, except issue or vent be given in this hollow axletree, whereby the imprisoned spirit may get forth †.

What strange things may be done by such extractions, I know not, and therefore dare not condemn this relation as impossible; but methinks it sounds rather like a chymical dream, than a philosophical truth. It seems this imprisoned spirit is now set at liberty, or else is grown weary, for the instrument (as I have heard) hath stood still for many years. It is here considerable that any force is weakest near the centre of a wheel; and therefore though such a spirit might of itself have an agitation, yet it is not easily conceivable how it should have strength enough to carry the wheels about with it. And then the absurdity of the author's citing this, would make one mistrust his mistake; he urges it as a strong argument against Copernicus, as if because Dreble did thus contrive in an engine the revolution of the heavens, and the immoveableness of the earth, therefore it must needs follow that it is the heavens which are moved, and not the earth. If his relation were no truer than his consequence, it had not been worth the citing.

* Epist. ad Jacobum Regem.
† Philosophical Dialogue, Confer. 2. cap. 3.

CHAP. X.

Of subterraneous lamps; divers historical relations concerning their duration for many hundred years together.

UNTO this kind of chymical experiments, we may most probably reduce those perpetual lamps, which for many hundred years together have continued burning without any new supply in the sepulchres of the ancients, and might (for ought we know) have remained so for ever, All fire, and especially flame, being of an active and stirring nature, it cannot therefore subsist without motion; whence it may seem, that this great enquiry hath been this way accomplished: and therefore it will be worth our examination to search further into the particulars that concern this experiment. Though it be not so proper to the chief purpose of this discourse, which concerns mechanical geometry, yet the subtilty and curiosity of it may abundantly requite the impertinency.

There are sundry authors, who treat of this subject on the by, and in some particular passages, but none that I know of (except Fortunius Licetus*) that hath writ purposely any set and large discourse concerning it: out of whom I shall borrow many of those relations and opinions, which may most naturally conduce to the present enquiry.

For our fuller understanding of this, there are these particulars to be explained:

1. ὅτι, or *quod sit.*

2. διότι $\begin{cases} cur\ sit. \\ quomodo\ sit. \end{cases}$

1. First then, for the ὅτι, or that there have been such lamps, it may be evident from sundry plain and undeniable testimonies: St. Austin † mentions one of them in a temple

---

* Lib. de reconditis Antiquorum Lucernis.

† De Civitat. Dei, l. 21. c. 6.

dedicated to Venus, which was always exposed to the open weather, and could never be consumed or extinguished. To him assents the judicious Zanchy *. Pancyrollus † mentions a lamp found in his time, in the sepulchre of Tullia, Cicero's daughter, which had continued there for about 1550 years, but was presently extinguished upon the admission of new air. And it is commonly related of Cedrenus, that in Justinian's time there was another burning lamp found in an old wall at Edessa ‡, which had remained so for above 500 years, there being a crucifix placed by it, whence it should seem, that they were in use also amongst some christians.

But more especially remarkable is that relation celebrated by so many authors, concerning Olybius's lamp, which had continued burning for 1500 years. The story is thus: as a rustic was digging the ground by Padua, he found an urn or earthen pot, in which there was another urn, and in this lesser, a lamp clearly burning; on each side of it there were two other vessels, each of them full of a pure liquor; the one of gold, the other of silver. *Ego chymiæ artis, (simodo vera potest esse ars chymia) jurare ausim elementa et materiam omnium,* (saith Maturantius, who had the possession of these things after they were taken up.) On the bigger of these urns there was this inscription;

Plutoni sacrum munus ne attingite fures.
  Ignotum est vobis hoc quod in orbe latet,
Namque elementa gravi clausit digesta labore
  Vase sub hoc modico, Maximus Olybius.
Adsit fœcundo custos sibi copia cornu,
  Ne tanti pretium depereat laticis.

The lesser urn was thus inscribed:

  Abite hinc pessimi fures,
Vos quid vultis, vestris cum oculis emissitis?
Abite hinc, vestro cum Mercurio
Petasato caduceatoque,
Donum hoc maximum, Maximus Olybius
Plutoni sacrum facit.

* De Operibus Dei, pars 1. l. 4. c. 12.   † De deperd. Tit. 35.
‡ Or Antioch. Licetus de Lucernis, l. 1. c. 7.

Whence we may probably conjecture that it was some chymical secret, by which this was contrived.

Baptista Porta * tells us of another lamp burning in an old marble sepulchre, belonging to some of the ancient Romans, inclosed in a glass vial, found in his time, about the year 1550, in the isle Nesis, which had been buried there before our Saviour's coming.

In the tomb of Pallas, the Arcadian who was slain by Turnus in the Trojan war, there was found another burning lamp, in the year of our Lord 1401 †. Whence it should seem, that it had continued there for above two thousand and six hundred years: and being taken out, it did remain burning, notwithstanding either wind or water, with which some did strive to quench it; nor could it be extinguished till they had spilt the liquor that was in it.

Ludovicus Vives ‡ tells us of another lamp, that did continue burning for 1050 years, which was found a little before his time.

Such a lamp is likewise related to be seen in the sepulchre of Francis Rosicrosse, as is more largely expressed in the confession of that fraternity.

There is another relation of a certain man, who upon occasion digging somewhat deep in the ground did meet with something like a door, having a wall on each hand of it; from which having cleared the earth, he forced open this door, upon this there was discovered a fair vault, and towards the further side of it, the statue of a man in armour, sitting by a table, leaning upon his left arm, and holding a sceptre in his right hand, with a lamp burning before him; the floor of this vault being so contrived, that upon the first step into it, the statue would erect itself from its leaning posture; upon the second step it did lift up the scepter to strike, and before a man could approach near enough to take hold of the lamp, the statue did strike and break it to

* Mag. Natural. l. 12. cap. ult.
† Chron. Martin. Fort. Licet. de Lucern. l. 1. c. 11.
‡ Not. ad August. de Civit. Dei, l. 21. c. 6.

pieces: such care was there taken that it might not be stolen away, or discovered.

Our learned Cambden in his description of Yorkshire * speaking of the tomb of Constantius Chlorus, broken up in these later years, mentions such a lamp to be found within it.

There are sundry other relations to this purpose. *Quod ad lucernas attinet, illæ in omnibus fere monumentis inveniuntur*, (saith Gutherius †.) In most of the ancient monuments there is some kind of lamp, (though of the ordinary sort:) but those persons who were of greatest note and wisdom, did procure such as might last without supply, for so many ages together. Pancirollus ‡ tells us, that it was usual for the nobles amongst the Romans, to take special care in their last wills, that they might have a lamp in their monuments. And to this purpose they did usually give liberty unto some of their slaves on this condition, that they should be watchful in maintaining and preserving it. From all which relations, the first particular of this enquiry, concerning the being or existence of such lamps, may sufficiently appear.

CHAP. XI.

Several opinions concerning the nature and reason of these perpetual Lamps.

THERE are two opinions to be answered, which do utterly overthrow the chief consequence from these relations.

1. Some think that these lights so often discovered in the ancient tombs, were not fire or flame, but only some of those bright bodies which do usually shine in dark places.

---

* Pag. 572.   † De Jure Manium, l. 2. c. 32.
‡ De perdit. Tit. 62.

2. Others grant them to be fire, but yet think them to be then first enkindled by the admission of new air, when these sepulchres were opened.

1. There are divers bodies (saith Aristotle *) which shine in the dark, as rotten wood, the scales of some fishes, stones, the glowworm, the eyes of divers creatures. Cardan † tells us of a bird in New Spain, called cocoyum, whose whole body is very bright, but his eyes almost equal to the light of a candle, by which alone in a dark night, one may both write and read: by these the Indians (saith he) used to eat their feasting suppers.

It is commonly related and believed, that a carbuncle does shine in the dark like a burning coal, from whence it hath its name ‡. To which purpose there is a story in Ælian ‖ of a stork, that by a certain woman was cured of a broken thigh, in gratitude to whom, this fowl afterwards flying by her, did let fall into her lap a bright carbuncle, which (saith he) would in the night time shine as clear as a lamp. But this and the like old relations are now generally disbelieved and rejected by learned men: *doctissimorum omnium consensu, hujusmodi gemmæ non inveniuntur*, (saith Boetius de Boot §) a man very much skilled in, and inquisitive after such matters; nor is there any one of name that does from his own eye-sight or experience, affirm the real existence of any gem so qualified.

Some have thought that the light in ancient tombs hath been occasioned from some such bodies as these ¶. For if there had been any possibility to preserve fire so long a space, it is likely then that the Israelites would have known the way, who were to keep it perpetually for their sacrifices.

But to this opinion it might be replied, that none of these noctilucæ, or night-shining bodies have been observed in any of the ancient sepulchres, and therefore this is a mere

* De Anima, l. 2. c. 7.   † Subtil. l. 9.
‡ Carlo Pyropus.   ‖ Historia Anim. l. 8.
§ De Lapid. et Gemmis, l. 2. c. 8.
¶ Vide Licet. de Lucern. l. 2.

imaginary conjecture; and then besides, some of these lamps have been taken out burning, and continued so for a considerable space afterwards. As for the supposed conveniency of them, for the perpetuating of the holy fire amongst the Jews, it may as well be feared lest these should have occasioned their idolatry, unto which that nation was so strongly addicted, upon every slight occasion; nor may it seem strange, if the providence of God should rather permit this fire sometimes to go out, that so by their earnest prayers, being again renewed from heaven, (as it sometimes was *) the people's faith might be the better stirred up and strengthened by such frequent miracles.

2. It is the opinion of Gutherius †, that these lamps have not continued burning for so long a space, as they are supposed in the former relations; but that they were then first enflamed by the admission of new air, or such other occasion, when the sepulchres were opened: as we see in those fat earthy vapours of divers sorts, which are oftentimes enkindled into a flame. And it is said, that there are some chymical ways, whereby iron may be so heated, that being closely luted in a glass, it shall constantly retain the fire for any space of time, though it were for a thousand years or more; at the end of which, if the glass be opened, and the fresh air admitted, the iron shall be as red hot as if it were newly taken out of the fire.

But for answer to this opinion, it is considerable that some urns have had inscriptions on them, expressing that the lamps within them were burning, when they were first buried. To which may be added the experience of those which have continued so for a good space afterwards; whereas the inflammation of fat and viscous vapours does presently vanish. The lamp which was found in the isle Nesis, did burn clearly while it was inclosed in the glass, but that being broken, was presently extinguished. As for that chymical relation, it may rather serve to prove that

---

* Levit. ix. 24. 2 Chron. vii. 1. 1 Kings xviii. 38.
† De Jure Manium, l. 2. c. 32.

fire may continue so many ages, without consuming any fewel.

So that notwithstanding the opposite opinions, yet it is more probable that there have been such lamps as have remained burning, without any new supply, for many hundred years together; which was the first particular to be explained.

2. Concerning the reason why the ancients were so careful in this particular, there are divers opinions. Some think it to be an expression of their belief, concerning the soul's immortality, after its departure out of the body; a lamp amongst the Egyptians being the hieroglyphic of life. And therefore they that could not procure such lamps, were yet careful to have the image and representation of them engraved on their tombs.

Others conceive them to be by way of gratitude to those infernal deities, who took the charge and custody of their dead bodies, remaining always with them in their tombs, and were therefore called *dii manes.*

Others are of opinion, that these lamps were only intended to make their sepulchres more pleasant and lightsome, that they might not seem to be imprisoned in a dismal and uncomfortable place. True indeed, the dead body cannot be sensible of this light, no more could it of its want of burial; yet the same instinct which did excite it to the desire of one, did also occasion the other.

Licetus * concludes this ancient custom to have a double end. 1. Politic, for the distinction of such as were nobly born, in whose monuments only they were used. 2. Natural, to preserve the body and soul from darkness; for it was a common opinion amongst them, that the souls also were much conversant about those places where the bodies were buried.

* De Lucernis, l. 3. c. 8.

CHAP. XII.

The most probable conjecture, how these lamps were framed.

THE greatest difficulty of this enquiry doth consist in this last particular, concerning the manner how, or by what possible means any such perpetual flame may be contrived.

For the discovery of which, there are two things to be more especially considered.

1. The snuff, or wick, which must administer unto the flame.

2. The oil, which must nourish it.

For the first, it is generally granted that there are divers substances which will retain fire without consuming: such is that mineral which they call the salamanders wool, saith our learned Bacon *. *Ipse expertus sum villos salamandræ non consumi,* saith Joachimus Fortius †. And Wecker ‡, from his own knowledge, affirms the same of plumeallum, that being formed into the likeness of a wick, will administer to the flame, and yet not consume itself. Of this nature likewise was that which the ancients did call *linum vivum* ‖, or *asbestinum:* of this they were wont to make garments, that were not destroyed, but purified by fire; and whereas the spots or foulness of other clothes are washed out, in these they were usually burnt away. The bodies of the ancient kings were wrapped in such garments, when they were put in the funeral pile, that their ashes might be therein preserved, without the mixture of any other §. The materials of them were not from any herb or vegetable, as other textiles, but from a stone called amiantus; which

---

* Nat. Hist. Exper. 774.   † Lib. Exper.
‡ De Secretis, l. 3. c. 2.
‖ Or linum carpasium.   Plutarch. de Oracul. Defectu.
§ Plin. Hist. l. 19. c. 1.

being bruised by a hammer, and its earthly nature shaken out, retains certain hairy substances, which may be spun and woven, as hemp or flax. Pliny says, that for the preciousness of it, it did almost equal the price of pearls. Pancirollus * tells us, that it was very rare, and esteemed precious in antient times, but now is scarce found or known in any places, and therefore he reckons it amongst the things that are lost. But L. Vives † affirms, that he hath often seen wicks made of it at Paris, and the same matter woven into a napkin at Lovaine, which was cleansed by being burnt in the fire.

It is probable from these various relations, that there were several sorts of it; some of a more precious, other of a baser kind, that was found in Cyprus, the deserts of India, and a certain province of Asia; this being common in some parts of Italy, but is so short and brittle, that it cannot be spun into a thread; and therefore is useful only for the wicks of perpetual lamps; saith Boetius de Boot ‡. Some of this, or very like it, I have upon enquiry lately procured and experimented; but whether it be the stone asbestus, or only plumeallum, I cannot certainly affirm; for it seems they are both so very like, as to be commonly sold for one another (saith the same author.) However, it does truly agree in this common quality ascribed unto both, of being incombustible, and not consumable by fire: but yet there is this inconvenience, that it doth contract so much fuliginous matter from the earthly parts of the oil, (though it was tried with some of the purest oil which is ordinary to be bought) that in a very few days it did choke and extinguish the flame. There may possibly be some chymical way, so to purify and defecate this oil, that it shall not spend into a sooty matter.

However, if the liquor be of a close and glutinous consistency, it may burn without any snuff, as we see in camphire, and some other bituminous substances. And it is

* De perd. Tit. 4.   † In August. de Civit. Dei, l. 21. c. 6.
‡ De Lapid. et Gemmis, l. 2. c. 204.

probable that most of the ancient lamps were of this kind, because the exactest relations (to my remembrance) do not mention any that have been found with such wicks.

But herein will consist the greatest difficulty, to find out what invention there might be for their duration: concerning which there are sundry opinions.

St. Austin * speaking of that lamp in one of the heathen temples, thinks that it might either be done by magic, (the devil thinking thereby to promote the worship and esteem of that idol to which it was dedicated) or else, that the art of man might make it of some such material, as the stone asbestus, which being once kindled, will burn without being consumed †. As others (saith he) have contrived as great a wonder in appearance, from the natural virtue of another stone, making an iron image seem to hang in the air, by reason of two loadstones, the one being placed in the ceiling, the other in the floor.

Others are of opinion, that this may be effected in a hollow vessel, exactly luted or stopped up in all the vents of it: and then, if a lamp be supposed to burn in it but for the least moment of time, it must continue so always, or else there would be a vacuum, which nature is not capable of. If you ask how it shall be nourished, it is answered, that the oil of it being turned into smoke and vapours, will again be converted into its former nature; for otherwise, if it should remain rarified in so thin a substance, then there would not be room enough for that fume which must succeed it; and so on the other side, there might be some danger of the penetration of bodies, which nature doth as much abhor. To prevent both which, as it is in the chymical circulations, where the same body is oftentimes turned from liquor into vapour, and from vapour into liquor again; so in this experiment, the same oil shall be turned into fume, and that fume shall again convert into oil. Always provided, that this oil which nourishes the lamp, be

* De Civ. Dei, l. 21. c. 6.
† Zanch. de Operibus Dei, par. 1. l. 4. c. 12.

Supposed of so close and tenacious a substance, that may slowly evaporate, and so there will be the more leisure for nature to perfect these circulations. According to which contrivance, the lamp within this vessel can never fail, being always supplied with sufficient nourishment. That which was found in the isle Nesis, inclosed in a glass-vial, mentioned by Baptista Porta, is thought to be made after some such manner as this.

Others conceive it possible to extract such an oil out of some minerals, which shall for a long space serve to nourish the flame of a lamp, with very little or no expence of its own substance *. To which purpose (say they) if gold be dissolved into an unctuous humour, or if the radical moisture of that metal were separated, it might be contrived to burn (perhaps for ever, or at least) for many ages together, without being consumed. For, if gold itself (as experience shews) be so untameable by the fire, that after many meltings and violent heats, it does scarce diminish, it is probable then, that being dissolved into an oily substance, it might for many hundred years together continue burning.

There is a little chymical discourse, to prove that urim and thummim is to be made by art. The author of this treatise affirms that place, Gen. vi. 16. where God tells Noah, a window shalt thou make in the ark, to be very unfitly rendered in our translation, a window; because the original word צהר signifies properly splendour, or light: and then besides, the air being at that time so extremely darkened with the clouds of that excessive rain, a window could be but of very little use in regard of light, unless there were some other help for it. From whence he conjectures, that both this splendour, and so likewise the urim and thummim were artificial chymical preparations of light, answerable to these subterraneous lamps; or in his own phrase, it was the universal spirit fixed in a transparent body.

---

* Wolphang. Lazius, l. 3. c. 18. Camb. Brit. p 572.

It is the opinion of Licetus*, (who hath more exactly searched into the subtilties of this enquiry) that fire does not need any humour for the nourishment of it, but only to detain it from flying upwards: for, being in itself one of the chief elements (saith he out of Theophrastus) it were absurd to think that it could not subsist without something to feed it. As for that substance which is consumed by it, this cannot be said to foment or preserve the same fire, but only to generate new. For the better understanding of this, we must observe, that there may be a threefold proportion betwixt fire, and the humour, or matter of it. Either the humour does exceed the strength of the fire, or the fire does exceed the humour; and according to both these, the flame doth presently vanish. Or else lastly, they may be both equal in their virtues, (as it is betwixt the radical moisture, and natural heat in living creatures) and then neither of them can overcome, or destroy the other.

Those ancient lamps of such long duration, were of this latter kind: but now, because the qualities of heat or cold, dryness or moisture in the ambient air, may alter this equality of proportion betwixt them, and make one stronger than the other; therefore to prevent this, the ancients did hide these lamps in some caverns of the earth, or close monuments. And hence is it, that at the opening of these, the admission of new air unto the lamp does usually cause so great an inequality betwixt the flame and the oil, that it is presently extinguished.

But still, the greatest difficulty remains how to make any such exact proportion betwixt an unctuous humour, and such an active quality as the heat of fire ; or this equality being made, it is yet a further difficulty, how it may be preserved. To which purpose, Licetus thinks it possible to extract an inflammable oil from the stone asbestus, amiantus, or the metal gold; which being of the same pure and homogeneous nature with those bodies, shall be so proportioned unto the heat of fire, that it cannot be consumed by it ;

* De Lucernis, c. 20, 21.

but being once inflamed, should continue for many ages, without any sensible diminution.

If it be in the power of chymistry to perform such strange effects, as are commonly experimented in that which they call aurum fulminans, one scruple of which shall give a louder blow, and be of greater force in descent, than half a pound of ordinary gunpowder in ascent; why may it not be as feasible by the same art, to extract such an oil as is here enquired after? since it must needs be more difficult to make a fire, (which of its own inclination shall tend downwards) than to contrive such an unctuous liquor, wherein fire shall be maintained for many years without any new supply.

Thus have I briefly set down the relations and opinions of divers learned men, concerning these perpetual lamps; of which, though there have been so many sundry kinds, and several ways to make them, (some being able to resist any violence of weathers, others being easily extinguished by any little alteration of the air, some being inclosed round about within glass, others being open;) yet now they are all of them utterly perished amongst the other ruins of time; and those who are most versed in the search after them, have only recovered such dark conjectures, from which a man cannot clearly deduce any evident principle, that may encourage him to a particular trial.

CHAP. XIII.

Concerning several attempts of contriving a perpetual motion by magnetical virtues.

THE second way whereby the making of a perpetual motion hath been attempted, is by magnetical virtues; which are not without some strong probabilities of proving effectual to this purpose: especially when we consider, that the heavenly revolutions, (being as the first pattern imitated and aimed at in these attempts) are all of them performed by the help of these qualities. This great orb of earth, and all the other planets, being but as so many magnetical globes, endowed with such various and continual motions, as may be most agreeable to the purposes for which they were intended. And therefore most of the authors *, who treat concerning this invention, do agree, that the likeliest way to effect it, is by these kind of qualities.

It was the opinion of Pet. Peregrinus, and there is an example pretended for it in Bettinus, (Apiar. 9. Progym. 5. pro. 11.) that a magnetical globe, or terella, being rightly placed upon its poles, would of itself have a constant rotation, like the diurnal motion of the earth : but this is commonly exploded, as being against all experience.

Others † think it possible, so to contrive several pieces of steel and a loadstone, that by their continual attraction and expulsion of one another, they may cause a perpetual revolution of a wheel. Of this opinion were Taisner ‡, Pet. Peregrinus ||, and Cardan §, out of Antonius de Fantis. But D. Gilbert, who was more especially versed in magnetical experiments, concludes it to be a vain and groundless fancy.

But amongst all these kind of inventions, that is most likely, wherein a loadstone is so disposed, that it shall draw unto it on a reclined plane, a bullet of steel, which steel as it ascends near to the loadstone, may be contrived to fall down through some hole in the plane, and so to return unto the place from whence at first it began to move; and being there, the loadstone will again attract it upwards, till coming to this hole, it will fall down again; and so the motion shall be perpetual, as may be more easily conceivable by this figure.

* Gilbert de Magnet. Cabæus Philos. Magnet. l. 4. c. 20.
† Athanas. Kircher, de Arte Magnet. l. 1. par. 2. prop. 13. item l. 2. p. 4.
‡ Tract. de motu continuo.
|| De Rota perpetui Motus, par. 2. c. 3.
§ De Variet. Rerum, L 9. c. 48.   De Magnet. L 2. c. 35.

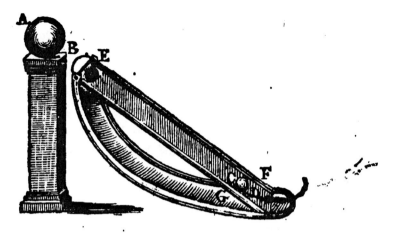

Suppose the loadstone to be represented at A B, which, though it have not strength enough to attract the bullet C directly from the ground, yet may do it by the help of the plane E F. Now, when the bullet is come to the top of this plane, its own gravity (which is supposed to exceed the strength of the loadstone) will make it fall into that hole at E; and the force it receives in this fall, will carry it with such a violence unto the other end of this arch, that it will open the passage which is there made for it, and by its return will again shut it; so that the bullet, (as at the first) is in the same place whence it was attracted, and consequently must move perpetually.

But however this invention may seem to be of such strong probability, yet there are sundry particulars which may prove it insufficient: for,

1. This bullet or steel must first be touched, and have its several poles, or else there can be little or no attraction of it. Suppose C in the steel to be answerable unto A in the stone, and to B; in the attraction, C D must always be directed answerable to A B, and so the motion will be more difficult, by reason there can be no rotation, or turning round of the bullet, but it must slide up with the line C D, answerable to the axis A B.

2. In its fall from E to G, which is *motus elementaris*, and proceeds from its gravity, there must needs be a rotation of it, and so it is odds but it happens wrong in the rise, the poles in the bullet being not in the same direction to

those in the magnet: and if in this reflux, it should so fall out, that D should be directed towards B, there should be rather a flight than an attraction, since those two ends do repel, and not draw one another.

3. If the loadstone A B have so much strength, that it can attract the bullet in F when it is not turned round, but does only slide upon the plane, whereas its own gravity would roll it downwards; then it is evident, the sphere of its activity and strength would be so increased when it approaches much nearer, that it would not need the assistance of the plane, but would draw it immediately to itself without that help; and so the bullet would not fall down through the hole, but ascend to the stone, and consequently cease its motion: for, if the loadstone be of force enough to draw the bullet on the plane, at the distance F B, then must the strength of it be sufficient to attract it immediately unto itself, when it is so much nearer as E B.   And if the gravity of the bullet be supposed so much to exceed the strength of the magnet, that it cannot draw it directly when it is so near, then will it not be able to attract the bullet up the plane, when it is so much further off.

So that none of all these magnetical experiments, which have been as yet discovered, are sufficient for the effecting of a perpetual motion, though these kind of qualities seem most conducible unto it, and perhaps hereafter it may be contrived from them.

CHAP. XIV.

The seeming probability of effecting a continual motion by solid weights, in a hollow wheel or sphere.

THE third way whereby the making of a perpetual motion hath been attempted, is by the natural affection of gravity; when the heaviness of several bodies is so contrived, that the same motion which they give in their descent, may be able to carry them up again.

But, (against the possibility of any such invention) it is thus objected by Cardan *. All sublunary bodies have a direct motion either of ascent, or descent; which, because it does refer to some term, therefore cannot be perpetual, but must needs cease, when it is arrived at the place unto which it naturally tends.

I answer, though this may prove that there is no natural motion of any particular heavy body, which is perpetual, yet it doth not hinder, but that it is possible from them to contrive such an artificial revolution, as shall constantly be the cause of itself.

Those bodies which may be serviceable to this purpose, are distinguishable into two kinds.

1. Solid and consistent, as weights of metal, or the like.

2. Fluid, or sliding; as water, sand, &c.

Both these ways have been attempted by many, though with very little or no success. Other men's conjectures in this kind you may see set down by divers authors †. It would be too tedious to repeat them over, or set forth their draughts. I shall only mention two new ones, which (if I am not over-partial) seem altogether as probable as any of these kinds that have been yet invented; and till experience had discovered their defect and insufficiency, I did certainly conclude them to be infallible.

The first of these contrivances was by solid weights being placed in some hollow wheel or sphere, unto which they should give a perpetual revolution: for (as the philosopher ‡ hath largely proved) only a circular motion can properly be perpetual.

But for the better conceiving of this invention, it is requisite that we rightly understand some principles in trochilics, or the art of wheel-instruments: as chiefly; the relation betwixt the parts of a wheel, and those of a balance; the several proportions in the semidiameter of a wheel,

---

* Subtil. l. 17. De Var. Rerum, l. 9. c. 48.

† D. Flud. Tract. 2. pars 7. l. 2. c. 4. et 7.

‡ Arist. Phys. l. 8. c. 12

being answerable to the sides in a balance, where the weight·is multiplied according to its distance from the centre *.

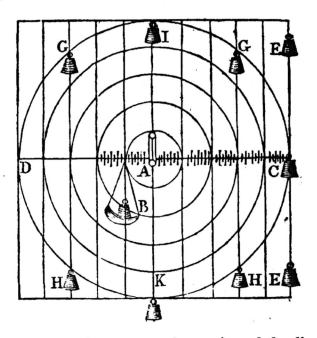

Thus, suppose the centre to be at A, and the diameter of the wheel D C to be divided into equal parts (as is here expressed) it is evident, according to the former ground, that one pound at C will equiponderate to five pound at B, because there is such a proportion betwixt their several distances from the centre. And it is not material, whether or no these several weights be placed horizontally; for though B do hang lower than C, yet this does not at all concern the heaviness; or though the plummet C were placed much higher than it is at E, or lower at F, yet would it still retain the same weight which it had at C; because these plummets (as in the nature of all heavy bodies) do tend downwards by a strait line: so that their several gravities are to be measured by that part of the horizontal semidiameter, which is directly either below or above them. Thus when the plummet C shall be moved either to G· or

* Arist, Mechan. c. 2. De ratione libræ ad circulum.

H, it will lose. ⅓ of its former heaviness, and be equally ponderous as if it were placed in the balance at number 3 ; and if we suppose it to be situated at I or K, then the weight of it will lie wholly upon the centre, and not at all conduce to the motion of the wheel on either side. So that the strait lines which pass through the divisions of the diameter, may serve to measure the heaviness of any weight in its several situations.

These things thoroughly considered, it seems very possible and easy for a man to contrive the plummets of a wheel, that they may be always heavier in their fall, than in their ascent ; and so consequently, that they should give a perpetual motion to the wheel itself; since it is impossible for that to remain unmoved, as long as one side in it is heavier than the other.

For the performance of this, the weights must be so ordered, 1. That in their descent they may fall from the centre, and in their ascent may rise nearer to it. 2. That the fall of each plummet may begin the motion of that which should succeed it. As in this following diagram:

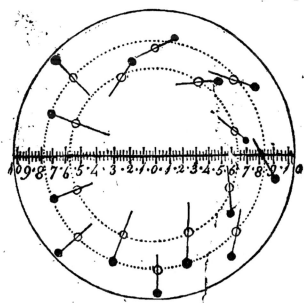

Where there are 16 plummets, 8 in the inward circle, and as many in the outward, (the inequality being to arise from their situation, it is therefore most convenient that the number of them be even.)   The 8 inward plummets are supposed to be in themselves so much heavier than the other, that in the wheel they may be of equal weight with those above them, and then the fall of these will be of sufficient force to bring down the other.   For example, if the outward be each of them four ounces, then the inward must be five; because the outward is distant from the centre five of those parts, whereof the inward is but four.   Each pair of these weights should be joined together by a little string or chain, which must be fastened about the middle, betwixt the bullet and the centre of that plummet which is to fall first, and at the top of the other.

When these bullets in their descent are at their farthest distance from the centre of the wheel, then shall they be stopped, and rest on the pins placed to that purpose; and so in their rising, there must be other pins to keep them in a convenient posture and distance from the centre, lest approaching too near unto it, they thereby become unfit to fall, when they shall come to the top of the descending side.

This may be otherwise contrived with some different circumstances, but they will all redound to the same effect. By such an engine it seems very probable, that a man may produce a perpetual motion.   The distance of the plummets from the centre increasing their weight on one side, and their being tied to one another, causing a constant succession in their falling.

But now, upon experience I have found this to be fallacious, and the reason may sufficiently appear by a calculation of the heaviness of each plummet, according to its several situation; which may easily be done by those perpendiculars that cut the diameter, (as was before explained, and is here expressed in five of the plummets on the descending side.)   From such a calculation it will be evident, that both the sides of this wheel will equiponderate; and so consequently that the supposed inequality whence the motion should proceed, is but imaginary and groundless.   On the descending side, the heaviness of each plummet may be measured according to these numbers, (supposing the diameter of the wheel to be divided into twenty parts, and each of those sub-divided into four.)

The outward plummets.   The inward plummets.

$$\left.\begin{cases} 7 & 0 \\ 10 & 0 \\ 7 & 0 \end{cases}\right\} \text{The sum 24.} \qquad \left.\begin{cases} 1 & 0 \\ 7 & 2 \\ 7 & 2 \\ 3 & 0 \end{cases}\right\} \text{The sum 19.}$$

On the ascending side, the weights are to be reckoned according to these degrees.

The outward.   The inward.

$$\left.\begin{cases} 1 & 3 \\ 7 & 2 \\ 9 & 0 \\ 5 & 3 \\ 0 & 0 \end{cases}\right\} \text{The sum 24.} \qquad \left.\begin{cases} 4 & 1 \\ 7 & 0 \\ 5 & 2 \\ 2 & 1 \end{cases}\right\} \text{The sum 19.}$$

The sum of which last numbers is equal with the former, and therefore both the sides of such a wheel, in this situation will equiponderate.

If it be objected, that the plummet A should be contrived to pull down the other at B, and then the descending side will be heavier than the other.

For answer to this, it is considerable,

1. That these bullets towards the top of the wheel, cannot descend till they come to a certain kind of inclination.

2. That any lower bullet hanging upon the other above it, to pull it down, must be conceived, as if the weight of it were in that point where its string touches the upper; at which point this bullet will be of less heaviness in respect of the wheel, than if it did rest in its own place: so that both the sides of it, in any kind of situation may equiponderate.

CHAP. XV.

Of composing a perpetual motion by fluid weights. Con-
cerning Archimedes's water-screw. The great probabi-
lity of accomplishing this enquiry by the help of that;
with the fallibleness of it upon experiment.

THAT which I shall mention as the last way, for the
trial of this experiment, is by contriving it in some
water-instrument; which may seem altogether as probable
and easy as any of the rest; because that element by reason
of its fluid and subtle nature (whereby of its own accord it
searches out the lower and more narrow passages) may be
most pliable to the mind of the artificer.   Now the usual
means for the ascent of water, is either by suckers or forces,
or something equivalent thereunto: neither of which may
be conveniently applied unto such a work as this, because
there is required unto each of them so much or more
strength, as may be answerable to the full weight of the
water that is to be drawn up; and then besides, they move
for the most part by fits and snatches, so that it is not easily
conceivable, how they should conduce unto such a motion,
which by reason of its perpetuity must be regular and
equal.

But amongst all other ways to this purpose, that invention
of Archimedes is incomparably the best, which is usually
called cochlea, or the water-screw; being framed by the
helical revolution of a cavity about a cylinder.   We have
not any discourse from the author himself concerning it,
nor is it certain whether he ever writ any thing to this purpose.   But if he did, yet as the injury of time hath deprived
us of many other his excellent works, so likewise of this
amongst the rest.

Athenæus* speaking of that great ship built by Hiero,
in the framing of which, there were three hundred carpen-

* Deipnosop. l. 5.

ters employed for a year together, besides many other hire-
lings for carriages, and such servile works; mentions this
instrument as being instead of a pump for that vast ship;
by the help of which, one man might easily and speedily
drain out the water, though it were very deep.

Diodorus Siculus* speaking of this engine, tells us, that
Archimedes invented it when he was in Egypt, and that it
was used in that country, for the draining of those pits and
lower grounds, whence the waters of Nilus could not return. Φιλοτεχνυ δ' οντος τυ οργανυ καθ' υπερβολην, (saith the
same author.) It being an engine so ingenious and artificial, as cannot be sufficiently expressed or commended.
And so (it should seem) the smith in Milan conceived it to
be, who having without any teaching or information found
it out, and therefore thinking himself to be the first inventor, fell mad with the mere joy of it †.

The nature and manner of making this, is more largely
handled by Vitruvius ‡.

The figure of it is after this manner:

Where you see there is a cylinder A A, and a spiral cavity or pipe twining about it, according to equal revolutions

---

* Biblioth. l. 1.   † Cardan. Subtil. l. 1. De Sapient. l. 5.
‡ Architect. l. 10. c. 11.

B B. The axis and centers of its motions are at the points C D; upon which being turned, it will so happen, that the same part of the pipe which was now lowermost, will presently become higher, so that the water does ascend by descending; ascending in comparison to the whole instrument, and descending in respect of its several parts. This being one of the strangest wonders amongst those many wherein these mathematical arts do abound, that a heavy body should rise by falling down, and the farther it passes by his own natural motion of descent, by so much higher still shall it ascend; which though it seem so evidently to contradict all reason and philosophy, yet in this instrument it may be manifested both by demonstration and sense.

This pipe or cavity, for the matter of it, cannot easily be made of metal, by reason of its often turnings; but for trial, there might be such a cavity cut in a column of wood, and afterwards covered over with tin-plate.

For the form and manner of making this screw, Vitruvius does prescribe these two rules:

1. That there must be an equality observed betwixt the breadth of the pipe, and the distance of its several circumvolutions.

2. That there must be such a proportion betwixt the length of the instrument, and its elevation, as is answerable to the pythagorical trigon. If the hypotenusal, or screw be five, the perpendicular or elevation must be three, and the basis four *.

However, (with his leave) neither of these proportions are generally necessary, but should be varied according to other circumstances. As for the breadth of the pipe in respect of its revolutions, it is left at liberty, and may be contrived according to the quantity of water which it should contain. The chief thing to be considered, is the obliquity or closeness of these circumvolutions. For the nearer they are unto one another, the higher may the instrument

* David Rivalt. Com. in Archim. opera exter.

be erected; there being no other guide for its true elevation but this.

And because the right understanding of this particular is one of the principal matters that concerns the use of this engine, therefore I shall endeavour with brevity and perspicuity to explain it. The first thing to be enquired after, is, what kind of inclination these helical revolutions of the cylinder have unto the horizon; which may be thus found out.

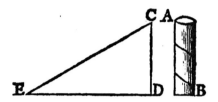

Let A B represent a cylinder with two perfect revolutions in it, unto which cylinder the perpendicular line C D is equal: the basis D E being supposed to be double unto the compass or circumference of the cylinder. Now it is certain, that the angle C E D, is the same with that by which the revolutions on the cylinder are framed, and that the line E C, in comparison to the basis E D, does shew the inclination of these revolutions unto the horizon. The grounds and demonstration of this are more fully set down by Guidus Ubaldus, in his Mechanics, and that other treatise De Cochlea, which he writ purposely for the explication of this instrument, where the subtilties of it are largely and excellently handled.

Now if this screw which was before perpendicular, be supposed to decline unto the horizon by the angle F B G, as in this second figure;

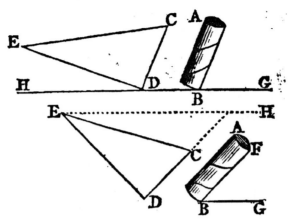

then the inclination of the revolutions in it will be increased by the angle E D H; though these revolutions will still remain in a kind of ascent, so that water cannot be turned through them.

But now, if the screw be placed so far declining, that the angle of its inclination F B G, be less than the angle E C D, in the triangle; as in this other diagram under the former; then the revolutions of it will descend to the horizon, as does the line E C; and in such a posture, if the screw be turned tound, water will ascend through its cavity. Whence it is easy to conceive the certain declination, wherein any screw must be placed for its own conveyance of water upwards. Any point betwixt H and D being in descent, but yet the more the screw declines downwards towards D, by so much the more water will be carried up by it.

If you would know the just quantity of water which every revolution does contain and carry, according to any inclination of the cylinder; this may be easily found, by ascribing on it an ellipsis, parallel to the horizon; which ellipsis will shew how much of the revolution is empty, and how much full *.

The true inclination of the screw being found, together with the certain quantity of water which every helix does contain; it is further considerable, that the water by this instrument does ascend naturally of itself, without any

* See a further explication of this in Ubaldus de Cochlea, l. 2. prop. 25.

violence or labour; and that the heaviness of it does lie chiefly upon the centres or axis of the cylinder, both its sides being of equal weight saith Ubaldus * : so that (it should seem) though we suppose each revolution to have an equal quantity of water, yet the screw will remain with any part upwards, (according as it shall be set) without turning itself either way. And therefore the least strength being added to either of its sides, should make it descend, according to that common maxim of Archimedes † ; any addition will make that which equiponderates with another, to tend downwards.

But now, because the weight of this instrument, and the water in it does lean wholly upon the axis, hence is it (saith Ubaldus) that the grating and rubbing of these axes against the sockets wherein they are placed, will cause some ineptitude and resistency to that rotation of the cylinder ; which would otherwise ensue upon the addition of the least weight to any one side ; but (saith the same author) any power that is greater than this resistency which does arise from the axis, will serve for the turning of it round.

These things considered together, it will hence appear, how a perpetual motion may seem easily contrivable. For if there were but such a water-wheel made on this instrument, upon which the stream that is carried up may fall in its descent; it would turn the screw round, and by that means convey as much water up as is required to move it ; so that the motion must needs be continual, since the same weight which in its fall does turn the wheel, is by the turning of the wheel carried up again.

Or if the water falling upon one wheel, would not be forcible enough for this effect, why then there might be two or three, or more, according as the length and elevation of the instrument will admit: by which means, the weight of it may be so multiplied in the fall, that it shall be equiva-

* Ubaldus de Cochlea, l. 3. prop. 4.

† De Æquipond. Suppos. 3.

R

lent to twice or thrice that quantity of water which ascends. As may be more plainly discerned by this following diagram: ·

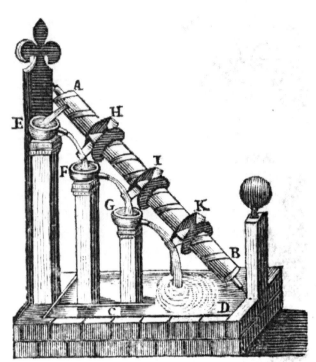

Where the figure L M, at the bottom, does represent a wooden cylinder with helical cavities cut in it; which at A B, is supposed to be covered over with tin-plates, and three water-wheels upon it H I K. The lower cistern which contains the water being C D. Now this cylinder being turned round, all the water which from the cistern ascends through it, will fall into the vessel at E, and from that vessel being conveyed upon the water-wheel H, shall consequently give a circular motion to the whole screw : or if this alone should be too weak for the turning of it, then the same water which falls from the wheel H, being received into the other vessel F, may from thence again descend on the wheel I; by which means the force of it will be doubled *. And if this be yet insufficient, then may the water which falls on the second wheel I, be received into the other vessel G, and from thence again descend on the third wheel at K: and so for as many other wheels as the instrument is capable of. So that besides the greater distance of these three streams from the centre or, axis, by which they are made so much heavier, and besides, that the fall of this outward water is forcible and violent, whereas the ascent of that within is natural; besides all this, there is thrice as much water to turn the screw, as is carried up by it.

But on the other side, if all the water falling upon one wheel, would be able to turn it round, then half of it would serve with two wheels; and the rest may be so disposed of in the fall, as to serve unto some other useful delightful ends.

. When I first thought of this invention, I could scarce forbear with Archimedes to cry out ευρηκα, ευρηκα, it seeming so infallible a way for the effecting of a perpetual motion, that nothing could be so much as probably objected against it: but upon trial and experience I find it altogether insufficient for any such purpose, and that for these two reasons:

1. The water that ascends will not make any considerable stream in the fall.

2. This stream (though multiplied) will not be of force enough to turn about the screw.

1. The water ascends gently, and by intermissions; but it falls continuately, and with force; each of the three vessels being supposed full at the first, that so the weight of the water in them might add the greater strength and swiftness to the streams, that descend from them. Now this swiftness of motion will cause so great a difference betwixt them, that one of these little streams may spend

---

* There is another like contrivance to this purpose in Pet. Bettin. Apiar. 4. Pogym. 1. Prop. 10. but with much less advantage than it is here proposed.

R 2

more water in the fall, than a stream six times bigger in the
ascent, though we should suppose both of them to be continuate : how much more then, when as the ascending
water is vented by fits and intermissions ; every circumvo-
lution voiding only so much as is contained in one helix?
and in this particular, one that is not versed in these kind
of experiments, may be easily deceived.

But secondly, though there were so great a disproportion,
yet notwithstanding, the force of these outward streams
might well enough serve for the turning of the screw ;
if it were so, that both its sides would equiponderate the
water being in them (as Ubaldus hath affirmed.)   But now,
upon farther examination, we shall find this assertion of
his to be utterly against both reason and experience.
And herein does consist the chief mistake of this contrivance : for the ascending side of the screw is made by
the water contained in it, so much heavier than the descending side, that these outward streams thus applied,
will not be of force enough to make them equiponderate,
much less to move the whole ; as may be more easily
discerned by this fig.

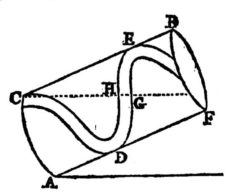

Where A B represents a screw covered over, C D E one
helix, or revolution of it, C D the ascending side, E D the
descending side, the point D the middle.   The horizontal
line C F, shewing how much of the helix is filled with water, viz. of the ascending side, from C the beginning of the
helix, to D the middle of it ; and on the descending side,

from D the middle, to the point G, where the horizontal does cut the helix. Now it is evident, that this latter part D G, is nothing near so much, and consequently not so heavy as the other D C. And thus is it in all the other revolutions; which, as they are either more or larger, so will the difficulty of this motion be increased. Whence it will appear, that the outward streams which descend, must be of so much force, as to countervail all that weight whereby the ascending side in every one of these revolutions does exceed the other. And though this may be effected by making the water-wheels larger, yet then the motion will be so slow, that the screw will not be able to supply the outward streams.

There is another contrivance to this purpose, mentioned by Kircher de Magnete, l. 2, p. 4, depending upon the heat of the sun, and the force of winds; but it is liable to such abundance of exceptions, that it is scarce worth the mentioning, and does by no means deserve the confidence of any ingenious artist.

Thus have I briefly explained the probabilities and defects of those subtle contrivances, whereby the making of a perpetual motion hath been attempted. I would be loth to discourage the inquiry of any ingenious artificer, by denying the possibility of effecting it with any of these mechanical helps * : but yet (I conceive) if those principles which concern the slowness of the power, in comparison to the greatness of the weight, were rightly understood, and thoroughly considered, they would make this experiment to seem (if not altogether impossible) yet much more difficult than otherwise perhaps it will appear. However, the inquiring after it cannot but deserve our endeavours, as being one of the most noble amongst all these mechanical subtleties. And (as it is in the fable of him who dug the vineyard for a hid treasure, though he did not find the money, yet he thereby made the ground more fruitful; so) though we do not attain to the effecting of this particular, yet our

* Treated of before, l. 1. c.

searching after it may discover so many other excellent subtleties, as shall abundantly recompense the labour of our
inquiry.

And then besides, it may be another encouragement, to
consider the pleasure of such speculations which do ravish
and sublime the thoughts with more clear angelical content-
ments. Archimedes was generally so taken up in the delight of these mathematical studies of this familiar siren, (as
Plutarch * stiles them) that he forgot both his meat and
drink, and other necessities of nature; nay, that he neglected
the saving of his life, when that rude soldier, in the pride
and haste of victory, would not give him leisure to finish
his demonstration. What a ravishment was that, when
having found out the way to measure Hiero's crown, he
leaped out of the bath, and (as if he were suddenly pos-
sessed) ran naked up and down, crying ευρηκα, ευρηκα ! It
is storied of Thales, that in his joy and gratitude for one of
these mathematical inventions, he went presently to the
temple, and there offered up a solemn sacrifice. And Pythagoras, upon the like occasion, is related to have sa-
crificed a hundred oxen. The justice of providence having
so contrived it, that the pleasure which there is in the success of such inventions, should be proportioned to the
great difficulty and labour of their inquiry.

* Οικιας και συνοικυ σειρην⊙. Plutarch. Marcell. Joan. Tzetzes, Chil. 2,
Hist. 35. Valer. Maxim. l. 8. c. 7.

AN

ABSTRACT OF DR. WILKINS's ESSAY

TOWARDS A

REAL CHARACTER,

AND

A PHILOSOPHICAL LANGUAGE.

Which was printed by order of the Royal Society, 1668.

IT appears by the author's dedication to the president, council, and fellows of the royal society, that they had several times required his papers of him relating to this subject, and that in obedience to their orders, he had reduced them into method. He tells them, he was not so vain as to think he had finished this great undertaking with all the advantages of which it was capable: nor was he so diffident of his essay, but that he thought it sufficient for what it pretended to, viz. the distinct expression of all things and notions that fall under discourse. He was sensible of sundry defects in several parts of the book, and therefore desired they would appoint some of their number to consider the whole, and to offer their observations as to what they thought fit to be amended. Accordingly several of the society, as appears by the Philosophical Transactions of Monday, May 18, 1668, were appointed to answer his desire, for the furthering and facilitating the practice of what he aimed at. But what progress they made in it does not appear. Our author was sensible that his design might lie neglected as other good designs had done; and the only expedient he could think of to prevent it, was, that it might be sent abroad with the approbation of the royal society, which might provoke at least the learned part of the world to take notice of, and encourage it, according as they should think it deserved.

The advantages proposed by this philosophical language were, the facilitating of mutual commerce among the several nations of the world; the improving of natural knowledge; and the propagation of religion: our author was also of opinion, that it might contribute much to the clearing of some modern differences in religion, by unmasking many wild errors that shelter themselves under the disguise of affected phrases: which being philosophically unfolded, and rendered according to the genuine and natural importance of words, would appear to be inconsistencies and contradictions; and several of these pretended mysterious, profound notions, expressed in big swelling words, by which men set up for reputation, being this way examined, would either appear to be nonsense, or very jejune. But whatever might be the issue of this attempt, as to the establishing of a real character, and bringing it into common use among several nations of the world, of which our author had but very slender expectations, yet of this he was confident, that the reducing of all things and notions to such kind of tables as he proposed, were it as completely done as it might be, would prove the shortest and plainest way for the attainment of real knowledge, that had yet been offered to the world. To which he added, that he thought his tables, as now they are, were a much better and readier course for training up men in the knowledge of things, than any other way that he knew of. And indeed since his design of the real character is wholly neglected, that seems now to be the principal use of the book, and alone makes it truly valuable.

In his preface to the reader he gives an account how he came to engage in this work, viz. that by his converse with Dr. Seth Ward, then bishop of Salisbury, upon the various desiderata, proposed by learned men to be still wanting to the advancement of several parts of learning, he found this of an universal character, to be one of the principal and most feasible, if regularly prosecuted; but most of those who had attempted any thing like it, mistook their foundation, by proposing a character according to some particular language, without reference to the nature of things, and that common notion of them wherein mankind agrees: this suggestion gave him the first distinct apprehension of the proper course to be taken for advancing such a design.

He says it was a considerable time after this before he attempted it; and the first occasion of it was; his desire to assist another person in framing a real character from the natural notion of things. In order to promote that person's design, he drew up the tables of substances, or the species of natural bodies, reduced under their several heads, much the same as they are published in this Essay. But the person thinking this method of too great a compass, and conceiving that he could provide for all the chief radicals in a much shorter and easier way, he did not make use of the doctor's tables. Our author however being convinced that this was the only way to effect such a work, and being unwilling to lose so much pains, he went on with the other tables of accidents, and then attempted the reduction of all other words in the dictionary to these tables, either as they were synonimous to them, or to be defined by them; which was a true way to try the fulness of those tables; and likewise a help to learners, who without such a direction, might not perhaps be able at first to find out the true place and notion of many words.

For the farther compleating of this work, our author found it necessary to frame such a natural grammar, as might be suited to the philosophy of speech, abstracting from many unnecessary rules belonging to instituted languages.

He takes notice of the assistance he received from his learned friends in several faculties; particularly from Mr. Francis Willoughby, as to the several species of animals; from Mr. John Ray, as to the tables of plants; and for the other principal difficulties from Dr. William Lloyd, than whom he knew none fitter, because of his accurate judgment in philology and philosophy; and to him particularly he owed the suiting the tables to the dictionary, and the drawing up of the dictionary itself, which he doubts not will be found the most perfect ever yet made for the English tongue.

It is observable however, that though he mentions others of his friends by name, from whom he had any light or help towards this design, he does not at all name Mr. George Dalgarno, a Scotch gentleman, born at Aberdeen, and bred in the university there, who printed a book upon the same subject, and with the same view, before him. This is the more remarkable, because Dr. Wilkins's own name is printed in the margin of King Charles the Second's letter, prefixed to Mr. Dalgarno's book, as one of those who informed his majesty of Mr. Dalgarno's design ; and " approved it as a thing that might be of singular use to facilitate an intercourse between people of different languages, and consequently a proper and effectual means for advancing all the parts of real and useful knowledge, civilizing barbarous nations, propagating the gospel, and increasing traffic and commerce ; which prevailed with his majesty to grant his said letters of recommendation to as many of his subjects, especially the clergy, as were truly apprehensive and sensible of the defectiveness of art, chiefly in this particular of language, what a great loss mankind is at thereby, how acceptable it would be before God, and praiseworthy among men, to encourage and advance those ways of learning, wherein the general good of mankind is intended ; that such persons would, as their affections shall incline them, and their places enable them, put their helping hands to the bringing forth this (as yet) infant design, now sticking in the birth."

These are the words of his majesty's letters, wherein he was pleased to declare he would give some token of his royal favour for the helping forward that so laudable and hopeful enterprize.

There is no conjecture to be made why the Bishop should have forborne to name this gentleman, but what is to be collected from his own epistle, and from Mr. Dalgarno's book. In the former it appears that the Bishop had formed his tables for the assistance of another person in so worthy an undertaking; but that person did not think fit to make use of those tables. And by Mr. Dalgarno's book, it is evident that he was in his judgment against those tables, as being too tedious and difficult, and such as philosophers were not agreed in, and by consequence other men of different languages and nations, could not have the same ideas about them; by which it is probable he gave the Bishop some disgust, which might be the occasion why he did not mention his name.

The title of Mr. Dalgarno's book is, *Ars Signorum, vulgo Character Universalis et Lingua Philosophica. Qua poterunt, homines diversissimorum idiomatum, spatio duarum septimanarum, omnia animi sui sensa (in rebus familiaribus) non minus intelligibiliter, sive scribendo, sive loquendo, mutuo communicare, quam linguis propriis vernaculis. Præterea, hinc etiam poterunt juvenes philosophiæ, principia et veram logicæ praxin, citius et facilius multo imbibere, quam ex vulgaribus philosophorum scriptis.*

This is enough to shew that Mr. Dalgarno's design, though he differed in the method, was the same, in the main, with the Bishop's, to which we now return. He divides his book into four parts; the first contains the prolegomena, and is divided into five chapters. The first chapter hath four sections: the first contains the introduction; the second, the original of languages; wherein he delivers his opinion, that the first language was concreated with our first parents. The rise of the confusion of languages is well enough known, but what number of languages sprung up at that confusion, is not certain; the most received conjecture is, that they were seventy, or seventy-two, though there be strong probabilities to prove that there were not so many, and that the first dispersion did not divide mankind into so many colonies. But the languages now used in the world do far exceed this number. Pliny and Strabo make mention of three hundred nations of different languages, from whence people resorted to Dioscuria, a great mart town in Colchos;

which considering the narrow compass of traffic, before the invention of the magnetic needle, must needs be but a small proportion, in comparison to the rest of the world. Some American histories say, that in every eighty miles of that country, the inhabitants speak a different language. Joseph Scaliger reckons eleven mother tongues in Europe, which have no dependance on one another; but they are so well known, that we need not insist upon them. Besides this difference of languages in their first derivation, every particular tongue has its several dialects in one and the same nation. The Hebrew is by many learned men supposed to be the first mother tongue of those now known in the world. When the Jews were captives at Babylon, their language was mixed with the Chaldean; and after the captivity, the pure Hebrew ceased to be vulgar, and remained only amongst learned men, as we find by Nehemiah, viii. 7, 8. And the pure Hebrew now in being is only that of the Old Testament; which though sufficient to express what is there intended, is not so for conversation, and therefore is guessed not to be the same which was concreated with our first parents, and spoken in paradise.

The second chapter consists of four sections. The first concerns the various changes to which all vulgar tongues are obnoxious. The second gives proofs of such changes in the English tongue in the Lord's prayer, from the year of Christ 700, to 1537. The third section determines in the affirmative, that several of the ancient languages are lost, since it is evident from the instance of our own, that in some few hundreds of years, a language may be so changed, as to be scarce intelligible. The fourth section accounts for the rise and occasion of new languages; which he says proceeds from commerce, and mixture of people by conquests, marriage of princes, or otherwise, and instances in that called the Malayan tongue, the newest in the world, and as common among the natives of the East Indies, as Latin and French in Europe. It was invented or occasioned by a concourse of fishermen from Pegu, Siam, Bengala, and other nations at Malacca, where they built the town of that name, and agreed upon a distinct language made up of the easiest words belonging to each nation.

The third chapter consists of four sections. The first treats of the original of letters and writing. Our author tells us, it is most generally agreed that Adam in process of time, upon his experience of the great necessity of letters, did first invent the ancient Hebrew character; but he rejects those particular alphabets which are by some ascribed to Adam, Enoch, and Noah; and adds, that it has been abundantly cleared by learned men, that the ancient Hebrew character has the priority before any now known. And it is none of the least arguments for the truth and divine authority of the holy scriptures, to consider the general concurrence of all manner of evidence for the antiquity of the Hebrew, and the derivation of all other letters from it. In the second section he gives us the opinion of many of the ancients, to confirm the derivation of other letters and languages from the Hebrew. In the third, he shews us that the use of letters is less ancient, and the kinds of them less numerous than the languages themselves. He proves this by several instances, that many nations do not yet understand the use of letters, and that though the German and French tongues be ancient, it is not much above four hundred years since books began to be writ in those languages; and the reason why letters are less numerous than languages, is, that several nations borrowed the use of letters from their neighbours, and adapted them to their own languages. In the fourth section, he gives us an account of the hieroglyphics of the ancients, which was a mere shift they were put to for want of letters, and was a slight and imperfect invention, suitable to those first and ruder ages. He treats also of the secret and occult ways of writing, taught by the abbot Trithemius, for which he was falsely accused of magic. He gives us some hints about letters or marks used by the ancients for brevity sake; of which nature is shorthand, so common in England. In the fifth section, he gives an account of some ancient attempts towards a real character, to signify things and notions. And in the sixth informs us, that no alphabet now in being, was invented at once, or by rules of art; but all of them, except the Hebrew, were taken up by imitation.

The fourth chapter consists of six sections. The first treats of the defects in the common alphabet, as to their true order, which is inartificial and confused, the vowels and consonants being huddled together without any distinction; whereas the vowels and consonants should be reduced into classes, according to their several kinds. In the second section, he takes notice of the redundancy and deficiency of the Hebrew alphabet, and likewise of the Greek and Latin. In the third section, he shews that they are very uncertain as to their powers and signification; of which he gives several instances in our own language. In the fourth section, he takes notice that the names of the letters in most alphabets are very improperly expressed by words of several syllables. In this respect, the Roman and English alphabet are more convenient than the rest, though not without some defects of the same nature. In the fifth section, he says their figures do not correspond sufficiently with their natures and powers, and observes that the manner of writing the oriental tongues from right to left is as unnatural as to write with light on the wrong side. In the sixth section, he takes notice of the defects of words as well as letters; some of them being equivocal, others synonimous, besides the irregularities in grammar, and the difference betwixt writing and pronouncing words. On this occasion, he takes notice of the endeavours of Sir Thomas Smith and others, to rectify our English orthography, though we still obstinately retain the errors of our ancestors.

The fifth chapter has three sections. The first maintains, that neither letters nor languages have been regularly established by rules of art: nor could it be otherwise, because grammar (by which they should be regulated) is of a much later invention than the languages themselves; as is evident from the Hebrew; which, though the oldest of all, was not reduced into order of grammar till the year 1040. In the second, he treats of the natural ground and principle of the everal ways of communication among men; where he tells us, that as they generally agree in the same principle of reason, they likewise agree in the same internal notion or apprehension of things; and those internal notions they communicate to the ear by sounds, and particularly by words, and to the eye they communicate them by motion and figure, &c. and more particularly by writing: so that if men should generally agree upon the same way of expression as they agree in the same notion, we should then be free from that curse of the confusion of tongues, and all the unhappy consequences of it. This is only to be done by some one language and character to be universally practised, and enjoined by authority; which cannot be expected without an universal monarchy; and perhaps not then: or else by some method which (without such authority) might engage men to learn it, because of its facility and usefulness, which was the design of this Essay. The third section informs us, that in order to this, the first thing to be considered, was a just enumeration and description of such things as were to have marks or names assigned them, and to be so contrived, as to be full and adequate without redundancy or defect as to their number, and regular as to their place and order. And if every thing and notion had a distinct mark, with some provision to express grammatical derivations and inflections, it would answer one great end of a real character, to signify things and not words. And if several distinct words were assigned for the names of such things, with fixed rules for such grammatical derivations and inflections as are natural and necessary, it would make a more easy and convenient language than any yet in being.

Then if these marks or notes could be so contrived, as to have such a dependance upon, and relation to one another, as might suit the nature of the things and notions they represent; and likewise, if the names of things could be so ordered, as to contain such an affinity or opposition in their letters and sounds, as might some way answer the nature of the things they signify, it would be a further advantage, by which, besides helping the memory by natural method, the understanding would be improved; and by, learning the characters and names of things, we should likewise learn their natures.

Thus our author concludes the first part, and comes to the second; which contains a regular enumeration and description of all those things and notions to which names are to be assigned, and forms a system of universal philoso-phy. This part is divided into twelve chapters. The first contains six sections. The first section has a scheme of genus's, or more common heads of things belonging to this design. Then he shews how each of them may be subdi-vided by its peculiar differences, which for the better con-veniency of the design, he determines for most part to the number of six, except in the numerous tribes of herbs, trees, exanguious animals, fishes, and birds, which cannot be comprehended in so narrow a compass. Then he enu-merates the several species belonging to each of those dif-ferences, in such an order and dependance, as may contri-bute to define them, and determine their primary significa-tions. These species he commonly joins together in pairs, for helping the memory; and so likewise are some of the genus's and differences; those things which naturally have opposites, are joined with them, according to such opposi-tion, whether single or double; and those things that have no opposites, are commonly joined together with respect to some affinity which they have to one another, though sometimes those affinities are less proper and more remote; there being several things shifted into those places, because the author did not know how to provide for them better. The second section relates to the more general notions of things, and the difficulty of establishing those notions aright. The third treats of transcendentals general. The fourth of transcendental relations mixed. The fifth of transcenden-tal relations of action; and the sixth of the several notions belonging to grammar or logic. But these things being di-gested into tables, we must refer the reader to the book it-self, for a distinct idea of them.

The second chapter consists of two sections. The first

is concerning God; and the second concerning the several things and notions reducible under that collective genus of the world: which is also digested into tables.

The third chapter consists of three sections. The first is of elements and meteors; the second of stones; and the third of metals; digested also into tables.

The fourth chapter has seven sections. The first of plants; the second concerning a more general distribution of them; the third, fourth, and fifth, treat of herbs; considered according to their leaves, flowers, and seed-vessels. The sixth treats of shrubs; and the seventh of trees. All of them likewise in tables.

The fifth chapter has six sections. The first concerns animals, and the general distribution of them; the second is of exanguious animals; the third of fish; the fourth of birds; the fifth of beasts; and the sixth has a digression concerning Noah's ark: wherein he maintains the truth and authority of the scripture, against the objections of atheists and heretics, that a vessel of such dimensions could not contain so vast a multitude of animals, with the whole year's provision for them.

The sixth chapter relates to the parts of animate bodies; first, peculiar; secondly, general: and these are also digested into tables.

The seventh chapter relates to the predicament of quantity. 1. Of magnitude. 2. Of space. 3. Of measure. All digested into tables.

The eighth chapter relates to quality, and its several genus's. 1. Of natural power. 2. Of habit. 3. Of manners. 4. Of sensible quality. 5. Of diseases. With the various differences and species under each.

The ninth chapter treats of action, and its several genus's. 1. Spiritual. 2. Corporeal. 3. Motion. 4. Operation.

The tenth chapter concerns more private relation. 1. Of family relation; with the several kinds of things belonging to those in that capacity, either as possessions, or provisions.

The eleventh chapter concerns public relations; as civil, judiciary, naval, military, and ecclesiastical.

The twelfth chapter explains the design of the foregoing tables; gives particular instances of the six principal genus's of it; has some notes concerning opposites and synonymas; and an account of such things as ought not to be provided for in those tables.

The third part contains a philosophical grammar; and is divided into fourteen chapters.

The first chapter concerns the several kinds and parts of grammar. 2. Of etymology; and the more general scheme of integrals and particles. 3. Of nouns in general. 4. Of substantives common, denoting either things, actions, or persons. 5. Rules concerning nouns of action. 6. Of substantives abstracts. 7. Of adjectives, according to the true philosophical notion of them. 8. The true notion of a verb. 9. Of derived adverbs. 10. A general scheme of the forementioned derivations.

The second chapter concerns particles in general. 2. Of the copula. 3. Of pronouns more generally. 4. More particularly. 5. Of interjections more generally. 6. More particularly.

The third chapter treats of prepositions in general. 2. The particular kinds of them enumerated. 3. An explication of the four last combinations of them, relating to place or time.

The fourth chapter concerns adverbs in general. 2. The particular kinds of them. 3. Conjunctions.

The fifth chapter treats of articles. 2. Of Moods. 3. Of Tenses. 4. The most distinct way of expressing the differences of time.

The sixth chapter concerns transcendental particles, and the end and use of them. 2. The usual ways for enlarging the sense of words in instituted languages. 3. The general heads of transcendental particles.

The seventh chapter has instances of the great usefulness of those transcendental particles; with directions how they are to be applied.

The eighth chapter treats of the accidental differences of words. 1. Inflexion. 2. Derivation. 3. Composition.

The ninth chapter is of the second part of grammar, called syntax.

The tenth chapter is of orthography; and contains three sections. The first concerning letters; and the authors who have treated of this subject: of whom Dr. Wallis seems with the greatest accurateness and subtilty to have considered the philosophy of articulate sounds. The second contains a brief table of all such kinds of simple sounds, as can be framed with the mouths of men. The third contains a further explanation of this table, as to the organs of speech, and as to the letters framed by those organs.

The eleventh treats of vowels. The twelfth of consonants. The thirteenth of compound vowels and consonants. The fourteenth treats of the accidents of letters: 1. Their names. 2. Their order. 3. Affinities and oppositions. 4. Their figures; with a twofold instance of a more regular character for the letters: the latter of which may be esteemed natural. 5. Of pronunciation. 6. The several letters disused by several nations.

The fourth part contains a real character and philosophical language. This consists of six chapters: the first treats of a proposal of one kind of real character amongst many others which might be offered both for the integrals, whether genus's, differences, or species, together with the derivations and inflexions belonging to them; as likewise for all the several kinds of particles. Here our author acquaints us, that it were exceeding desirable that the names of things might consist of such sounds as should bear in them some analogy to their natures, and the figure or character of these names should bear some proper resemblance to those sounds; but he does not understand how this character can be adjusted any otherwise than by institution: and in the framing of those characters, he says, special regard must be had to these four properties. 1. That the figure be plain and easy, so as it may be made by one or at most by two strokes of the pen. 2. That they be sufficiently distinguished from one another. 3. Graceful to the eye. 4. Methodical. But we must refer to the book itself for our author's specimen.

The second chapter contains an instance of this real character in the Lord's prayer and creed.

The third shews how this character may be made affable in a distinct language, and what kind of letters or syllables may be conveniently assigned to each character.

The fourth has a comparison of the Lord's prayer and creed in this language, with 50 other languages as to the facility and euphony of it. The fifth contains directions for the more easy learning this character and language; with a brief table containing the radicals both integrals and particles, together with the character and language by which each of them are to be expressed.

The sixth is a comparison betwixt this natural philosophical grammar, and that of other instituted languages, particularly the Latin, in respect of the multitude of unnecessary rules, and of anomalisms. It treats also concerning the China character; the several attempts and proposals made by others towards a new kind of character and language, and the advantage in respect of facility which this philosophical language has above the Latin. In the last place comes an alphabetical dictionary wherein all English words according to their various significations, are either referred to their places in the philosophical tables, or explained by such words as are in those tables.

THE END.

C. Whittingham, Printer,
Dean-Street, Fetter-Lane, London.

CPSIA information can be obtained at www.ICGtesting.com
Printed in the USA
LVOW051930040213

318575LV00016B/885/P